Exploring Spoken English Learner Language Using Corpora

'Finally, some principled empirically-based information on qualities of spoken language in context! For several decades, a promise of second language (L2) corpus linguistics has been to revolutionize ways of teaching English to speakers of other languages. But prior to this book's publication, most L2 corpus resources have focused on genres of the written language. As a result, specialists in research and teaching of the spoken language have felt somewhat frustrated. We are intrigued by the great potential corpus tools offer since we witness the many exciting ways in which they are applied to the written language. Partly because spoken corpora are notably more difficult to generate and analyze, the infusion of corpus tools into research and teaching of the spoken language has been limited. This book goes far in alleviating such concerns since it expands the landscape of corpus studies to include several core genres of the spoken language.'

—John Murphy *Georgia State University, USA*

'This is a long-awaited volume presenting a brief introduction to corpus linguistics and a variety of excellent corpus-based studies on spoken learner language in the university setting. The authors provide a historical overview of the research in this area, offer a range of new approaches to the analysis, introduce accessible learner corpora, and discuss pedagogical applications. The reader finds a state-of-the-art picture of research and plenty of ideas for future directions to analyze spoken learner language. I highly recommend this volume to researchers and students alike.'

—Eniko Csomay *San Diego State University, USA*

Eric Friginal
Joseph J. Lee • Brittany Polat
Audrey Roberson

Exploring Spoken English Learner Language Using Corpora

Learner Talk

palgrave
macmillan

Eric Friginal
Applied Linguistics and ESL
Georgia State University
Atlanta, Georgia, USA

Brittany Polat
Georgia State University
Atlanta, Georgia, USA

Joseph J. Lee
Ohio University
Athens, Ohio, USA

Audrey Roberson
Hobart and William Smith Colleges
Geneva, New York, USA

ISBN 978-3-319-59899-4 ISBN 978-3-319-59900-7 (eBook)
DOI 10.1007/978-3-319-59900-7

Library of Congress Control Number: 2017946322

Printed on acid-free paper

This Palgrave Macmillan imprint is published by Springer Nature
The registered company is Springer International Publishing AG
The registered company address is: Gewerbestrasse 11, 6330 Cham, Switzerland

Summary

As second language (L2) corpus studies expand into their third decade, innovations in computational technology and corpus creation have facilitated unprecedented access to authentic language in the classroom, including among non-native speakers (NNSs) of English. This book focuses on corpus-based analyses of learner oral production in university-level English or English as a Second Language (ESL) classrooms. Our analyses highlight three specialized corpora collected for the three empirical parts of this book, explored using a range of corpus approaches and methods: (1) learner talk in the English for Academic Purposes (EAP) classroom, (2) learner talk in English language experience interviews, and (3) learner talk in peer response/feedback activities. Historical and methodological perspectives in exploring spoken learner corpora, pedagogical applications, and future directions in studying learner language are discussed. A synthesis of corpus-based research of spoken learner language, list of available corpora and online databases, and an introduction to corpus linguistics and corpus tools and approaches are provided in the first two chapters of the book.

Acknowledgement

We would like to thank our mentors and colleagues at the Department of Applied Linguistics and ESL at Georgia State University (GSU), especially Gayle Nelson, John Murphy, and Sara Cushing for their guidance and critical perspectives in developing the three empirical studies presented in this book. Thanks to Mike Cullom for his valuable insights and reviews of earlier drafts of this book, our Palgrave Macmillan commissioning editors and reviewers, and the staff of the Longview Public Library, Longview, WA. We recognize Douglas Biber and Randi Reppen at Northern Arizona University; Lucy Pickering at Texas A&M, Commerce; John Swales and Rita Simpson-Vlach at University of Michigan and for their work with MICASE; Laurence Anthony at Waseda University; and the Learner Corpus Association (Founding Members: Gaëtanelle Gilquin, Sylviane Granger, Fanny Meunier and Magali Paquot at the Centre for English Corpus Linguistics, Université Catholique de Louvain) for leading the way with their corpus tools and seminal studies of learner language. Much appreciation to our GSU colleagues: Diane Belcher, Stephanie Lindemann, Scott Crossley, Youjin Kim, Ute Römer, Jack A. Hardy, Pam Pearson, Nic Subtirelu, Cassie Leymarie, and many other collaborators who have assisted in the data collection and analyses in various parts of this book. We are grateful to all our study participants and especially the students, instructors, and administrators at GSU's Intensive English Program (Cheryl Delk-Le Good, John Bunting, Debra Snell, Louise

Gobron, and Alison Camacho). Data collection in Part 3 of this book was supported by grants from the Educational Testing Service (ETS) and *Language Learning*. Finally, we dedicate this book to our families and friends, and thank them for their love and support: Mike and Beth Cullom, Donna and Ela Friginal; Chang Keun Lee and Joanne Y. Lee, and Helen, Hetty, and Jules Lee; Ali, Guinevere, Thomas, and Charlie Polat; Susan and Jim Roberson, and Michael Mills.

Eric Friginal
Joseph J. Lee
Brittany Polat
Audrey Roberson

Contents

About the Authors

Eric Friginal is Associate Professor of Applied Linguistics at the Department of Applied Linguistics and ESL, and Director of International Programs, College of Arts and Sciences, at Georgia State University. He specializes in (applied) corpus linguistics, sociolinguistics, cross-cultural communication, and the analysis of spoken professional discourse. His recent books include *Talking at Work: Corpus-Based Explorations of Workplace Discourse* (2016, Palgrave Macmillan), co-edited with Lucy Pickering and Shelley Staples; *Studies in Corpus-Based Sociolinguistics* and *Corpus Linguistics for English Teachers* (2017–2018, Routledge).

Joseph J. Lee is the Assistant Director of the ELIP Academic & Global Communication Program, and Director of ELIP Center for Academic Communication: Tutoring Services in the Department of Linguistics, Ohio University. His research and teaching interests include ESP/EAP, genre studies, classroom discourse, advanced academic literacies, applied corpus linguistics, and teacher education. His recent publications include research articles in *English for Specific Purposes, Journal of English for Academic Purposes*, and *Journal of Second Language Writing.*

Brittany Polat is an independent ESL researcher based in Lakeland, Florida. Her research interests include second language acquisition, pragmatics, and corpus linguistics. Her research has appeared in journals such as *Applied Linguistics*, *Journal of Pragmatics*, and *Corpus Linguistics Research.*

Audrey Roberson is Assistant Professor of Education at Hobart and William Smith Colleges in Geneva, New York, where she oversees TESOL certification in the department's Teacher Education Program, as well as directs a certificate program in TEFL. Her research interests include language teacher preparation, applied corpus linguistics, interaction in second language learning, and second language writing. She has co-authored articles in *Corpora* and in the composition journal *Across the Disciplines*.

List of Figures

List of Tables

Part I

Introduction

1

Exploring Spoken English Learner Language Using Corpora

As second language (L2) corpus studies expand into their third decade, innovations in computational technology and corpus creation have facilitated unprecedented access to authentic language in the classroom, including among non-native speakers (NNSs) of English. NNS writing across various written contexts (e.g., school essays, standardized tests/proficiency tests, and laboratory or research reports) has been studied extensively in both journal article and book formats using corpora by applied linguists including Douglas Biber, Ken Hyland, John Swales, Rod Ellis, Susan Conrad, Eli Hinkel, and Sylviane Granger, to name only a few. Despite these impressive contributions, gaps still remain in our knowledge of spoken English L2 registers, even those that are quite important for NNSs to master. Classroom learner speech and face-to-face NNS interviews, for example, have been researched both qualitatively and quantitatively, primarily by utilizing the assessment of learner performance. However, extensive corpus-based analyses of these registers are still relatively few in number. Given that these oral learner skills are essential in high-stakes situations, such as admission to graduate programs, job interviews in English-speaking settings, or proficiency tests like the TOEFL (Test of English as a Foreign Language) or IELTS (International

E. Friginal et al., *Exploring Spoken English Learner Language Using Corpora*,
DOI 10.1007/978-3-319-59900-7_1

English Language Testing System), it is certainly useful and worthwhile to further investigate oral learner language systematically, and especially with corpora as part of the research methodology.

This book focuses on corpus-based analyses of learner oral production in university-level English or English as a Second Language (ESL) classrooms in the USA. Our overarching goal here is to provide an in-depth discussion and analysis of learner spoken language, with specific pedagogical impetus and applications. Our analyses highlight three specialized corpora collected for the three analytical parts of the book, explored using a range of corpus approaches and (mixed) methods: (1) learner (and also teacher) talk in the English for Academic Purposes (EAP) classroom; (2) learner talk in English language experience interviews; and (3) learner talk in peer response/feedback activities in the classroom. Pedagogical applications are discussed in each section and future directions in studying learner talk are provided in the concluding chapter (Chap. 14). A synthesis of corpus-based research of spoken learner language, list of available corpora and online databases, and an introduction to corpus linguistics and corpus tools and approaches are discussed in this first chapter of the book.

Studies of Spoken English Learner Language

Studies of spoken learner language are often situated in the field of Second Language Acquisition (SLA), with emphasis on the documentation and assessment of learner performance. For example, Ellis and Barkhuizen's (2005) *Analyzing Learner Language* highlighted the application of discourse and conversational analysis in exploring language learning as it takes place in interaction, but also covered the use of (written) learner corpora and contrastive analysis in SLA. In many experimental research settings, spoken learner language is evaluated from a variety of angles, focusing on the acquisition of L2 pronunciation and phonology; suprasegmental features of oral production; lexis and vocabulary development; and presentation, content, coherence, and delivery. Data are primarily extracted from audio and video recordings of real-world speech, transcriptions, and performance evaluations conducted by teachers. Learner speech in the classroom has also been measured according to quality and accuracy (e.g., accuracy of response to a teacher-initiated question), frequency of participation, conversational coherence, and usage and recall. Over the years, SLA research has produced meaningful data characterizing English learner speech across a range of speech events with clearly guided pedagogical implications.

The role of conversational interaction in SLA has been extensively studied utilizing a range of methodologies, most of them in experimental research settings. As briefly reviewed in some parts of this book, L2 learners' conversational interaction studies have been motivated by a few iterations of the interaction hypothesis from, for example, seminal works by Gass (1997), Long (1983, 1996), and especially Pica et al. (1989). As discussed by Saito and Akiyama (2017), the main focus of the hypothesis involves adult SLA which is facilitated and promoted through conversational interaction with NSs and NNSs. Such settings provide many opportunities for interactants to impact various aspects of conversation and the acquisition of conversational skills and competence. This is especially effective when interlocutors work together on negotiating and solving miscommunication.

The interaction–acquisition connection in spoken L2 has often been examined using a pretest–posttest design. With this approach, researchers are able to control various features of L2 interaction as independent variables and test their impact on L2 development (Plonsky and Gass 2011). In several studies, L2 learners improved their grammatical and lexical performance when given opportunities to negotiate meaning through interaction rather than through mere exposure to simplified input (Mackey 1999). Various opportunities for learners to respond to real-world questions, ask or clarify for comprehension, and engage extensively in the conversation have proven to be beneficial in improving oral production and performance in spoken tasks. Learners' "efficacy of interaction" also increased when they had sufficient proficiency with the target structures or if they had relatively high aptitude, especially when measured through working memory (Goo 2012). Other constructs such as pedagogically elaborated feedback (Sheen 2007), interlanguage development (Ziegler 2015) and specific location (e.g., laboratory vs. classroom settings) (Gass et al. 2005) have been explored in SLA, producing conclusive information underscoring the importance of conversational interaction on the acquisition of L2 spoken discourse features.

More recent studies of learner interaction (within experimental settings) have looked at video-based conversational interaction with a more longitudinal design. Saito and Akiyama (2017), for example, analyzed L2 production by college-level Japanese English-as-a-foreign-language (EFL) learners. Learners in the experimental group were asked to participate in weekly dyadic conversation with native speakers (NSs) in the USA. The NSs were trained to provide interactional feedback (recasts) when the Japanese learners' responses had comprehensibility issues. Learners in the comparison group received "regular" EFL instruction without any interaction with NSs. Saito and Akiyama's video data showed that the experimental group developed skills related to improving many linguistic domains of language, likely in response to their NS interlocutors' interactional feedback (recasts, negotiation) during the video-based interaction. The pretest–posttest data of the students' spontaneous production showed that they made significant gains in the dimensions of comprehensibility, fluency, and lexicogrammar but not in production areas such as accentedness and pronunciation.

Clearly, recorded data from this type of experiment may be further analyzed, and the texts compiled to form a corpus of conversational interaction. The corpus approach will provide additional insights into the linguistic characteristics of NNS and NS interaction that may add supporting evidence of the importance of conversational interaction and the unique linguistic features of interlanguage speech. What are the characteristic features of L2 negotiation? How are video-based interactions similar or different from face-to-face conversation (e.g., from a corpus of study groups or classroom feedback sessions)? Questions such as these may be answered by utilizing a corpus approach, given that parameters are already aligned to facilitate successful corpus compilation.

Studies of learner comprehension and how they modify speech (e.g., in providing comprehensible input) from repetitions, emphasizing slower speech rate, and the rephrasing of utterances with more frequent and simple words have all been examined in experiments, but these may also be analyzed from a comprehensive, well-developed corpus. From simple word counts to more advanced frequencies of reformulations, various corpus methods may also allow for distributions that can be used alongside test results. Corpora will further describe the linguistic features of L2 negotiation strategies (e.g., confirmation checks, clarification requests, recasts, or information packaging). These descriptions may be used to develop testing and teaching materials, and NNSs may also be induced to notice and understand the gap between their own L2 speech system and those of other learners, NSs, and their classroom instructors.

Finally, in addition to SLA, the related sub-fields of English for Specific Purposes (ESP) and, more specifically, English for Academic Purposes (EAP) have increasingly used corpora to systematically analyze and examine spoken learner language. Spoken texts (i.e., transcriptions of oral language) are carefully designed, with additional emphasis on quantity and representation of various associated registers. The corpus approach is limited, in that phonological features (segmental and supra-segmental features of speech) may not be directly included (and assessed) in the analysis. Up to this point, transcriptions of speech have been primarily verbatim, capturing word- and sentence-level features and distributions, for the most part. Although there are attempts at more in-depth annotation of spoken texts, the process to phonologically transcribe a corpus is still in its infancy.

Exploring Spoken English Learner Language Using Corpora

Corpus-based analysis of learner language has historically focused on written rather than spoken texts. Various collections of academic written language, from popular online databases, such as the Michigan Corpus of Upper-Level Student Papers (MICUSP), the British Academic Written English (BAWE), International Corpus of Learner English (ICLE) (and many other ICLE-inspired collections), and various learner written texts from corpora including the American National Corpus (ANC) and the Santa Barbara Corpus, have been widely used to compare registers of written L2 texts. Written corpora are certainly easier and less costly to compile, especially with the internet and advanced computational techniques. Corpus-based EAP research on written genres has flourished to a greater extent in the past few years than comparable research on spoken registers (Simpson-Vlach 2013).

Pioneering efforts to also focus sufficient attention on corpus-based analysis of spoken learner language, especially in English, have been initiated in the late 1990s and early 2000s. A recognition of the importance of spoken EAP corpora paved the way for the creation of the TOEFL 2000 Spoken and Written Academic Language (T2K-SWAL) Corpus (written and spoken texts combined), compiled by Douglas Biber and his colleagues at Northern Arizona University, Georgia State University, Iowa State University, and California State University, Sacramento (Biber et al. 2004). A corpus of academic speech, the Michigan Corpus of Academic Spoken English (MICASE), developed and collected by (applied) linguists from the University of Michigan (Simpson et al. 2002) focused exclusively on speech that represents oral language in a university setting (see the MICASE section in Chap. 2 for additional description of this corpus). Simpson-Vlach (2013) noted that:

> Prior to the development of spoken language corpora, the study and teaching of spoken academic language relied heavily on some combination of written academic discourse, conversational speech, or intuition to provide models of spoken language in academic contexts. With the availability of specialized corpora of academic speech, researchers and teachers gained access to resources that permit investigations of specific questions about grammar, lexis, usage, and discourse patterns as these actually occur in spoken academic contexts. These research inquiries have begun to fill in the gaps in our knowledge about the characteristics of academic speech as a specialized language genre. Results from such investigations are of interest to both applied linguists generally as well as EAP teachers and materials writers who can use such insights to better inform their teaching and materials development. A judiciously sampled spoken academic corpus constitutes a valuable research resource and set of models characterizing the spoken language that students will encounter and need to produce in the course of their academic endeavors. (p. 453)

Both MICASE and T2K-SWAL include L2 speech, especially from learner presentations and study groups, but these corpora of spoken academic texts focus more on spoken language in academia in general than upon an in-depth learner oral production. L2 speech is tangentially represented and can be extracted, but may still be limited when it comes to fully illustrating a learner-centered speech event in US universities. The advantage in using MICASE and T2K-SWAL is that both corpora include a wide range of speech events from classroom lectures (primarily on teacher-led lectures and discussions), laboratory sessions, tutorials, advising sessions, research interviews, dissertation defenses, public colloquia, meetings, and academic service encounters. As Simpson-Vlach (2013) argued, these spoken academic corpora are valuable collections of previously unavailable data that constitute an important resource for EAP and corpus practitioners. Nevertheless, within the larger world of corpus-based research, SLA, and ESL in the classroom, these seminal corpora are still relatively limited as far as how comprehensively they represent L2 speech.

There have been encouraging and important additions to MICASE and T2K-SWAL, with specialized collections targeting very specific groups of learners and sub-registers (e.g., interviews, computer-mediated communication, and peer response). It appears that the trend is to continue exploring learner talk through very specialized corpora and register-centered analysis. For example, Oral Proficiency Interviews (OPIs), which are widely used to measure speaking ability in a second or foreign language, are also now being explored using data from, for example, The Michigan English Language Assessment Battery (MELAB) speaking assessment (which is an OPI used for academic and professional purposes around the world). A study by Staples et al. (2017) shows that the MELAB has similarities with conversation in its use of stance and is closely aligned with academic registers and nurse–patient interactions in the use of language for informational exchange.

Overall, texts in these corpora, especially those collected in the classroom, are still comparatively restricted in number of speakers and total number of words, but more qualitative evidence may be utilized from accompanying audio/video files and researcher data (e.g., teacher observation reports, test results, student papers/reflections). Triangulating corpus-based distributions with results from qualitative data sources may produce meaningful results and relevant pedagogical implications. In this book, Parts II (learner talk in the classroom), III (learner talk in English language experience interviews), and IV (learner talk in peer response/feedback activities) all utilize specialized corpora that highlight, more than other collections of learner language, L2 speech in use within a very specific language teaching and learning contexts. The numbers, overall, are still low and could be beneficially increased in future related studies, but we present a clear model of corpus-based analysis (including semantic and psychosocial analytical constructs), with results that are descriptive of the register and potentially useful in aiding L2 spoken pedagogy.

Corpus Linguistics: A Brief Introduction

Corpus linguistics, primarily a *research approach* in the study of spoken and written texts, has evolved over a few decades to support empirical investigations of naturally occurring language-in-use. From (macro) collections of millions of texts to very specialized (micro) corpora, the corpus approach has been instrumental in providing in-depth descriptions of the linguistic characteristics of spoken and written discourse. Biber et al. (2010) emphasize that corpus linguistics is not, in itself, a model of language but a methodological approach that can be characterized as follows:

- It is empirical, analyzing the actual patterns of use in natural texts
- It utilizes a large and principled collection of natural texts, known as a *corpus* (pl. *corpora*), as the basis for analysis
- It makes extensive use of computers for analysis, employing both automatic and interactive techniques
- It relies on the combination of quantitative and qualitative analytical techniques.

Corpus-based researchers argue that language use is systematic and can be extensively described using empirical, quantitative, and frequency-based methods (Biber 1988). Corpora and corpus-based research provide extensive numerical data, but these will then have to be functionally interpreted meaningfully and accurately. Biber, as cited in Friginal

(2013), notes that quantitative patterns discovered through corpus analysis should always be subsequently interpreted in functional terms. Clearly, these patterns of linguistic variation exist because they reflect underlying functional differences. With corpus data, then, descriptions of written and oral production of L2 learners in the classroom may have greater generalizability and validity, producing a range of supporting evidence that could be further examined in research settings. Results and interpretations of these findings may be used to inform pedagogy—the creation of learning and teaching materials and L2 teaching lessons utilizing corpus tools.

What Is a *Corpus*?

> " … a corpus is a large and principled collection of natural texts." (Biber et al. 1998, p. 12)

> "A corpus is a collection of pieces of language text in electronic form, selected according to external criteria to represent, as far as possible, a language or language variety as a source of data for linguistic research." (Sinclair 2005)

> "… a corpus is a collection of (1) machine readable (2) authentic texts (including transcripts of spoken data) which is (3) sampled to be (4) representative of a particular language or language variety." (McEnery et al. 2006, p. 5)

> "Corpora may encode language produced in any mode—for example, there are corpora of spoken language and there are corpora of written language. In addition, some video corpora record paralinguistic features such as gesture (Knight et al. 2009) and corpora of sign language have been constructed (Johnston and Schembri 2006; Crashborn 2008)." (McEnery and Hardie 2012, p. 3)

> " … is a collection of spoken or written texts to be used for linguistic analysis and based on a specific set of design criteria influenced by its purpose and scope." (Weisser 2016, p. 13)

From the definitions above, a *corpus* (Latin, "body," *corpora*, plural) can be briefly defined as a **systematically designed electronic collection of naturally occurring *texts*.** The word text, as used in corpus-based research, is not limited to describing language that was initially written. Hence, a text can also be a transcription of spoken language. Even in the age of computers, the transcription of speech is still quite labor-intensive. Capturing various features of spoken language (e.g., dysfluent markers, repeats and reformulations, overlaps and backchannels, and many others) may require extensive hand coding and annotation. Although there have been recent advancements in dictation tools and "speech to text" technology (similar to the technology used in subtitles and close captioning on live television), the transcription of spoken data, especially by teachers and student researchers, is still primarily conducted manually.

A corpus is, by definition, computerized, stored electronically, and searchable by computer programs. Corpora and corpus approaches in the study of speech patterns may offer relevant options to search for a wide variety of data on vocabulary use, commonly used markers, and potential errors as they occur in transcripts. The advantage of creating spoken corpora is that they can be designed with a purpose. Researchers compile corpora and search for existing constructs or speech patterns which are identified as relevant and measurable. A corpus provides the opportunity to measure tendencies and distributions across registers and genres of speech. For example, if a lexicographer is interested in the use of oral respect markers (e.g., use of *sir* or *ma'am*, use of titles—*Dr. Williams, Atty. Johnson*) in task-based interaction by a particular group of people, he or she may construct a corpus of naturally occurring speech from speakers of the target group. If the corpus is **representative** of that group, the researcher can find the distributions of these respect markers and describe the tendencies of those patterns (Friginal and Hardy 2014).

An important distinction among corpora is the number of groups (e.g., native vs. non-native speakers, advanced L2 vs. beginning level learners) and types of language production they are designed to represent. Corpora can, therefore, be constructed to reflect the language used by very large groups of people or learners, or researchers may focus on a particular type of language user or classroom situation. Most large-scale corpora (i.e., **general** corpora) such as those representing national varieties of English (e.g., British English from the British National Corpus or BNC) contain millions of words and texts representing a range of spoken and written registers. In the early 1980s, a corpus of 1 million words was considered large (e.g., seminal corpora such as Brown and LOB corpora both had 1 million total words). In comparison, today, there are corpora of hundreds of millions of words. The size of the corpus does not necessarily make it a general (or reference) corpus. It is, instead, the inclusion and distribution of multiple registers and groups of speakers and writers that does. Note that while the Brown and LOB included many registers of English, they crucially lacked spoken language. If the goal of a corpus is to attempt to represent the language as a whole, it must also necessarily include samples of texts transcribed from speech. The BNC's latest edition is made up of nearly 97 million orthographic words, but only about 10 percent of this corpus is from spoken data, primarily because of the enormous time and manpower needed to record and transcribe naturally occurring speech. A variety of forms of written language, such as books, newspapers, and advertisements were included in the BNC to give the sample breadth across genres. The BNC's spoken texts include multiple types of speaking from education, business, public life, and leisure from three geographical regions in Great Britain (2.64% of the spoken texts came from speakers of unknown location) (Friginal and Hardy 2014).

Another popular general corpus is the Corpus of Contemporary American English (COCA). COCA is a database of more than 450 million words and is readily searchable online (http://corpus.byu.edu/coca). Mark Davies of Brigham Young University designed and developed COCA as well as his other collections including COHA (Corpus of Historical American English) and the 1.9-billion-word GloWbE (Corpus of Web-Based Global English). These freely available corpora are great resources for register-based research in contemporary and historical American English, and in the case of GloWbE, varieties of English collected from the global internet. However, spoken registers are also still not well represented in these collections. For example, COCA separates groups of texts "representing" spoken data, but these are limited to television interview transcripts (e.g., interviews from talk shows like the *Oprah Show*) and news reports. Clearly, the pattern here is that recording and transcribing speech samples may not be comprehensively represented, even in large-scale and highly regarded general collections.

For the most part, classroom-based research data may come from a limited number of sources whose context is as important to describe as the larger language domain itself. Data that have been collected in this more focused, individualized setting may allow the researcher to more clearly understand the discourse domain and target group (or groups) of speakers and writers. In corpus linguistics, this dataset is referred to as **specialized corpus**. Specialized spoken corpora like MICASE and T2K-SWAL are large enough to provide opportunities for statistical computations of significance, but are still relatively small in overall size, especially with their total number of words, text files, and registers.

Specialized spoken corpora collected from classrooms provide teachers and researchers the ability to control for many more variables to study and include in the analysis. These are designed to represent a particular register (e.g., lecture vs. small group discussion), domain, or variety of the language. This is useful especially when moving from the analysis of results to the discussion of 'generalizing' towards a bigger population, after further analysis. Overall, this is a question of scope. What is being investigated? What spoken texts are included? What are teacher and learner backgrounds? These are interesting questions, but they may be very difficult to answer as it would be problematic to collect a spoken corpus that includes an equal **representation** of all classroom talk from multiple geographic areas, groups of learners, and classroom tasks. Not only would such a corpus be difficult to collect, but also if all relevant variables are not represented in the corpus, the researcher would be unable to make valid generalizations based on his results to the population as a whole. Instead, a narrowing of scope may be necessary to ask a realistic and specific set of questions (Friginal and Hardy 2014). The classroom-based and learner interview corpora we analyze in this book are very specialized and could still be further redesigned and developed to include other settings and groups of learners and teachers. Interview questions, language activities (in the classroom and peer response activities), and other learner demographics may be added to fully represent classroom talk in US universities.

A Brief Historical Overview of Corpus Linguistics

The following is a brief historical overview of corpus linguistics adapted and synthesized from Friginal and Hardy's *Corpus-Based Sociolinguistics: A Guide for Students* (Routledge, 2014) and Biber, Reppen, and Friginal's 'Research in Corpus Linguistics' from the *Oxford Handbook of Applied Linguistics* (Oxford University Press, 2010):

The focus on collecting naturally occurring texts has been essential in corpus linguistics and recognized as an important methodological approach. Some may think that corpus-based research emerged only in the 1980s and 1990s, along with developments in desktop computing technology (Biber et al. 1998). In fact, the standard practice in language research up until the 1950s was to base language descriptions on analyses of collections of natural texts from those collected by ethnographers and field linguists. Many of these collected text samples have been used to describe the structure of languages and produce dictionaries. Dictionaries have been primarily based on the analysis of word use in natural utterances taken from interviews with speakers representing a particular dialect region. For example, the *Oxford English Dictionary*, which was published in 1928, was based on around 5,000,000 citations from natural texts (totaling approximately 50 million words), compiled by over 2,000 volunteers for more than a 70-year period. Samuel Johnson's *Dictionary of the English Language*, published in 1755, was developed from a collection of 150,000 natural sentences written on slips of papers to illustrate the natural usage of words (Biber et al. 2010).

Pre-electronic corpora of texts such as newspaper writing, short stories, and academic essays were collected to study vocabulary use empirically and also to inform grammar studies and grammar teaching in English. Influential grammar books used actual sentences taken from novels and newspapers to show various structures of formal, grammatically correct sentences and syntactic items such as verb phrases and clauses. In the 1960s and 1970s, most research in linguistics moved to what Biber (1988) referred to as *intuition-based methods* (i.e., intuition vs. empirical analysis in research), which maintained that language was a mental construct and that empirical analyses of corpora were not relevant for describing language competence. Nevertheless, some linguists continued to believe in the utility and validity of empirical linguistic analysis.

Work on large electronic corpora had actually begun in the 1960s with Kučera and Francis' (1967) compilation of the **Brown Corpus**, a 1 million word corpus of published American English written texts. The Brown Corpus (or in full, The Brown University Standard Corpus of Present-Day American English) was collected to catalogue a wide variety of types of American English, all of which were written in 1961. A total of 500 samples of approximately 2000 words each were collected for this project, coming from 15 different genres. News, religious texts, biographies, official documents, academic prose, humor, and various styles of fiction were included (see Kučera and Francis 1967). A parallel corpus of British English written texts, the **LOB Corpus** (London-Oslo-Bergen also *Lancaster*-Oslo-Bergen), followed in the 1970s.

Major studies of language use based on large electronic corpora did not begin to appear, however, until the 1980s, when these corpora became more accessible as a result of the increasing availability of computational tools to facilitate linguistic analysis. For example, in 1982, Francis and Kučera provided a frequency analysis of the words and grammatical part-of-speech categories found in the Brown Corpus. Johansson and Hofland (1989) followed with a similar analysis of the LOB Corpus. Also during this period, book-length descriptive studies of linguistic features began to appear, e.g., Granger (1983) on passives; de Haan (1989) on nominal post-modifiers; and the first multi-dimensional studies of register variation, e.g., Biber (1988). This period also saw the emergence of English language learner dictionaries such as the Collins CoBuild English Language Dictionary (1987) and the Longman Dictionary of Contemporary English (1987), which were based on the analysis of large electronic corpora. Since the 1980s, most descriptive studies of linguistic variation in and usage of English have utilized analyses of electronic corpora, either a large, standard corpus such as the British National Corpus (BNC), or a smaller, study-specific corpus such as a corpus of 20 biology research articles constructed for a genre analysis.

Collecting and Analyzing Large-Scale Spoken Corpora

Most analyses of spoken corpora, in general, have come from sociolinguistic studies of interactions. For example, Sali A. Tagliamonte from the University of Toronto follows a tradition of recording and transcribing spoken data from groups of interactants in comfortable, unmonitored speech. Her focus is on capturing real language-in-use, or the kind of language style that speakers use when paying minimal attention to how they are speaking. This type of language, known as the **vernacular** in sociolinguistics, is important because it offers insight into the baseline, real-world style for speakers (Friginal and Hardy 2014). This model is also very useful in classroom-based research of spoken learner language, ensuring that learners (especially NNSs) engaged in various learning situations are recorded in actual stages of oral production. Learners' responses to teacher questions, their minimal responses to each other in small group activities, and reformulations of phrases and sentences provide important variable data for detailed analysis. In Tagliamonte's model, more identified components defining the spoken corpus are considered. The components of Tagliamonte's (2006) variationist research are: (1) recording media, audio-tapes (analogue, digital, or other formats), (2) interview reports (hard copies) and signed consent forms, (3) transcription files (ASCII, Word, .txt), (4) a transcription protocol (hard copy and soft copy), (5) a database of information (FileMaker, Excel, etc.), and (6) analysis files (Goldvarb files, token, cel, cnd, and res).

Allowing for multiple data points for each participant is important in recording classroom interactions. Having a carefully defined and efficient system for retrieving and connecting data will certainly help during the interpretive stages of corpus-based analysis. After processing the transcripts for linguistic distributions, the ability to return to the audio (or video, if available) files to confirm observations or make correlations with learner information is vital in formulating conclusions and implications. In SLA studies, recall activities, delayed post-tests, and student reflections are added to triangulate data. Teacher impressions (e.g., through journals or annotated lesson plans) may also provide important confirmatory materials relative to corpus-based distributions.

The Santa Barbara Corpus of Spoken American English (SBCSAE) consists of various speech events, including face-to-face conversation, sermons, telephone conversations, and discourse from tour guides. The SBCSAE is relatively large (with almost a quarter million words) and has been used in various comparisons of large-scale register variation studies (e.g., comparing US vs. British English from the BNC). Other spoken English corpora are recorded and transcribed from workplace settings. As noted previously, these projects are often with the sub-field of English for Specific Purposes (ESP), and, specifically, the English for Occupational Purposes (EOP). Workplace interactions in New Zealand were identified as target context for the Wellington Corpus of Spoken New Zealand English (WSC), containing multiple types of speech events with over 1 million words and counting. The WSC is well balanced, consisting of news monologues, sports commentary, judicial summaries, lectures, conversations, telephone conversations, interviews, radio conversations, political debate, and meetings. This corpus was also annotated for variables frequently studied in ESP/EOP and sociolinguistics. For example, gender, ethnicity, and age are speaker variables included in the corpus (Friginal and Hardy 2014; Vine 2016). Related to the WSC is the Language in the Workplace (LWP) corpus which has been analyzed specifically to explore cross-cultural pragmatics, speakers' gender and ethnicity and language use in the workplace, humor, small talk, and speech acts, e.g., directives from multiple discourse perspectives (Holmes 2006; Marra 2012; Stubbe et al. 2003; Vine 2009). Two recent studies by Vine (2016, forthcoming) using the LWP explore the use of the pragmatic markers *you know, eh*, and *I think*; and *actually, just*, and *probably* in office-based interactions using a theory of cultural dimensions (Hofstede 2001) to locate New Zealand workplaces on a continuum of power and formality (from informal conversations to formal unscripted monologues). Other well-known corpora of spoken workplace discourse include:

- AAC and Non-AAC User Workplace Corpus (ANAWC): ANAWC (Pickering and Bruce 2009) is a highly specialized corpus representing machine-based language production from users of Augmentative and

Alternative Communication (AAC) devices in the workplace their non-AAC counterparts. This corpus is annotated for communicative items such as pauses and wait times, small talk markers, POS-tags, and transitions/overlaps. Participants in eight target workplaces in the USA were given voice-activated recorders to be used for a full week of data collection, capturing a range of workplace events. The ANAWC broadly interprets the definition of office-based settings, and recordings range from IT offices to warehouse floors (Friginal et al. 2016).

- American and British Office Talk Corpus (ABOT): ABOT comprises primary "informal, unplanned workplace interactions between co-workers in office settings" (Koester 2010, p. 13). Koester has taken a primarily discourse approach to corpus-based analysis, investigating the performance of communicative functions in the workplace using speech acts and relational sequences ("transactional-plus-relational talk") using conversation analysis.
- Call Center Interaction Corpus: This corpus (Friginal 2008–2013) has over 400 transcribed telephone conversations (N of words = 346,789) provided by an outsourced call center located in the Philippines serving callers based in the USA. This corpus has, in part, been used in a variety of other research and has appeared in publications such as Friginal (2009, 2013). Transcriptions details include agent and caller turns, markers of dysfluencies, and some minor pausing and overlapping indicators. Details about the agents, including gender, length of experience with the company, and an overall in-house quality rating for each agent were included with the corpus.
- The Cambridge and Nottingham Business English Corpus (CANBEC): CANBEC is a 1-million word sub-corpus of the Cambridge English Corpus (CEC) covering a range of business settings from large companies to small firms and both transactional (e.g., formal meetings and presentations) and interactional (e.g., lunchtime or coffee room conversations) language events. Some studies using the CANBEC have focused on the distribution of multi-word units and discursive practices in business meetings (McCarthy and Handford 2004; Handford 2010).
- The Hong Kong Corpus of Spoken English (prosodic) (HKCSE): HKCSE was collected between 1997 and 2002 and includes a

sub-corpus of business English of approximately 250,000 words (Cheng et al. 2008; Warren 2004). The HKCSE contains various types of formal and informal office talk, service encounters in hotels, business presentations and conference calls. As a cross-cultural corpus, the two main cultural groups communicating in many of the workplaces are Chinese speakers from Hong Kong and native and non-native English speakers from many different countries. The HKCSE is unique in that it is transcribed for prosodic features using Brazil's (1985/1997) model of discourse intonation. A concordancing program—iConc—was specifically developed for the corpus and allows quantitative analyses of intonational features (Cheng et al. 2006).

- Various Corpora of Health Care Interactions: There are many specialized corpora of spoken interactions in health care collected to examine the differences in the use of particular lexicogrammatical features across settings such as doctor-patient interactions in primary care settings and simulated nurse-patient interactions in a hospital setting (Staples 2015). Staples (2015, 2016), for example, investigated the frequency and function of interactive features (e.g., pronouns and conditionals), narrative features (e.g., past tense), and stance features (e.g., modals and stance adverbs) in health care interactions. She found that, in part, the differences in roles (doctor vs. patient) and settings (primary care clinic vs. hospital) were reflected in the frequency and function of linguistic features used by interactants. Doctors use more *wh*-questions to open the encounter (e.g., *so, what can we do for you today?*) while nurses use a balance of *wh-* and *yes/no* questions (e.g., *are you still having chest pain?*).

Corpus Tools

Analyses of corpora can be accomplished using relatively simple (some are free), yet powerful, computer programs. These include **concordancers** such as *AntConc 3.4.3* (Anthony 2014) *WordSmith Tools 6* (Scott 2012), and *MonoConc Pro* (Barlow 2012). Concordancers are programs that can extract words (or key words) as they appear in the corpus. Their frequencies can be easily obtained and the contexts within which these words are used can also be collected by taking words that appear before and after these key words in the corpus (known as Key Word in Context or **KWIC**). Advanced corpus researchers and computational linguists may need to use very specialized computer programs designed to extract particularly unique patterns that are not provided by concordancers.

The freeware *AntConc* is a concordancer that works with Windows, Mac, and Linux operating systems created and maintained by Laurence Anthony at Waseda University in Japan. With a relatively easy-to-use interface, *AntConc* is a good tool for beginners. In addition, there are many video tutorials on how to use the various functions of the program. It is important to know that *AntConc* does not house a corpus. Instead, users will have to upload files into the program to be analyzed.

Taggers/Parsers: The Biber Tagger, Sketch Engine, CLAWS, LIWC

- **The Biber Tagger** is a POS-tagger created by Douglas Biber from Northern Arizona University, which combines computerized dictionaries with the identification of word sequences as instances of a linguistic feature (e.g., noun + WH pronoun and not preceded by the verb *tell* or *say* = "relative clause") (Biber 1988). There are over 150 POS-tagged categories in this tagger's output which includes grammatical and some syntactic elements. Tag accuracy is around 95 percent for written texts. Accuracy goes down a little bit for spoken text, especially those that are not consistently transcribed. Unfortunately, access is an issue with this tool, since the Biber Tagger is not commercially available or accessible online. However, researchers may contact The Corpus Linguistics Research Program at Northern Arizona University for information about corpus tagging and analysis using the Biber Tagger.
- **Coh-Metrix** is a sophisticated computational/corpus tool that rates readability and also provides frequency counts for a range of linguistic aspects such as Descriptive, Connectives, Syntactic Pattern Density, Word Information, and Readability sections. The Coh-Metrix tagset is generally similar to the Biber Tagger, with additional features focusing on lexical diversity and specificity markers. Data and related research

from Coh-Metrix, including contact information for potential tagging requests, are located at: http://cohmetrix.memphis.edu/cohmetrixpr/index.html.

- **The Constituent Likelihood Automatic Word-tagging System (CLAWS)** is a POS-tagger that was used to tag the BNC and is available for user licenses as well as copies for single sites. CLAWS has over 160 different POS- and semantic tags (current version: CLAWS7) developed by the University Centre for Computer Corpus Research on Language (UCREL). The CLAWS team from Lancaster University offers tagging services, and charges depending on the amount of text being tagged (http://ucrel.lancs.ac.uk/claws). This program has consistently achieved 96–97% accuracy which may vary based on the type of text or transcription convention.
- **The Linguistic Inquiry and Word Count** (LIWC, pronounced *Luke*) (Pennebaker et al. 2007) utilizes a dictionary with 80 preset categories in order to analyze the linguistic composition of texts. The output includes linguistic dimensions (e.g., percentage of words in the text that are pronouns, articles, auxiliary verbs, etc.), word categories tapping psychological constructs (e.g., affect, cognition, biological processes), personal concern categories (e.g., work, home, leisure activities), paralinguistic dimensions (e.g., assents, fillers, nonfluencies), and punctuation categories (periods, commas, etc.). LIWC is available for purchase (http://www.liwc.net/). See Part III, Chaps. 9 and 10 for our two LIWC-based studies.
- **Sketch Engine** is a new addition to the growing number of onlinecorpus tools that uses multi-billion word samples of authentic corpora to provide linguistic data on POS features, grammatical categories (e.g., singular/plural, present/past, passive verbs),collocations, andconcordances. The database contains 400 'ready-to-use corpora' in 80 different languages, each with a size of up to 20 billion words. Sketch Engine users can create their own corpora by allowing the tool to find and download relevant texts online or by uploading their own corpus. A free 30-day access is available, but a monthly charge is required for regular users. [See pricing information here: https://www.sketchengine.co.uk/price-list]

- **The Stanford Parser** and the **Stanford Tagger** (http://nlp.stanford.edu/software/lex-parser.shtml) may also be used to obtain POS-tagged data, although the current tagsets for these tools are limited to primary POS counts of 30–40 linguistic features (e.g., nouns, verbs, modal verbs, prepositions).
- **Wmatrix** is a tagging program designed to grammatically and semantically tag corpora from Lancaster University (Rayson 2003, 2008) (http://ucrel.lancs.ac.uk/wmatrix). This tool combines the CLAWS tagger and a semantic annotation system. Many recent studies have been conducted using this program because of its extensive tagset and accessibility.
- **Various Manual 'Tagging' Software:** Manual coding and annotations of classroom texts may be required in highly specialized collections that focus more on individual features that are difficult to automatically extract. Coding software tools typically used for qualitative analysis may also be used in corpus-based research to synthesize coded themes or categories together with text samples. ATLAS.ti (http://www.atlasti.com/index.html) and NVivo (http://www.nvivo10.com) are two coding software packages that incorporate corpus technology for qualitative research.

Linguistic Analysis of Corpora

The following sub-sections provide a brief discussion of common linguistic constructs typically investigated using corpora, software tools, and corpus-based techniques. These constructs can all be applied to examine data from L2 spoken discourse in the classroom, especially when comparing a range of variables from well-designed corpora with a variety of speakers (teachers and learners) and learning contexts.

Frequency

Determining the frequency of linguistic items from corpora is one of the most basic types of analysis in corpus-based research. Questions such as *what words are the most frequently used in a language (or a particular setting)* or *what are the top 100 most common verbs spoken by learners in the classroom* are easy to extract from corpora. The former simply requires running the wordlist function of a software like *AntConc*, and the latter will require a corpus that is tagged or annotated for part-of-speech (POS), i.e., the researcher will have to utilize a POS-tagger to obtain the frequency of most common nouns in the corpus. Frequency is important for teachers in describing the features of language varieties (including academic language) and also in determining what to focus on when considering how to teach vocabulary or grammatical features. Popular wordlists such as Coxhead's (2000, 2011) or Nation's (2001) "Academic Word Lists" have been used in developing teaching and learning materials for students in many academic writing/speaking classes.

Biber (2006a) noted that although most ESP/EAP studies have focused on written academic discourse, more recently, researchers have also turned their attention to university classroom discourse and combined frequencies of various linguistic features. In addition to individual counts and frequency distributions (e.g., counts for how many pronouns, *okay*, or *however*), exploring the distribution of functional features, such as the study of stance and evaluation, informational discourse, and hedging in speech has provided relevant results for comparison across academic registers. For example, MICASE has been used to extract and examine the uses of *kind of* and *sort of* as hedges (Poos and Simpson 2002); the functions of *just* for metadiscourse and hedging (Lindemann and Mauranen 2001); the functions of evaluative adjectives and intensifiers (Swales and Burke 2003); and the expression of evaluation and other kinds of metadiscourse (Mauranen 2003) (see Chaps. 3, 4, 5, and 6 for a related discussion of these features).

Concordances and KWIC

Computer-based concordances are now frequently used in many academic settings to show real-world vocabulary usage especially in teaching and research areas (e.g., data-driven learning). The traditional concordance with which most are familiar is a reference book comprised of an alphabetical listing of all significant content words in the source material, excluding grammatical and functional words (e.g., prepositions, articles, adverbial phrases). This alphabetized index of primary words from the source text is accompanied by a secondary list of words that co-occur before or after the primary word elsewhere in the text. The concordance can, therefore, show the typical contextual meaning(s) of each word as it is used in the material. In the pre-computer era, concordances were created manually by scholars of the Bible, the Qu'ran, and other important historical and religious documents. For example, teaching or study versions of the Bible may contain concordances as featured appendices or footnotes. Editions with concordances of early literary works, such as those by Socrates, Homer, and Shakespeare, enable easier cross-indexing of relevant terms, unique words, and repetition of word usage. These concordances help identify key words and, very importantly, define the specific nuances and semantic meanings intended by the authors in the various, particular contexts. Additional author commentaries, biographer footnotes, and editor narratives are also often provided in these concordances (Friginal 2015).

Concordances from digital text files, which could represent shared meanings from groups of speakers (and writers), contribute comparative qualitative and quantitative data about the actual language used by these individuals. Concordances can be extracted primarily to identify the different usage and frequency of a content word; examine word collocations; explore the distribution of key terms and phrases; and create a list of multi-word units, lexical bundles (or N-grams), and word frames (see the sections below). These additional features can be produced immediately from *AntConc*, and resulting concordance lines can be saved for extended qualitative coding and analyses. A cross-comparison of these concordances and their distributions across groups of speakers/writers may be invaluable in intercultural communication research. Text Sample 1.1 shows KWIC lines for *I think* from small group discussions (study groups) in the T2K-SWAL corpus.

Text Sample 1.1. Concordance Lines for *I think* in Study Groups

1	...yeah, all right, yeah, the,	**I think** that's the topic I'm interested in or I'd like to
2	special about this country, is	**I think** is that got to hate the the Spanish and
3	... and this was it <laughs>	I don't **think** so cos we are not very close friends now
4	yes yes <stops laughing>	**I think** I am ready but (erm). the first association the
5	es she know what, oh no, no	I don't **think** so cos she is (erm) ... she is disappointed
6	<overlap> doesn't like it, it,	**I think** so yes is it okay if I consider that as a
7	(mhm) eight years ago	**I think** and it was my first going to a Protestant
8	well I don't know that ...	**I think** (eh) . it has been . it has somewhat calmed
9	down for the last two years	**I think** it's a good sign but .. still I do not know
10	in terms of her hairstyle	**I think** . and probably of her dress also well well it's

Collocations

Firth (1957) has influenced the way linguists examine discrete elements such as words and phrases that often co-occur across a range of datasets. Instead of seeing these units as independent from rules and other words, Firth famously wrote, "You shall know a word by the context it keeps" (p. 11) (Friginal and Hardy 2014). The corpus approach allows for the determination of the statistical significance of word combinations (i.e., word collocations) and how these combinations are distributed across registers. Collocations can also be found using more objective measurements from statistical results obtained from reference corpora. Prediction models of what might follow or precede a word, a noun, or a verb can be measured based on their expected frequencies.

AntConc's first left and first right collocations for the word *know* is provided in Table 1.1 from a spoken American English conversation corpus. The distributions here are based on the transcription conventions of the corpus. The top right collocate of know is "s," which, in the corpus

Table 1.1 Collocations of the word *know* (first left and first right)

Rank	Freq	Freq (Left)	Freq (Right)	Collocate
1	245	6	239	['s]
2	239	0	0	let
3	22	22	0	okay
4	19	19	0	well
5	13	13	0	[unclear]
6	9	9	0	uh
7	8	8	0	yeah
8	7	7	0	now
9	6	6	0	so
10	6	6	0	say
11	6	6	0	and
12	5	5	0	oh
13	5	5	0	[laugh]
14	5	5	0	is
15	4	4	0	um

indicated an end of turn (e.g., "I know <s>"). These sequences appeared in the corpus 239 times. Features of speech such as discourse markers (*okay, well, so*), short responses (*yeah*), filled pauses (*uh, um*), and transcription features (unclear, laugh) were top collocates of *know* in spoken interactions.

Keyword Analysis

Keyness draws from word frequency data, but instead of descriptive statistics as in numerical frequencies or averages, inferential statistics is used to determine if a word is more or less likely to occur in one corpus versus another. Specifically, a keyword analysis identifies significant differences in the distribution of words used by speakers or writers between two groups of texts or two corpora. Scott (1997) defines a keyword as "a word which occurs with unusual frequency in a given text" (p. 236). This "unusual frequency" is based on the likelihood of occurrence of the word in a target corpus from a process called cross-tabulation. Comparisons provide an interesting look at the unique features of one type of discourse, language variety, or register compared to another. Keywords can be extracted easily using *AntConc* and *WordSmith Tools*.

Barbieri's (2008) keyword analysis compared two sub-corpora comparing younger and older speakers from an American Conversation corpus from the Longman Corpus of Spoken and Written English. The two sub-corpora were of relatively similar sizes: the Younger Corpus had 195,400 words, while the Older Corpus has a total of 204,200 words. These sub-corpora comprised conversations from 139 speakers: 85 speakers aged 15–25 (46 males and 39 females) and 54 speakers aged 35–60 (17 males and 37 females) from approximately 57 hours of conversation. Barbieri analyzed up to 450 words from two keyword lists: one generated using the Younger Corpus as main corpus and the Older Corpus as comparison corpus, and vice versa. Listed below are the first 20 keywords from the Younger Corpus (target) compared to the Older Corpus (reference corpus):

1.	like	11.	m
2.	unclear*	12.	really
3.	you	13.	I
4.	fucking	14.	cool
5.	um	15.	Wayne
6.	mhm	16.	shit
7.	Ayesha	17.	right
8.	man	18.	no
9.	dude	19.	fucked
10.	fuck	20.	totally

*unclear refers to the use of words in the transcript that was undecipherable. Barbieri implied that, based on this outstanding number of words which were unclear to the transcribers, younger speakers' talk may be faster or more "dysfluent" than older speakers' speech

The list of keywords from the two groups was then used as a springboard for more detailed qualitative comparisons of lexical features of age-based variation. In summary, Barbieri's (2008) qualitative analyses showed that, based on outstanding keywords, younger speakers favored the adverbs *totally*, *really*, and *seriously*, all of which were adverbs of degree that intensified intended meanings. This finding suggested that intensifier use varied across age groups. Other significant age-based differences were found to include the use of personal pronouns, modal verbs, quotative verbs, attitudinal adjectives, stance adverbs, inserts and discourse markers, and slang.

Multi-word Units (MWU)

As with collocations, some words frequently co-occur as linear, formulaic strings, like a prefabricated "chunk" of language. MWUs cover a range of studies on extended strings of language, and there are various ways and operationalizations (including definition of terms) to explore this construct of formulaic language using corpus tools. Three of the commonly used approaches to MWUs are n-grams, lexical bundles, and p-frames.

- **N-grams:** The most basic construct associated with MWUs is that of the **n-gram**. The N stands for any number variable (e.g., 4-gram = *on the other hand*). N-grams can also be extracted using most basic corpus packages—both *AntConc* and *WordSmith Tools 6* have commands for n-gram extraction. Table 1.2 shows a comparison of the 20 most common 4-grams from call-takers and callers from a corpus of spoken telephone-based interaction in business call centers (Friginal 2013).

Table 1.2 Comparison of the most common 4-grams in call-taker and caller interaction in business call centers

Rank	Frequency (Call-takers)	Call-takers' 4-word units (4-grams)	Frequency (Callers)	Callers' 4-word units (4-grams)
1	543	*thank you for calling*	337	*I don't know*
2	227	*may I help you*	141	*I don't have*
4	178	*how may I help*	95	*I'm trying to*
5	156	*can I help you*	80	*you want me to*
6	153	*let me just check*	79	*don't know if*
7	151	*thank you so much*	74	*don't know what*
8	145	*may I have your*	71	*I don't think*
9	141	*how can I help*	67	*that's what I*
10	138	*can I have your*	67	*uh I don't*
12	128	*thank you very much*	60	*thank you very much*
13	125	*I help you today*	48	*I'm not sure*
14	118	*put you on hold*	45	*and I don't*
15	118	*you so much for*	41	*do you want me*
16	116	*first and last name*	39	*don't have a*
18	106	*your first and last*	37	*I don't see*
19	103	*I please have your*	35	*you know what I*
20	100	*may I please have*	33	*I'm sorry I*

- **Lexical bundles:** Lexical bundles are a type of N-grams, but there are additional specifications as to how they are extracted or categorized. Traditionally, lexical bundles consist of at least three words (tri-grams) that occur frequently across a corpus of at least 1 million words. This is determined by a count per one million words. The frequency, however, can be determined by the researcher. Another important criterion for labeling MWUs as lexical bundles is that they surface in at least five different texts in the corpus (i.e., they are common in other registers as well). This is necessary to avoid any idiosyncratic language usages (Cortes 2004).
- **P-frames**: Researchers have also moved beyond looking only at uninterrupted strings of language to also examine frequent, patterned constructions. P-frames are phraseological structures that allow for variability in one position of the phrase frame. An example of a p-frame, found by Römer (2010), is *it would be * to*, in which the asterisk represents an open slot. Grammatically, any number of adjectives might go into the blank slot in this example. Römer found that the most frequent words (using a corpus of student essays) in that fill blank slot were *interesting*, *useful*, *nice*, and *better*, accounting for 77 percent of all the variants in the corpus.

Vocabulary Usage: Complexity and Sophistication

Vocabulary development in spoken and written discourse has been documented as critical in the literacy development of L2 learners. The mastery of academic vocabulary has been identified as an important determinant of academic success; to be successful academically, students need to develop the specialized and sophisticated vocabulary of academic discourse that is distinct from conversational language (Francis et al. 2006). Corpus tools are used to extract and then interpret the nature of vocabulary usage by learners across levels of proficiency. The changes in vocabulary usage from general language to specific language, and then to specialized or technical language that is required in processing or responding to a situation have been examined in multiple settings. Many corpus-based studies of academic language have looked at predictive or correlational data showing the relationship between individual textual features and quality of test/performance scores given by instructors or raters. A substantial number of studies have identified linguistic features (e.g., subordination, prepositions, linking adverbials, etc.) that are predictive of scores given by instructors/raters and features that distinguish differences between students' disciplines (Römer and Wulff 2010) and various demographic factors (e.g., language proficiency levels, graduate vs. undergraduate) (e.g., Grant and Ginther 2000; Hinkel 2002).

The identification of linguistic features found to be statistically significant indicators of speech and writing quality has interested researchers because of its obvious pedagogical import. Linguistic complexity is important as it may refer to the amount of discourse produced by learners, the types and variety of grammatical structures, the organization and cohesion of ideas and, at the higher levels of language proficiency, the use of text structures in specific genres. These features may be defined and operationalized to aid in the development of teaching materials in the classroom. Computational measures such as t-units, clause constructions, type/token ratio, and markers of information density and elaboration have all been used to create lessons and test prompts in the L2 classroom, especially in the university setting.

Linguistic Co-occurrence and Multi-dimensional Analysis

The concept of linguistic co-occurrence suggests that the linguistic composition of a particular language or discourse domain, such as face-to-face classroom interaction or a study group, may have higher frequencies of questions and responses, inserts, dysfluent markers (e.g., filled pauses—*uh, um*), and backchannels (e.g., *uh-huh*) used often by speakers compared to other settings. Conversely, these features may not be common in extended and prepared lectures, news reports, or formal speech. Linguistic features such as pronouns, past tense verbs, and nouns, often occur together whenever speakers engage in everyday conversations or talk about their previous experiences and recent events. These same features could also appear together with very high frequency in written, first person narratives or soliloquies about past events. In order to capture and document these co-occurring features from corpora, a simple KWIC search will no longer be sufficient. A more advanced statistical framework is necessary to identify the composition of features that are frequently found together within a corpus.

Biber's (1988) *Variation across Speech and Writing* introduced corpus-based multi-dimensional analysis (MDA) as a research methodology for exploring linguistic variation in spoken and written English texts. Biber's primary research goal was to conduct a unified linguistic analysis of spoken and written registers from 23 sub-registers of the LOB (for written texts) and London-Lund Corpus (for spoken texts). By using a multivariate statistical procedure to identify intrinsic linguistic co-occurrence patterns across POS-tagged texts, Biber was able to substantially redefine a range of register characteristics of spoken/written discourse. Subsequently, he was able to establish a model of corpus-based research that could be applied to more specialized contexts. MDA output is derived from Factor Analysis (FA), which considers the sequential, partial, and observed correlations of a wide-range of variables in order to produce groups of co-occurring factors. Biber's Factor 1 (Table 1.3), interpreted as *Involved vs. Informational Production,* shows the combination of private verbs (e.g., *think, feel*), demonstrative pronouns, first and second person pronouns, and adverbial qualifiers in how speakers (or writers) talk about his/her personal ideas, sharing opinions, and involving an audience (the use of *you* or *your*). The discourse is also informal and hedged (*that* deletions, contractions, *almost, maybe*). On the other side, features combine to focus on the giving of information ("Informational Production") as a priority in the discourse. There are many nouns and nominalizations (e.g., *education, development, communication*), prepositions, and attributive adjectives (e.g., *smart, effective, pretty*)—appearing together with very few personal pronouns. This suggests that informational data and descriptions of topics are provided without particular focus on the speaker or writer. More unique and longer words are used (higher type/token ratio and average word length) and the texts appear to be formal in structure and focus. In our brief discussion of the LINDSEI corpus below, we provided a sample application of the MDA approach in the study of L2 interviews from Friginal and Polat (2015). See also an application of the MDA approach using data from LIWC in Chap. 9.

Table 1.3 Biber's (1988) co-occurring features in Factor 1

Factor	Co-occurring features—Positive side	Co-occurring features—Negative side
1	Private Verb (e.g., *believe, feel, think*) *'That'* Deletion Contraction Verb (uninflected present, imperative and third person) Second Person Pronoun/Possessive Verb *'Do'* Demonstrative Pronoun Adverb/Qualifier—Emphatic (e.g., *just, really, so*) First Person Pronoun/Possessive Pronoun *'it'* Verb *'Be'* (uninflected present tense, verb and auxiliary) Subordinating Conjunction—Causative (e.g., *because*) Discourse Particle (e.g., *now*) Nominal Pronoun (e.g., *someone, everything*) Adverbial—Hedge (e.g., *almost, maybe*) Adverb/Qualifier—Amplifier (e.g., *absolutely, entirely*) Wh- Question Modals of Possibility (*can, may, might, could*) Coordinating Conjunction—Clausal Connector Wh- Clause Stranded Preposition	Noun Word Length Preposition Type/Token Ratio Attributive Adjective (Place Adverbial) (Agentless Passive) (Past Participial WHIZ Deletion) (Present Participial WHIZ Deletion)

2

Corpora of Spoken Academic Discourse and Learner Talk: A Survey

This chapter lists and briefly discusses seminal and recently collected corpora of spoken academic discourse and learner oral language (in English). We also provide descriptions of the texts and types of student oral language in these collections and some examples of corpus-based studies utilizing these corpora. Most are publicly available (e.g., MICASE, VOICE, LINDSEI, ELFA) and some may be purchased online from their developers. Table 2.7, which lists specialized spoken texts from L2 learners collected by various research groups globally, suggests a growing interest in this area of corpus-based research in the classroom and the important merging of SLA and corpus-informed approaches.

The Michigan Corpus of Academic Spoken English

The Michigan Corpus of Academic Spoken English (MICASE) (Simpson et al. 2002) is accessible online with a searchable interface that functions as a concordance program. MICASE's original audiotapes are housed at the University of Michigan's English Language Institute and may be

E. Friginal et al., *Exploring Spoken English Learner Language Using Corpora*,
DOI 10.1007/978-3-319-59900-7_2

used by researchers after obtaining permission. The MICASE database (transcripts) is available at the MICASE website (http://quod.lib.umich.edu/m/micase/), and a MICASE users' guide (Simpson-Vlach and Leicher 2006) is also available in book form, published by the University of Michigan Press.

The MICASE team had two primary research questions that guided their research design and collection: (1) What are the characteristics of contemporary academic speech—its grammar, its vocabulary, its functions and purposes, its fluencies and dysfluencies? (2) Are these characteristics different for different academic disciplines and for different classes of speakers? As MICASE focused on recording a range of academic speech, the team's sampling goals spanned 15 different types of speech events and four major academic divisions within those types (Humanities and Arts, Social Sciences, Biological and Health Sciences, and Physical Sciences). They followed a stratified, random sampling procedure, with each recording classified according to speech event type, a pre-assigned number indicating the academic discipline, two letters representing the majority of participants in the event (e.g., junior undergraduate, senior faculty, staff), and a final three-digit sequence to track chronologically when the tape was recorded. MICASE recordings had two researchers who attended most speech events in order to identify speakers and facilitate transcription by taking field notes on non-verbal contextual information. Small group events (e.g., advising sessions, office hours, study groups), where an observer's presence would have been intrusive, did not include research assistants after the recording equipment was set up (Simpson-Vlach and Leicher 2006).

MICASE provides examples of speech events ranging in length from 19 to 178 minutes, with word counts ranging from 2805 words to 30,328 words. Clearly, this indicates that academic discourse varies with respect to both length and form. In MICASE, academic speech is defined as "that speech which occurs in academic settings." This means that academic discourse is not pre-defined as something like a scholarly discussion. Simpson-Vlach (2013) noted that, in academic settings, speech acts such as jokes, confessions, and personal anecdotes co-occur with definitions, explanations, and intellectual justifications.

Table 2.1 MICASE word counts by speech event type and student/faculty and staff 'participation' percentages

Speech Event Type	Words	% Faculty &/or Staff	% Students
Advising (2)	35,275	70%	30%
Colloquia (14)	157,333	89%	11%
Discussion Sections (9)	74,904	33%	67%
Dissertation Defenses (4)	56,837	37%	63%
Interviews (3)	13,015	56%	44%
Labs (8)	73,815	32%	68%
Large Lectures (30)	251,632	94%	6%
Small Lectures (32)	333,338	78%	22%
Meetings (6)	70,038	38%	62%
Office Hours (14)	171,188	29%	71%
Seminars (7)	138,626	65%	35%
Study Groups (8)	129,725	0%	100%
Student Presentations (11)	143,369	22%	78%
Service Encounters (2)	24,691	40%	60%
Tours (2)	21,768	39%	61%

Source: Simpson-Vlach and Leicher (2006)

The MICASE website has 152 transcripts (totaling 1,848,364 words). Table 2.1 shows the breakdown of speech event types, total number of words, and faculty and/or staff and student participation percentage within each event type. The most useful event types for investigating student speech are study groups (eight events, 100% student), student presentations (11 events, 78% student), labs (eight events, 68% student), and discussion sections (nine events, 67% student).

However, only 12% of MICASE came from non-native speakers of English, and this percentage also includes some faculty and staff. Table 2.2 shows a detailed description of MICASE demographic groups. The range of speech events includes monologic and interactive speech; undergraduate and graduate students; junior faculty, senior faculty, and staff; and native, near-native, and non-native speakers of English.

Several papers on MICASE have focused specifically on teaching applications intended for L2 learners in US academia. For example, grammar-based studies of academic speech conducted by John Swales and his students and colleagues included topics such as plural versus singular nouns; the use of *among* and *between*; modal contractions with

Table 2.2 Demographic groups in MICASE

Speaker Category				Total Speakers	Total Words	% of Total Corpus
Gender	Male			729	786,487	46%
	Female			842	909,053	54%
Academic Role	Faculty			160	825,829	49%
		Male		84	446,925	26%
		Female		76	378,904	22%
	Students			1039	742,348	44%
		Undergraduates		782	368,433	22%
			Male	336	142,102	8%
			Female	446	226,331	13%
		Graduates		257	373,915	22%
			Male	121	158,696	9%
			Female	136	215,219	13%
Language Status	Native Speakers			1449	1,493,586	88%
	Non-Native Speakers			122	201,954	12%
Totals				1571	1,695,540	

Source: Simpson-Vlach and Leicher (2006)

will; the use of vocatives; and anaphoric *so* (Simpson-Vlach 2013). Swales and Malczewski (1999) also examined clusters of discourse markers and reported how often clusters such as *okay*, *so*, and *now* were used to signal topic transitions in academic speech, and how they contribute to the cognitive task of discourse management. Simpson-Vlach and Leicher's (2006) *The MICASE Handbook* (University of Michigan Press) also featured a collection of pedagogical suggestions for incorporating MICASE data and corpus-based exercises and research findings in the classroom.

TOEFL 2000 Spoken and Written Academic Language Corpus

The TOEFL 2000 Spoken and Written Academic Language (T2K-SWAL) Corpus was also designed to represent the range of spoken and written registers that university students encounter in the USA. The project was sponsored by the Educational Testing Service and the Test of English as a Foreign Language (TOEFL), with the primary goal of providing a basis for test construction and validation (see Biber et al. 2004) and also to provide descriptive data on spoken and written registers in US universities. The spoken and written texts in the T2K-SWAL Corpus were carefully sampled from six major disciplines (Business, Education, Engineering, Humanities, Natural Science, Social Science), three levels of education (lower division undergraduate, upper division undergraduate, graduate), and four universities (Northern Arizona, Iowa State, California State Sacramento, Georgia State). These texts have been collected from four major regions in the USA and from four different types of academic institutions: a teacher's college, a mid-size regional university, an urban research university, and a Research 1 university.

Thus, the resulting corpus could be taken as a reasonably representative sample of university language in the early to mid-2000s. Recent developments, especially those from online registers of university discourse, could be added for future upgrade of the T2K-SWAL Corpus. Technology-mediated discourse such as emails, online courses, Skype lessons, course online discussion posts (or similar posts from social media like Facebook or Twitter), and language from course management systems (e.g., iCollege, D2L, WebNet, and related Blackboard applications commonly used by US universities) will have to be included (most of these are written registers) in future collections due to their major prevalence in everyday academia.

The T2K-SWAL Corpus is relatively large (2.7 million words) as well as representative of the range of university registers that university students must listen to or read in and out of the university setting. The register categories chosen for the corpus are sampled from across the full range of spoken and written activities associated with university life, including classroom teaching, office hours, study groups, on-campus service encounters, textbooks, course packs, and other written materials (e.g., university catalogs, brochures). Table 2.3 shows the composition of the spoken component of the T2K-SWAL Corpus.

Actual student speeches are recorded across all spoken registers of the corpus but the dataset is not coded specifically to separate NS and NNS students. NNSs participated in office hours, class sessions, study groups,

Table 2.3 Composition of the T2K-SWAL Corpus (spoken texts)

Register	# of texts	# of words
Class sessions	176	1,248,800
Classroom management	40	39,300
Labs/In-class groups	17	88,200
Office hours	11	50,400
Study groups	25	141,100
Service encounters	22	97,700
Total	251	1,665,500

and labs/in-class groups. Unlike MICASE, the T2K-SWAL Corpus is not publicly available (and there is no designated online database or published manual). However, there have been many studies utilizing data from the T2K-SWAL Corpus, primarily focusing on EAP and academic discourse comparisons. Biber's (2006a) *University Language: A Corpus-Based Study of Spoken and Written Registers* (John Benjamins) provides an in-depth analysis of data from the T2K-SWAL Corpus across topics such as vocabulary use, grammatical variation, lexical bundles, and linguistic co-occurrence patterns.

Biber (2006b) examined modal verbs as stance markers in academic discourse utilizing sub-corpora from the T2K-SWAL Corpus. As shown in Fig. 2.1, modals are by far the most common grammatical device (as compared to adverbs and complement clauses) used to mark stance in university registers and are especially more common in the spoken registers than in written registers. However, modals are also strongly associated with management/directive purposes, especially in writing. Biber found that there are also differences in the use of certain modal classes across university registers, particularly classroom teaching and class management (spoken) and textbook, and course management (written). Prediction/volition modals (e.g., *will* and *would*) are the most common modal class, especially in the management registers. Possibility modals (e.g., *can, could, may*) are moderately common in all four registers, but they are more common in speech than writing. Necessity modals (*must, should*) are the least common class, but they are more common in written course management than in any other register. These results have been used in the classroom particularly to show NNSs the varying forms and functions of modal verbs coming from their teachers' utterances in

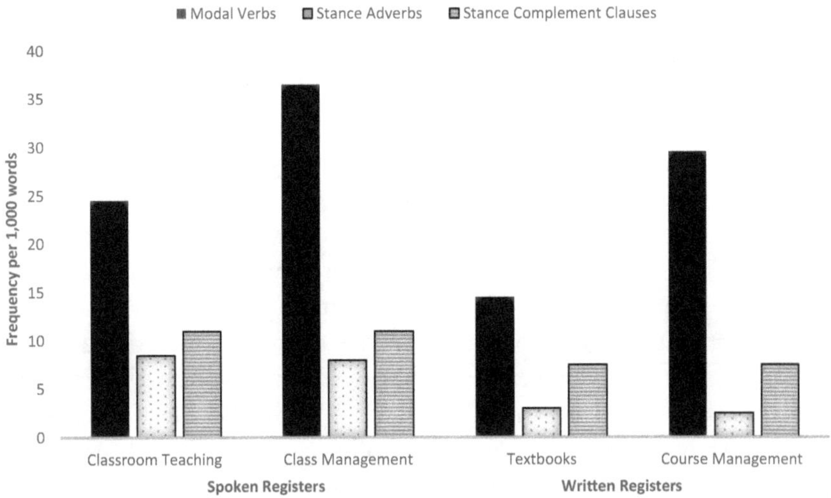

Fig. 2.1 Major stance features across registers (Adapted from Biber 2006a)

class teaching and class management events (see also Parts 2 and 4 of this book). Learners may notice, for example, that the more "traditional" definition of *could* as the past tense of *can* (that they may have learned previously from textbooks) may not necessarily be the most frequent function. *Could* in classroom management was used more frequently as a request marker (e.g., *could you please check the date?*).

The British Academic Spoken English Corpus

Both British Academic Spoken English Corpus (BASE) and BASE Plus corpora are housed at the Universities of Warwick and Reading and were collected between 2000 and 2005 under the leadership of Hilary Nesi (Warwick) and Paul Thompson (Reading). The BASE corpus has 160 lectures and 40 seminars recorded and transcribed from a variety of academic departments in these two universities. Overall, the BASE corpus contains 1,644,942 tokens (from lectures and seminars) available through the Oxford Text Archive (http://www2.warwick.ac.uk/fac/soc/al/research/collections/base/).

BASE Plus is a much larger and more current collection of British academic speech with the original tagged transcripts of BASE, video and audio recordings of lectures and seminars, video recordings of academic conference presentations, and interviews with academic staff "on aspects of their academic work and field (audio recordings, transcripts, and interview notes)." BASE Plus may be compared with MICASE and the T2K-SWAL for dialect comparisons of academic discourse. As is the case with MICASE and T2K-SWAL, BASE Plus represents language in academia which does not necessarily feature a large amount of L2 learner output. The BASE Plus video recordings have been used in material development projects at the University of Warwick, most notably the Essential Academic Skills in English (EASE) series (EASE: Seminar Discussions and EASE: Listening to Lectures are available online) (British Academic Spoken English and BASE Plus Collections 2017).

Vienna-Oxford International Corpus of English

Vienna-Oxford International Corpus of English (VOICE) is a structured collection of interactions capturing spoken English as a Lingua Franca (ELF). ELF is widely known to be most accurate and comprehensive representative of the contemporary use of English globally, employed by speakers from different first-language (L1) backgrounds as a common means of communication (Seidlhofer 2007, 2012) across various locations and contexts (e.g., business, education, tourism). The VOICE project was developed and collected by research teams from the Department of English at the University of Vienna (Barbara Seidlhofer, Project Director), funded by the Austrian Science Fund, with support from Oxford University Press. VOICE currently has over 1 million words of transcribed spoken ELF (120 hours of transcribed speech, 23 recordings of speech events) from professional, educational, and leisure domains.

VOICE features transcripts of naturally occurring, non-scripted face-to-face ELF interactions from 1250 mostly European speakers. These speakers are primarily "experienced ELF speakers" from a wide range of L1 backgrounds (49 total). Interactions or speech events include interviews, press conferences, service encounters, seminar discussions, working group discussions, workshop discussions, meetings, panels, question-answer sessions, and conversations. These speech events may also include code-switches into non-English speech (e.g., German, French). VOICE 2.0 Online (which is based on VOICE 2.0 XML) is freely available on the VOICE Project's website: http://www.univie.ac.at/voice.

VOICE obviously is not classroom-based, but the corpus is certainly relevant as a potential target corpus for many comparative studies of L2 speech across contexts. ELF texts from VOICE may, in fact, be considered as the type of English student-learners may aspire to in communicating successfully in English across specific tasks.

English as a Lingua Franca in Academic Contexts

Also developed in the early 2000s and around the same time as text collections for the initial version of VOICE is the English as a Lingua France in Academic Contexts (ELFA) corpus. This corpus was compiled in Finland under the leadership of Anna Mauranen (University of Tampere). The ELFA corpus recognizes that English has established itself as the global lingua franca, and NNSs have increasingly outnumbered NSs in many global universities. Within academic contexts, the English language constitutes the primary medium of communication for a great number of international students, especially in communities with speakers from different language backgrounds (Simson-Vlach 2013).

The ELFA corpus, with 1 million words of transcribed speech from a variety of speakers, provides an important resource for studying the linguistic features of this speech community both as a language variety in its own right and as an important component of academic speech. Mauranen (2003) argues that the applications of theoretical and descriptive work on ELF are of considerable practical significance in global academia. She noted that,

> An international language can be seen as a legitimate learning target, a variety belonging to its speakers. Thus, deficiency models, that is, those stressing the gap that distinguishes NNSs from NSs, should be seen as

> inadequate for the description of fluent L2 speakers and discarded as the sole basis of language education in English. Moreover, learners with a lingua franca target should be particularly sensitized to interpersonal aspects of language and intercultural competence (as distinct from familiarity with the target culture) because the expected intercultural encounters are much less predictable than those in which L1 speakers (especially of a given nation or culture) constitute the other party. (p. 517)

ELFA's collection of texts (of speech events) was based on (1) prototypicality: the extent to which genres are shared and named by most disciplines, for example, lectures, seminars, thesis defenses, and conference presentations; (2) influence: genres that affect a large number of participants (or are widely consumed), for example, introductory lecture courses, examinations, and consultation hours; and (3) prestige: genres with high status in the discourse community, for example, guest lectures, plenary conference presentations, and opening/closing speeches. The ELFA team also included dialogic events alongside lectures, seminars, and conference presentations.

The Louvain International Database of Spoken English Interlanguage

The Louvain International Database of Spoken English Interlanguage (LINDSEI) is an 800,000-word corpus of learner interviews, with 554 NNSs of English (Gilquin et al. 2010) and their NS interviewers. Because LINDSEI also captures the interactions of NNS students with NS interlocutors, it provides an excellent approximation of the language that L2 learners might choose to use in real-world interview contexts. LINDSEI represents learners from 11 different L1 backgrounds: Bulgarian, Chinese, Dutch, French, German, Greek, Italian, Japanese, Polish, Spanish, and Swedish, which allows for direct comparison of linguistic variation across L1 groups. The primary interview tasks in LINDSEI may illustrate how learners shift their use of various linguistic features, covering a range of discourse domains such as descriptions of places and events, the reconstruction or creation of a story from picture prompts, or development of a more formal or academic expository response. Other learner demographics (e.g., number of years of English at school, number of months living in an English-speaking country) are also available as bases of comparisons.

LINDSEI represents one of the first and most important collections of learner spoken interviews (Gilquin et al. 2010). The corpus is especially well suited to investigations of learner talk because of its large size, representativeness (as noted earlier, 11 L1 backgrounds with approximately 50 interviews each), and the consistency of its implementation. Each interview was conducted by a native English speaker, who first asked each participant to discuss a subject of his or her choice, from three possible choices. The interviewer then continued the conversation informally by asking follow-up questions from the student's discussion, and the interview concluded with a picture-strip narration. Interviews lasted approximately 15 minutes, and each was transcribed orthographically according to specific guidelines. Background information is also noted for each speaker, including age, gender, L1, and English learning experience. The text sample below shows an excerpt of a LINDSEI interview with a Bulgarian student participant.

Text Sample 2.1 LINDSEI Extract

<h nt="BG" nr="BG005">
<A> I'd like to: have an informal chat with you about some things I hope will be of interest to you . to: get the conversation started . I'd like you to chose one of the following topics . and think a little . about what you are going to say . and then try to talk for . three to five minutes and we'll carry on the conversation from there . so you can take a look at the topics . and see what looks . interesting </A>
<B> thank you .. well I ... I choose the . third topic . and it's about a film: .. as a matter of fact . I think it's a very . <starts laughing> bad film <stops laughing> it's Speed . with Keanu Reeves and Sandra Bullock ... (mhm) I don't . think it's good because . the= there is nothing worthy .. in it just the typical ... story line of goodies and badies (erm) ... where ... there is a happy end and only beautiful actors having hard time nothing more <coughs> as a matter of fact and: as an action movie ... it has .

The development of large-scale learner language corpora such as LINDSEI has provided a wealth of information on how learners actually use language in interviews, as well as how their language use compares to that of native English speakers or across different L1 backgrounds. For example, discourse and pragmatic markers have been studied through LINDSEI, revealing that learners generally tend to *overuse* some pragmatic markers and *underuse* others compared to native English speakers (Aijmer 2011; Buysse 2012; Gilquin 2008; Mukherjee 2009). Other researchers have used LINDSEI to study fluency and accuracy in learner language (Brand and Götz 2011), grammatical phenomena such as articles and prepositions (Kaneko 2007, 2008), or word collocations (De Cock 2004; Mukherjee 2009). Clearly, LINDSEI is a rich data source for investigations of lexico-grammatical phenomena in L2 speech.

Friginal and Polat (2015) conducted an MDA study of LINDSEI specifically (1) to extract and identify the linguistic dimensions of English learner talk, (2) to functionally interpret the resulting dimensions, and (3) to compare how these dimensions are distributed across LINDSEI speakers' eleven L1 backgrounds. Their results show that the four primary functional dimensions of learner speech are (1) Involved Conversational Style versus Informational Production; (2) Complex Statement of Opinion; (3) Formal, Academic Focus of Discussion versus Informal, Non-Academic Discourse; and (4) Personal Narrative Prose versus Non-Narrative Discourse. The linguistic composition of Dim 4, interpreted as distinguishing between personal narrative prose and non-narrative discourse (in L2 learners' responses to interview questions), is shown in Table 2.4.

Learner interviews with positive Dim 4 scores are comprised of activity verbs (e.g., *go, walk, make, bringing*), place adverbs and nouns, size adjectives, and coordinating conjunctions. These features co-occur with first-person pronouns (especially *I* and *we*). These texts have the features of story-telling and discussion of past events experienced by students. Interviewers provide follow-up questions and backchannels that allow learners to give further details of their accounts of events. As shown in the excerpt below (Dim 4 Score = 12.272), a past-oriented narrative of going to a restaurant with friends is maintained for a stretch of turns describing the setting and the participants' reactions and observations (Friginal and Polat 2015).

Table 2.4 Linguistic composition of Dim 4 from LINDSEI (Friginal and Polat 2015)

Dimension 4	
Positive: Personal narrative prose	
Activity verb	0.67
Past tense verb	0.52
Verb (not including auxiliary verbs)	0.52
Place adverb	0.48
Noun—place	0.45
Time adverb	0.35
Noun—group	0.35
First person pronoun	0.34
Size adjective	0.34
Coordinating conjunction	0.31
⇳	
Negative: Non-narrative discourse	
That comp. clause with verb	−0.5
Noun—abstract	−0.42
That comp. clause with likelihood verb	−0.38
Preposition	−0.36
Noun—cognition	−0.36
Discourse particle	−0.3

Text Sample 2.2 GR018.txt (Dim Score = 12.272)

the way **we were behaving** or when **we went** to restaurants and **we were making** lo= . noise . and **we didn't know** what to eat and (eh) all that stuff and (em) . usually: the: waiters (em) . **tried** . (eh) . t= t= (eh) **were trying to explain** to us . what (er) . we should try to eat and (eh) . when (er) they **were bringing** us the: . the plates . **we thought** that (em) . it di= . (eh) okay the food (eh) . is not the same like here in Greece and **we thought** that . that **it was** . unusual . and (erm) . the first plate **I had I think it was** really disgusting and I couldn't eat it

In contrast, interviews with negative scores are typically personal opinions from interviewees and those that provide analyses of contexts in free-topic tasks. Past tense verbs are rarely used and the dominant co-occurring features include abstract and cognition nouns, prepositions, discourse particles, and *that* complement clauses controlled by verbs, especially likelihood verbs. Unlike narrative prose, negative segments of interviews are organized to provide supporting details for an idea or opinion guided by interviewer prompts. There are limited statements of recall or discussion of past events as shown in the excerpt below from an Italian student (Dim 4 Score = −8.076) in which the student provides a description of a favorite actress.

Text Sample 2.3 IT047.txt (Dim 4 Score = −8.076)

(er) I don't know I think she is a really good actress (eh) I like it (eh) I like her very much (erm) I think she's (eh) quite uncommon that is she's not the (mm) the typical (eh) vamp or particularly (eh) good-looking (eh) woman (eh) I think (eh) that (eh) (mm) her most important feature is not her look but her appearance but (eh) his her talent she (mm) I think (eh) she has (erm) expressions hi= her face is (eh) very expressive and (mm) (mm) I don't know (erm) she's (em) . I don't know how how to say it (eh) I think when one (erm) sees a film with her (erm) one cannot (eh) avoid (eh) following with with heart the film (erm) I don't know how to ex= to explain it (erm) you feel (eh) with her as as if you: you were in the film

The comparison scale in Fig. 2.2 shows that Greek (1.455), Japanese (1.417), and German (1.386) students had the highest average positive scores in Dim 4, while Italian (−2.227) and French (−2.143) students had the lowest negative scores.

The European Corpus of Academic Talk

The European Corpus of Academic Talk (EUROCAT) (http://www.eurocoat.es) is a 58,834-word highly specialized corpus (27 total transcripts) of office hours and student-faculty consultations carried out in English in five different European universities, collected by a team of researchers based in Spain. It is one of the newest collections of spoken transcripts primarily focused on dialogic speech between instructors and students. Detailed demographic information on all speakers is provided in the corpus, including gender, age, L1, work experience (for lecturers), and students' proficiency in English. The corpus was collected under the Erasmus Plus project, and the English language requirement for being awarded an Erasmus grant (which varies across Spanish universities) was

Fig. 2.2 Comparison of student texts in Dim 4: Personal narrative vs. non-narrative discourse (Adapted from Friginal and Polat 2015)

used to assess student proficiency levels. Other available student information includes the number of hours the student spends every day listening to and speaking in English while on Erasmus, how long the student has been living in the foreign country prior to the date of the conversation recorded, and whether the student recalls having spoken to this lecturer outside class prior to the recorded conversation (MacArthur et al. 2014).

EUROCAT is unique in its focus on additional annotation of speakers' positioning during the recording, comfort in being recorded, and other general observations. From information gathered from participant questionnaires after the recording had been made, the corpus also includes section reports on participants' assessments of how natural the conversation was, how comfortable they felt during the conversation, and how similar the conversation was to the kind of conversation they would have in ordinary office hours. Participant positioning (potentially useful in multi-modal studies) is provided by reporting how the participant was sitting (e.g., the predominant posture of the participant), what the participant was sitting on (e.g., the distinction is made between a swivel chair and a stable chair), the position of the participant with regard to the camera view (e.g., the participant's location, whether to the left, right, or in the middle of the camera view), and who or what the participant was facing (e.g., toward whom or in what direction the participant's body was facing throughout most of the recording). Annotations of the physical environment include details of the immediate surroundings in which the interaction took place: the background and foreground of the office structure (e.g., doors and windows), office furniture, office equipment, office supplies, and objects in view (MacArthur et al. 2014).

The EUROCAT team also included references to objects that were relevant to and used throughout the conversation (e.g., a student's work on printed paper, mug, pen, etc.). And finally, specific annotations of transcriber/researcher observations include observations of situations, consistent and/or peculiar participant behavior, other relevant behavioral occurrences (e.g., computer, papers, etc.), background noises (e.g., music, people speaking, car sirens, etc.), and eye gaze (e.g., shifting gaze from one point to another).

The International Corpus of English

The International Corpus of English (ICE) project (http://ice-corpora.net/ice/) collects comparable corpora for varieties of English spoken around the world (Greenbaum 1996). Each corpus in ICE (e.g., ICE

India or ICE Jamaica) ideally has the same corpus design: a total size of 1 million words, with 500 texts of approximately 2000 words, each from the same registers (news, lectures, parliamentary debates, etc.). The authors and speakers are aged 18 or over, educated through the medium of English in their respective countries, and either born in the target country or moved there at an early age. The texts in the corpus date from 1990 or later (Nelson 1996). The ICE project was initiated in 1988 by the late Sidney Greenbaum, the then Director of the Survey of English Usage, University College London. Greenbaum and his team's three primary goals in collecting data for ICE were (1) to sample standard varieties from other countries where English is the first language, for example, Canada and Australia; (2) to sample national varieties from countries where English is an official additional language, for example India and Nigeria; and (3) to include spoken and manuscript English as well as printed English (Greenbaum 1996). The ICE project has various research teams in each of the following countries: Australia, Cameroon, Canada, East Africa (Kenya, Malawi, Tanzania), Fiji, Great Britain, Hong Kong, India, Ireland, Jamaica, Kenya, Malta, Malaysia, New Zealand, Nigeria, Pakistan, Philippines, Sierra Leone, Singapore, South Africa, Sri Lanka, Trinidad and Tobago, and the USA. Each ICE follows a common corpus design and a common annotation scheme. Table 2.5 lists the spoken and written registers collected for the ICE by its research teams.

The ICE was intended primarily for comparative studies of emerging Englishes all over the world alongside "native-Englishes." The Asian varieties of English available for free download from the ICE website feature countries/territories where English has been used extensively as the language of business and education. Although academic spoken language is very limited in ICE, there are useful comparisons of spoken and written texts in professional settings that may directly relate to academic discourses. Transcripts of class lessons, often with teacher and student interactions (mostly from teacher lectures), may be extracted and compared across country groups. Below are two excerpts showing class interactions between teachers and students from India and the Philippines.

Table 2.5 Spoken and written registers of the International Corpus of English

Spoken texts (300 2000-word samples)	Written texts (200 2000-word samples)
Dialogues (180)	Student exams (10)
Spontaneous conversations (90)	Student essays (10)
Telephone conversations (10)	Social letters (15)
Class lessons (20)	Business letters (15)
Broadcast discussions (20)	Learned humanistic (10)
Broadcast interviews (10)	Learned social sciences (10)
Political debates (10)	Learned natural sciences (10)
Legal cross-examinations (10)	Learned technology (10)
Business transactions (10)	Popular humanistic (10)
Monologues (120)	Popular social sciences (10)
Spontaneous commentaries (20)	Popular natural sciences (10)
Unscripted speeches (30)	Popular technology (10)
Demonstrations (10)	Press reportage (20)
Legal presentations (10)	Administrative/regulatory directives (10)
Broadcast news (20)	Instructional skills/hobbies (10)
Broadcast talks (20)	Press editorials (10)
Scripted speeches (10)	Fiction (20)

Text Samples 2.4 Student-Teacher Classroom Interaction from ICE India and Philippines

INDIA

[Teacher] The ground water, I was talking about the rain water which enters which falls on the surface of the earth, is distributed in three ways. Now can you tell me the three ways in which it is distributed? Yes Naresh?

[Student] Uh, first it percolates, uh, means uh, it percolates

[Teacher] Where does it percolate?

[Student] Uh when it falls on the ground

[Teacher] Yes? What happens to it?

[Student] It gathers into ponds

[Teacher] Correct, and it falls as rain. Sit down. Which is the other one?

[Student] Miss it is evaporated

[Teacher] Okay, it evaporates. Third one? Which is the third way in which, the rain water is ...

[Student] It goes underground
[Teacher] Okay he said it goes underground. On slopes the streams are formed

PHILIPPINES
[Teacher] Thus far we have seen the uhm two kinds of knowledge, or judgement according to source namely
[Student] A priori </foreign> and <foreign> a posteriori </foreign>
[Teacher] Alright <foreign> a priori </foreign> and <foreign> a posteriori </foreign>If you were asked to, de, to define the two types of knowledge how would you
[Student] What is an <foreign> a priori </foreign> knowledge against an <foreign> a posteriori </foreign> knowledge
[Teacher] Yes Mister <unclear> word </unclear> Alright so it has something to do with what is the source of that knowledge where we uhm acquire this knowledge either from experience in which case it is <foreign> a posteriori </foreign> or from reason from the mind itself in which case it is <foreign> a priori </foreign> We have also uhm seen that there are two kinds of judgement according to the relationship <,> of a subject and a predicate. And what are they?
[Student] Either synthetic or analytic
[Teacher] Alright it could either be synthetic or analytic. And how would you differentiate them
[Student] Synthetic the predicate is <unclear> words </unclear>
[Teacher] So if the predicate is already contained in the subject you call it

Friginal and Hardy (2014) compared POS-tagged data from ICE India, Philippines, and Singapore—three parallel corpora of "Asian Englishes"—and reported a significant number of linguistic features that differed in average distributions across the three countries. For example, in Table 2.6, Indian spoken texts had consistently the fewest average private verbs, contractions, second-person pronouns, first-person pronouns, emphatics, *it* pronouns, and verb *be*. These results suggest that

Table 2.6 ICE components tagged results using the Biber Tagger (data normalized per 1000 words)

	1	2	3	4	5	6	7
ICE Component	typ/tokn	wrdlen	wrdcont	vrb_priv	that_del	contrctn	verb
India Spoken	46.82	4.30	2284.93	15.71	5.01	0.24	98.08
India Written	55.10	4.80	2224.38	6.80	1.16	0.11	59.50
Philippines Spoken	47.94	4.22	2258.32	18.36	6.32	1.05	90.13
Philippines Written	56.19	4.82	2250.31	8.02	1.76	0.04	60.75
Singapore Spoken	48.32	4.17	2215.82	22.88	8.34	0.88	104.51
Singapore Written	55.77	4.74	2186.85	9.28	1.78	0.15	65.61

	8	9	10	11	12	13	14
ICE Component	2nd pers	vrb_do	dem_pron	qual_emph	1st pers	it	vrb_be
India Spoken	17.98	1.44	5.48	3.88	33.39	14.04	2.40
India Written	5.44	0.47	2.22	1.86	11.77	8.72	1.80
Philippines Spoken	22.31	1.66	4.24	7.41	43.33	14.97	2.73
Philippines Written	4.95	0.48	2.75	2.84	14.69	8.97	1.88
Singapore Spoken	34.40	1.89	5.83	6.53	38.74	16.76	2.84
Singapore Written	9.37	0.59	2.96	2.87	16.06	9.85	2.43

Indian spoken discourse is more focused on informational production rather than personal and other-directed talk (typical in texts with a high number of pronouns, especially second-person *you/your*).

Other Specialized Spoken Learner Corpora

Finally in this section, we highlight the pioneering work of the Learner Corpus Association (LCA) which is an international association promoting learner corpus research and providing an interdisciplinary forum for researchers to share results of their studies, corpora, and related projects.

The LCA hosts a bi-annual international research conference and maintains a comprehensive website (http://www.learnercorpusassociation.org/) which serves as a repository of data and published materials and research tools for members and non-members alike. The group supports the compilation of learner corpora (both written and spoken) in a wide range of languages and the design of innovative methods and software. Members promote learner corpus research focusing on SLA theory and applications in fields including foreign or second language teaching, language testing, and natural language processing (e.g., automated scoring, spell- and grammar-checking, L1 identification). The founding members of the LCA are Gaëtanelle Gilquin, Sylviane Granger, Fanny Meunier and Magali Paquot, all based at the Centre for English Corpus Linguistics, Université Catholique de Louvain (Belgium). Recent publications by LCA scholars, such as *The Cambridge Handbook of Learner Corpus Research* (Granger et al. 2015), have covered emerging models in speech annotation of learner corpora, statistics for learner corpus research, and extensive historical overviews alongside future directions.

Related to the works of the LCA, Table 2.7 provides a list of spoken English learner corpora collected by various research teams all over the world. Most of these corpora have an online presence and additional information from manuals or "read me" files are available from the research teams. The data in Table 2.7 were adapted from "Learner Corpora around the World" developed by Amadine Dumont and Sylviane Granger (source: https://www.uclouvain.be/en-cecl-lcworld.html).

Table 2.7 Spoken English learner corpora from research groups around the world

Corpora	Additional Information	Learners' L1	Type of Task (or Text)	No. of Words (or length)
The Corpus of Writing, Pronunciation, Reading, and Listening by Learners of English as a Foreign Language	Project Location: School of Foreign Studies, Kansai Gaidai University	Japanese	Varied	Written: 30,000 Audio: 30 hours
The ANGLISH Corpus	Project Location: University of Provence, France [freely available]	French	Readings of texts and sentences; spontaneous oral language	
The Barcelona English Language Corpus (BELC) [University of Barcelona]	Longitudinal data (from children and young adults learning English)	Spanish, Catalan	4 tasks: written, composition, oral narrative, oral interview, and role-play	Both written and spoken data available
The Bilingual Corpus of Chinese English Learners (BICCEL) [National Research Center for Foreign Language Education Beijing Foreign Studies University, China]	Spoken and Written English Texts	Chinese	Spoken: National Oral English test Written: In-class assignments	2 million
The City University Corpus of Academic Spoken English (CUCASE)	Project Location: City University of Hong Kong Medium: Multimedia	Chinese Also includes data produced by English L1 speakers	Various types	2 million

(*continued*)

Table 2.7 (continued)

Corpora	Additional Information	Learners' L1	Type of Task (or Text)	No. of Words (or length)
The College Learners' Spoken English Corpus (COLSEC)		Chinese	National spoken English test for non-English majors	700,000
The Corpus of Young Learner Interlanguage (CYLIL)	Project Location: Vrije Universiteit Brussel, Belgium	Dutch, French, Greek, Italian	English L2 data elicited from European School pupils. Longitudinal data	500,000
The Eastern European English Learner Corpus	Project Location: Eberhard Karls University of Tübingen, Germany	Russian, Ukrainian, Polish, Slovak	Spontaneous spoken production data elicited by means of a semi-structured interview	60,000
The EFL Teacher Corpus (ETC)	Currently being developed	Korean	Teacher talks in language classrooms	123,000
The English Speech Corpus of Chinese Learners (ESCCL) [Nantong University, Beijing Foreign Studies University, Chinese Academy of Social Sciences]	Audio and transcripts of read speeches	Chinese	Dialogue reading-aloud	
The EVA Corpus of Norwegian School English	Project Location: University of Bergen, Norway	Norwegian	Picture-based tasks	35,000

(*continued*)

Table 2.7 (continued)

Corpora	Additional Information	Learners' L1	Type of Task (or Text)	No. of Words (or length)
The Giessen-Long Beach Chaplin Corpus (GLBCC) [University of Giessen, Germany]	Copy of the corpus may be requested from developers	German	Transcribed interactions between native English speakers, ESL and EFL speakers	350,000
The International Corpus Network of Asian Learners of English (ICNALE)	Project Location: Kobe University, Japan	Chinese, Indonesian, Japanese, Korean, Malay, and others	Controlled speeches and essays; L1 productions by 350 NS	1.8 million
The International Teaching Assistants Corpus (ITACorp)	Project Location: Penns State University, USA	Various	Learner (ITA) language from a variety of spoken classroom tasks: lectures, office hours, role plays, presentations, discussions	500,000
The ISLE Speech Corpus	CD-ROM available	German, Italian	Recorded utterances from several blocks of differing task types (reading simple sentences, using minimal pairs, giving answers to multiple choice questions)	18 hours of audio

(continued)

Table 2.7 (continued)

Corpora	Additional Information	Learners' L1	Type of Task (or Text)	No. of Words (or length)
The LeaP Corpus: Learning Prosody in a Foreign Language	The annotated corpus is available for research purposes [from the University of Augsburg and University Freiburg, Germany]	German	Four types of speech styles were recorded: nonsense word lists, readings of a short story, retellings of the story, free speech in an interview situation	12 hours of audio
A Learners' Corpus of Reading Texts	Freely available	French	Unprepared reading of English texts; texts are short abstracts of fiction or made-up dialogues	
The LONGDALE Project: LONGitudinal DAtabase of Learner English [Centre for English Corpus Linguistics Université Catholique de Louvain, Belgium]	Both spoken and written	Various	Range of text types/ task types; longitudinal data	Under development
The Multimedia Adult ESL Learner Corpus (MAELC)	Multimedia materials collected by researchers from Portland State University, USA	ESL setting	Videos of classroom interaction and associated written materials	Available to researchers [contact the PSU team]

(continued)

Table 2.7 (continued)

Corpora	Additional Information	Learners' L1	Type of Task (or Text)	No. of Words (or length)
The Neungyule Interlanguage Corpus of Korean Learners of English (NICKLE)	Spoken and written data from the Yonsei University, Seoul, Korea research team	Korean	Written: student essays Spoken: student interviews and oral speech tests transcriptions	Written: 890,000 Spoken: 100,000 Available to researchers
The Japanese Learner English Corpus (NICT JLE)	Project Location: National Institute of Information and Communications Technology, Kyoto, Japan.	Japanese	English oral proficiency interview test	2 million Available for download
The PELCRA Learner English Corpus (PLEC)	Spoken and written data Online search engine and corpus analysis tools accessible	Polish	Written: argumentative, descriptive, narrative and quasi-academic essays; formal letters	Under development Goal spoken: 200,000 Goal written: 2.8 million
The Qatar Learner Corpus	Project Location: Carnegie Mellon University, USA	Arabic (mostly from Qatar)	Spoken interviews with Qatari learners of English	Freely available

(*continued*)

Table 2.7 (continued)

Corpora	Additional Information	Learners' L1	Type of Task (or Text)	No. of Words (or length)
The Santiago University Learner of English Corpus (SULEC)	Spoken and written texts Project Location: Santiago University	Spanish	Written: compositions or argumentative essays Spoken: semi-structured interviews, short oral presentations and brief story descriptions	Goal: 1 million
Second Language Research Tasks (SLRT)	Spoken and written texts Project Location: Northern Arizona University, USA and Concordia University, Canada	Various	Written paragraphs; various oral tasks	300,000
The Spoken and Written English Corpus of Chinese Learners (SWECCL)	Spoken (SECCL) and Written (WECCL)	Chinese	Written: argumentative and narrative essays. Spoken: National Spoken English Test—longitudinal data	2 million

(continued)

Table 2.7 (continued)

Corpora	Additional Information	Learners' L1	Type of Task (or Text)	No. of Words (or length)
The TELEC Secondary Learner Corpus (TSLC)	Spoken and written texts Project Location: University of Hong Kong, Hong Kong	Chinese	Compositions from secondary classroom	2 million
The Young Learner Corpus of English (YOLECORE)	Project Location: Aristotle University of Thessaloniki, Greece	Greek	Pedagogic corpus of video-recorded EFL language classes	170 school hours (126 hours of videotaped data) 1.5 million
The COREIL Corpus	Project Location: Université Paris-Diderot, France	French, English		
The European Science Foundation Second Language Database (ESF Database) [Max Planck Institute, Nijmegen, Netherlands]	Multilingual: Dutch, English, French, German, Swedish	Punjabi, Italian, Turkish, Arabic, Spanish, Finnish	"Spontaneous interactions of 40 adult immigrant workers living in Western Europe and their communication with native speakers in their respective host countries"	Freely available

(*continued*)

Table 2.7 (continued)

Corpora	Additional Information	Learners' L1	Type of Task (or Text)	No. of Words (or length)
The Padova Learner Corpus [University of Padua, Italy]	Computer-mediated communication Multilingual: English, French, Spanish	Italian	Student work produced in blended language courses using FirstClass conferencing software Variety of genres: diaries, debate contributions, formal reports, résumés etc.; longitudinal data	Under development
The corpus **PAR**allèle **O**ral en **L**angue **E**trangère (PAROLE) [Université de Savoie, France]	Multilingual: English, French, Italian (Mainly L2 speakers but also includes data produced by L1 speakers)	Various	5 oral production tasks	Available online (with manual)
The University of Toronto Romance Phonetics Database (RPD)	Multilingual: English, French, Italian, Portuguese, Romanian, Spanish	Various (including English, Mandarin, Russian, Spanish, etc.)	Elicited production—sentence and passage reading, story narration, description of favorite meal	Accessible online upon request from research team

Part II

Learner Talk in the Classroom

3

Learner (and Teacher) Talk in EAP Classroom Discourse

Research on spoken classroom discourse has a comparatively long tradition in linguistics, applied linguistics, and education in general. This, of course, is due to the fact that communication is central to educational contexts. It is through language that teachers conduct their work and students display what they have acquired. Language use in L2/foreign language classrooms, however, serves a distinct purpose, one that is quite unique from that of other classrooms. In most L2 classrooms, language is not only the medium of instruction but also the objective of learning (Lee 2010; Long 1983). In other words, "the medium *is* the message" in language teaching (Hammadou and Bernhardt 1987, p. 302). While teachers who teach in students' L1 (e.g., teachers who teach Korean to L1 Korean speakers) also use the language as medium and object of instruction, one difference between L1 and L2 classrooms is the fact that, unlike L1 students, L2 learners in many cases have yet to develop high levels of proficiency in the target language. In order to gain a deeper appreciation of the complexity of L2 classroom discourse, researchers have used different analytical frameworks, including interaction analysis (e.g., Allen et al. 1984), discourse analysis (e.g., Cullen 2002), and conversation analysis (e.g., Lee 2007). The vast majority of research in these traditions, however, has mostly limited the analysis to the micro-levels of teacher-student

E. Friginal et al., *Exploring Spoken English Learner Language Using Corpora*,
DOI 10.1007/978-3-319-59900-7_3

interaction, focusing on the distribution and functions of teacher and student contributions to the three-part exchange structure: teacher *initiation*, student *response*, and teacher *feedback* (or IRF) (Sinclair and Coulthard 1975). Little research has examined L2 classroom discourse, particularly that of EAP classrooms, from a corpus linguistic perspective.

This chapter reviews the literature on L2 classroom discourse and describes the corpus used to investigate various linguistic dimensions of learner and teacher talk in EAP classrooms.

Approaches to L2 Classroom Discourse

One of the earliest approaches used to examine L2 classroom discourse is called interaction analysis. Rooted in behavioral psychology, researchers in this tradition have used different types of observation schemes for real-time coding of classroom interaction. The purpose of these observation systems is to describe classroom interaction in naturalistic conditions in order to assist teachers in improving their interactional behaviors. Several earlier schemes, such as Moskowitz's (1971) *FLint* (Foreign Language Interaction) and Fanselow's (1977) *FOCUS* (Foci for Observing Communications Used in Settings), were developed specifically for language teacher training. Departing from these systems, *COLT* (Communicative Orientation of Language Teaching) is a sophisticated observation schedule used to measure the degree to which classroom instruction is communicatively oriented and to examine the effects of instructional practices on L2 learning (Allen et al. 1984; Spada and Frölich 1995).

Grounded in structural-functional linguistics, another framework commonly used in the analysis of classroom discourse is referred to as discourse analysis, or more specifically the Birmingham School of Discourse Analysis (Sinclair and Coulthard 1975). This approach is based on the work of Sinclair and Coulthard on L1 British elementary school classrooms, who found, among other discourse features, a consistent three-part exchange structure known as the IRF. Utilizing their approach, researchers have examined the structural patterns and functional features of classroom discourse. The purpose of this approach is to subject classroom discourse to rigorous analysis; however, research in this tradition has offered suggestions for improving instructional practices. Researchers adopting this approach have made significant contributions to our understanding of the formal and functional properties of classroom interaction, revealing features of L2 classroom discourse that could affect L2 learning, such as teacher question strategies (e.g., Tsui 1985) and repair strategies (e.g., Cullen 2002).

From the ethnomethodological tradition, conversation analysis has also been used to examine the pervasive three-part IRF exchange. Conversation analysis permits researchers to analyze the moment-by-moment interactional patterns of the classroom. Rather than imposing *a priori* categories, this approach allows the participatory patterns to emerge from the data (Seedhouse 2004). Using conversation analysis, researchers have discovered more complex turn-taking, topic-nomination, and repair strategies in teacher-student interactions (e.g., Lee 2007; Seedhouse 2004).

However, these approaches have primarily focused on the distribution of student and teacher contributions to the tripartite IRF exchange, even in the discourse analytic framework, where the unit of analysis has extended beyond this interaction. Little attention has been devoted to describing the schematic structure or linguistic features of language lessons. Recently, researchers have adopted genre analysis and corpus-based methods to examine the rhetorical structure and lexicogrammatical aspects of L2 classroom lessons. Using Swales' (1990) move analysis, Lee (2016) examined the recurrent rhetorical moves and linguistic realizations of these movements in a corpus of EAP classroom lessons. Lee found that EAP lessons consist of three major phases, each with three distinct moves. In addition, using corpus-based methods, he found that EAP teachers used different lexical phrases to realize different phases and rhetorical moves. For instance, *we're going to/gonna* and *I'm going to/gonna* were found to be frequent in the opening phase used for housekeeping matters and for signaling a lesson's official start, respectively. On the other hand, *you're going to/gonna* and *I want you to* were commonly used in what Lee refers to as the activity cycle phase. These lexical phrases were predominantly used to set up classroom tasks. Based on Hyland's (2005) interpersonal model of metadiscourse, Lee and Subtirelu (2015) compared two corpora of teacher talk: EAP teachers and university lecturers. Specifically, they examined these teachers' use of interactive metadiscourse (i.e., linguistic resources for organizing discourse) and interactional metadiscourse (i.e., expressions of stance and engagement). Among other metadiscoursal features, Lee and Subtirelu found that, while both teacher groups used the personal pronoun *you* more commonly than *I* or *we*, EAP teachers used more *you* than academic lecturers at a significant level, most often to set up pedagogical tasks. They suggest that the inclusion of students in the discourse permits teachers to maintain learner engagement and participation. Combing conversation analysis and corpus linguistics methods, Yang (2014) examined the use of discourse markers (e.g., *okay, right*) in a corpus of Chinese college English as a foreign language (EFL) teacher talk for her doctoral dissertation. She found that these teachers not only frequently use discourse markers to manage their talk, but she also discovered a relationship between teachers' use of discourse markers and pedagogical functions.

These studies have contributed greatly to our understanding of L2 teacher talk from a corpus-based perspective, but what is lacking is an examination of learners' classroom language use. Although teachers are ultimately responsible for the construction of a lesson's structure, classroom discourse is a collaborative effort, one that is co-constructed by both learners and teachers. To the best of our knowledge, O'Boyle (2014) is the only study that has explored EAP learner talk using corpus-based methods. She compared the use of *you* and *I* in two corpora of classroom discourse: a corpus of various L1 university classroom genres and a corpus of L2 learner talk during group tasks. O'Boyle found that L1 and L2 students use *you* and *I* in different ways, and suggests that L2 learners' use of pronouns displays a lack of connection with the informational space of other class participants, although such an association is an important feature of university classroom discourse. However, O'Boyle's learner corpus is restricted to L2 learner-learner interactions in pedagogical tasks, and thus provides limited insight into L2 learners' use of language in relation to their teachers in the unfolding discourse of typical classroom instruction. According to van Lier (1996, p. 5), teacher-student "interaction is the most important element in the curriculum," as much of the learning occurs through such interactions. Therefore, examining how L2 learners, particularly EAP learners preparing for academic work, use various linguistic resources in the context of typical classroom lessons and how they compare with their teachers would allow us to better understand the classroom discourse behaviors of L2 learners.

L2 Classroom Discourse (L2CD) Corpus

To investigate learner talk in the classroom and how they compare with their teachers, we use the second language classroom discourse (L2CD) corpus created by Lee (2011). This corpus consists of 24 EAP lessons taught by four highly experienced EAP teachers: three female instructors and one male instructor (Burt, Mary, Lillian, and Baker—all pseudonyms). The teachers worked in an intensive English program (IEP) at a large US research university. The IEP was an EAP program for prematriculated, university-bound English as a second language (ESL) students, with an academic task-based curriculum utilizing authentic academic contents (e.g., business, history) to simulate academic tasks of typical university classes. At the time of data collection, Burt and Mary taught oral communication, Lillian taught reading and listening, and Baker taught structure and composition. Each teacher had at least an MA/MS in applied linguistics/TESL, and Burt and Mary were pursuing a PhD in applied linguistics. Including EAP settings, their extensive domestic and international teaching experience ranged from 13 to 21 years ($M = 17.5$; SD = 3.4).

Each EAP teacher's lessons were video-recorded six times over a 16-week semester, totaling 28 hours of recordings. The uneven distribution of hours was due to the length of the teachers' classes. Both Burt and Mary taught afternoon classes that met for 50 minutes (totaling five hours each). Lillian's was a morning class 75 minutes in length (eight hours in total), and Baker's was also a morning class of 100 minutes in length (a total of 10 hours). Both Lillian's and Mary's classes had 15 students each, Burt's class consisted of 13 learners, and Baker's had 17 students.

The video camera was positioned in the back corner of the classrooms. It recorded the teachers' linguistic and non-linguistic behaviors and learners' speech when they were interacting with the teachers in mostly whole classroom formats. Since the learners and teachers did not wear clip-on lavalier microphones, however, it was difficult to capture most of their speech when learners and teachers interacted during individual, pair, or group tasks. Additionally, while three of the classes included student presentations (i.e., oral communication and reading/listening classes), the lessons were recorded on those days involving more regular academic and language tasks such as vocabulary, grammar, reading, writing, and listening activities. Therefore, the recordings are mostly of instructor and learner talk during whole class interactions. The first recordings occurred in weeks 3 and 4, four consecutive lessons were then recorded in weeks 6–9, and the last recording occurred in weeks 11–14. All 24 video-recorded lessons were transcribed verbatim including dysfluencies (see Appendix A for transcription conventions). The transcripts of the video-recorded lessons made up the L2CD corpus. Table 3.1 provides a full description of the L2CD corpus. As previously mentioned, it consists of 24 complete lessons, and the size of the corpus is 179,638 tokens.

In order to examine learner and teacher talk in the L2CD, we divided the corpus into two sub-corpora: L2CD-S and L2CD-T (Table 3.2). The L2CD-S includes only learner contributions to the L2CD while the L2CD-T consists of only teacher contributions. To create these sub-corpora, we divided each lesson file into two files, one for the teacher and one for the learners. For instance, L2CD-1 was divided into L2CD-1-S, where only learner contributions to L2CD-1 were included, while L2CD-1-T consists only of the teacher's contribution to L2CD-1, in this case Baker. The learner files and teacher files were separately compiled to create the two sub-corpora. We then cleaned each file and removed all transcription elements that were not part of the teachers' or learners' speech, such as pauses (e.g., P:02 for 2 seconds of silence), laughter (i.e., <LAUGH>), and nonverbal actions (e.g., teacher nods). None of these were included in the final word count for either sub-corpus. As shown in Table 3.2, the L2CD-S consists of 25,261 tokens and the L2CD-T, 140,668 tokens. The table further shows that the learners only contributed approximately 15% of data to the L2CD, while the teacher contributions constitute nearly 85% of the L2CD. This stark contrast is mostly due to how the lessons were recorded, as mentioned above. However, it is also due to the number of words in teacher and learner turns in typical

Table 3.1 Description of the L2CD corpus (Lee 2011)

Teacher	Course	Level[a]	Class[b] size	Class[c] meeting	Class[d] time	Label	Tokens
Baker	Structure and composition	3	17	MWF	100 min	L2CD-1	8039
						L2CD-2	9977
						L2CD-3	10,178
						L2CD-4	10,528
						L2CD-5	11,448
						L2CD-6	9705
Burt	Oral communication	2	13	MWF	50 min	L2CD-7	7854
						L2CD-8	6843
						L2CD-9	6579
						L2CD-10	7671
						L2CD-11	6632
						L2CD-12	5591
Lillian	Reading and listening	3	15	TTH	80 min	L2CD-13	8392
						L2CD-14	6450
						L2CD-15	6369
						L2CD-16	5085
						L2CD-17	5146
						L2CD-18	7432
Mary	Oral communication	3	15	MWF	50 min	L2CD-19	6086
						L2CD-20	7163
						L2CD-21	5398
						L2CD-22	6849
						L2CD-23	6874
						L2CD-24	7349
Total							179,638

[a]Level refers to the proficiency level of the course: *2* low-intermediate, *3* intermediate
[b]Class size refers to the number of students in the course
[c]Class meeting refers to the days the course met: *M* Monday, *T* Tuesday, *W* Wednesday, *TH* Thursday, and *F* Friday
[d]Class time refers to the total meeting time per lesson

Table 3.2 Description of the L2CD-S and L2CD-T sub-corpora

Sub-corpora	No. of lessons	Range of contribution[a]	Ave. contribution[b]	Tokens	% of contribution[c]
L2CD-S	24	434–2037	1052.54	25,261	15.2
L2CD-T	24	3712–9526	5861.17	140,668	84.8

[a]Range of contribution refers to the range of tokens in each sub-corpus
[b]Ave. contribution refers to the average tokens in each sub-corpus
[c]% of contribution refers to the percentage of learner and teacher contributions to the larger L2CD corpus

lessons. The example below is illustrative of typical learner contributions in teacher-student interactions in the L2CD:

Text Sample 3.1 Learner Contributions in Teacher-Student Interactions in the L2CD (Lee 2011)

T: i want you to say a component. don't worry, we'll we'll we'll work with that. here.
S5: music.
T: good.
S5: music. dance.
T: some other ones from the audience. music. dance. okay. so let's see what we have from the group over there. traditions. behavior.
S3: subculture.
T: food. what what Azeem?
S3: subculture.
T: okay, we have. let's let's look at that, later. foods values beliefs language, behavior and speech.
S5: religion.
T: so we could say
S5: reli-
S4: religion
S5: religion is the is different.
T: let's put speech here.
S10: belief.
T: and we got behavior here. what else.

S10: i think religion is part of belief.
SU: religion?
S5: no n- no.
SU: x belief.
T: good. religious beliefs. what's a value.
S7: what is the value.
T: either give me an example or tell me what value means.
S16: honesty. honesty.
S10: individualism.
S6: collectivist.
S4: collectivist. collectivism.
T: wow. we have some experts in here, i can see.

Notice that nearly all learner contributions are one or two word utterances; only three students (S5, S7, S10) offer longer responses. Similar to previous findings (e.g., Csomay 2007; Walsh 2002), the learners took more turns than the teachers but their turns were short in length and quantity. Therefore, the fewer number of words in learner turns also contributes to the sizeable difference in the two sub-corpora.

To summarize, this chapter reviewed the literature on L2 classroom discourse and presented the L2CD-S and L2CD-T sub-corpora. Using these sub-corpora, Chaps. 4, 5, and 6 explore and compare different linguistics features of learner and teacher talk. In Chap. 4, we examine the issues of hedging and boosting in learner and teacher talk, while Chap. 5 focuses on personal pronouns (or person deixis), particularly first and second person pronouns, in the two sub-corpora. In Chap. 6, we further explore deixis in learner and teacher discourse, specifically concentrating on spatial deixis.

4

Hedging and Boosting in EAP Classroom Discourse

A key aspect of classroom interaction is the way teachers and students use evaluative language to express doubts, opinions, and judgment to establish meaning and to negotiate interpersonal relations. Through the use of evaluative language, particularly hedges and boosters, teachers and students are able to modify their assertions and indicate their stance toward the content and interlocutors. Hedges are linguistic devices (e.g., *might, seem*) used to express uncertainty, doubt, and caution toward propositional content and audience (Hyland 2005). Boosters, on the other hand, are expressions (e.g., *always, know*) used to convey certainty, strong conviction, and full commitment (Hyland 2005). Using these interpersonal resources, class participants are able to explicitly communicate their affective position toward course content and each other, and engage in interactive dialogues in an effort to establish rapport. Although numerous studies have examined hedges and boosters in academic written discourse, far less research has focused on these interpersonal features in learner and teacher talk. In this chapter, we report on a corpus-based comparative analysis of hedges and boosters in EAP learner and teacher discourse.

E. Friginal et al., *Exploring Spoken English Learner Language Using Corpora*,
DOI 10.1007/978-3-319-59900-7_4

Hedges and Boosters

With the increasing understanding that language serves both propositional and non-propositional functions, a considerable amount of research has been devoted to hedges and boosters, particularly in academic written discourse. Previous studies have examined these devices in, for example, research articles (e.g., Hyland 1996; Mur-Dueñas 2011), PhD dissertations and master's theses (e.g., Hyland 2004; Lee and Casal 2014), and undergraduate student essays (e.g., Hinkel 2002; Lee and Deakin 2016). These studies have investigated how hedges and boosters are employed across disciplines (e.g., Hyland 2004, 2005), learning contexts (e.g., Li and Wharton 2012), lingua-cultures (e.g., Lee and Casal 2014; Mur-Dueñas 2011), and genres (e.g., Hong and Cao 2014), in addition to their realizations in L1 and L2 writer texts (e.g., Hyland and Milton 1997; Lee and Deakin 2016). They show that the amount and lexicogrammatical realizations of these stance dimensions vary across educational levels, learning contexts, lingua-cultures, and genres. Further, they demonstrate that L1 and highly-proficient L2 writers of English use far more hedges than boosters in their writing, as displaying caution and modesty in presenting an argument is considered to be highly valued in Anglophone academic cultures (Li and Wharton 2012).

Comparatively speaking, however, little research has examined how hedges and boosters are employed in spoken discourse, specifically in the classroom. Most scholars who have examined these interactional elements in classroom discourse have focused on university lectures. For example, as previously mentioned, Swales and Burke (2003) examined evaluative adjectives and their corresponding boosters (e.g., *very interesting, really nice*) in MICASE (Simpson et al. 2002). Similarly, Mauranen (2001) investigated the relationships between hedges and what she calls discourse reflexivity (e.g., *let me just rephrase*) in lecturer discourse in MICASE. Looking more specifically at a particular linguistic realization of hedges, Lindemann and Mauranen (2001) focused on the forms and functions of *just* in MICASE (e.g., *I just wanna*). Also exploring MICASE, Poos and Simpson (2002) found high frequencies of *sort of/sorta* and *kind of/kinda* in instructor discourse, particularly in the humanities and social sciences. Biber et al. (2004) compared lexical bundles, or the most frequent multi-word sequences in a register, in university lectures, textbooks, conversations, and academic prose. They found that classroom discourse and conversations include far greater stance bundles (e.g., *I think it was*) than either of the written registers. Lin (2012) compared softeners and intensifiers in lecturer talk in MICASE and the BASE corpus of university lectures and seminars in the U.K. Although educational cultures appear to play a role in the distribution of these stance elements, she argues that lecturing style (i.e., monologic vs. interactive teaching) plays a much more central role in university classrooms. These studies have underscored the pervasiveness of stance features in the discourse practices of university instructors, and have made signification contributions to our understanding of how university lecturers express doubt and certainty.

Despite the importance of hedging and boosters in university lectures, surprisingly little attention has been devoted to how these stance features are enacted in EAP classrooms. We are aware of only one study that has examined these devices in this context. Lee and Subtirelu (2015) compared hedges and boosters, among other interpersonal dimensions, in EAP teacher and university lecturer speech. While no significant differences were found for either of these stance features between the teachers, they discovered that hedges were highly frequent in both university and EAP instructors. Boosters, however, played a lesser role in the teacher talk of either group. They argue that when it comes to hedges and boosters, the real-time context of the classroom overrides pedagogical foci and approaches.

Yet, while EAP teachers' work involves preparing academically-oriented learners, which includes helping students gain proficient control over these interpersonal dimensions of communication in order to be successful in university settings, little is known of how EAP learners use these resources in the classroom and how they compare with their teachers. In the following sections, we describe our analytical procedure for conducting this investigation and discuss our findings of the hedging and boosting characteristics of EAP learners and teachers.

Analytical Procedure

As discussed in Chap. 3, the data used for this analysis consist of EAP learner and teacher contributions to the L2CD corpus: L2CD-S and L2CD-T sub-corpora. This section outlines the analytical procedure used to examine hedges and boosters in the two sub-corpora. The departure point for our analysis was the list of hedges and boosters provided in Hyland (2005, pp. 221–223). Hyland's list, though comprehensive, was created principally for written discourse. Therefore, we added a few other hedging and boosting devices commonly found in spoken discourse and from our examination of both sub-corpora (e.g., *kind of, pretty, so, too*). Appendix B provides a complete list of hedges and boosters investigated. Although the lists are inclusive, they are obviously not exhaustive, as "it may not be possible to capture every interpersonal feature or [speaker] intention in a coding scheme" (Hyland 2005, p. 31). Nonetheless, these lists provide a means to compare how these resources are employed, for example, across speakers/writers, registers, genres, cultures, and communities.

The hedging and boosting devices were then classified into sub-functions, as delineated by Hyland (1996, 2005). In Hyland's framework, hedges are categorized into two main sub-functions: content-oriented and audience-oriented hedges.[1] According to Hyland (1996), content-oriented hedges "concern a statement's *adequacy conditions:* the relationship between proposition and a representation of reality" (p. 439). These hedges, in turn, are categorized into accuracy-oriented and speaker-oriented hedges. While accuracy-oriented hedges are used to express the uncertainty of the accuracy, precision, and reliability of the propositional content (e.g., *almost, could*), speaker-oriented hedges protect a speaker against threats of contradiction by reducing the speaker's commitment to the proposition (e.g., *assume, suppose*). On the other hand, audience-oriented hedges attend to a statement's *acceptability conditions*, or the acceptability of statements to the audience. These hedging devices proactively attend to an audience's judgment and potential objection and show respect and modesty (e.g., *in my view, would*).

Furthermore, Hyland (2005) classifies boosters into two sub-functions: emphatics and amplifiers. Emphatics (e.g., *certain, of course*) function to "reinforce [the] truth value" of a proposition (Hyland 2005, p. 130). In contrast, amplifiers (e.g., *a lot/lots, never*) serve to strengthen one's commitment by intensifying the meaning of a statement. Through the use of these emphatics and amplifiers, speakers are able to assert their conviction and commitment to a proposition.

Using *AntConc* (Anthony 2014), we searched electronically for every item listed in Appendix B in order to identify examples of hedges and boosters in the two sub-corpora. Each example was then manually examined in its context to ensure that all potential items were functioning as hedges and boosters rather than as propositions, and to exclude those that did not serve as hedges or boosters. For instance, in (1), the adverb *about* functions as a hedge to indicate the approximate amount of time the teacher wants the class to devote to the task. In (2), however, the learner uses the preposition *about* to signal that the subsequent proposition concerns a woman's grandfather.

Text Sample 4.1 (1–4) Examining Hedges and Boosters

(1) T: okay, let's take about two more minutes, and then we're gonna move on and i'll try to come to everybody. (L2CD-T-1)

(2) T: okay yeah she's not happy she wants something better for the future anything else that you remember?
S: she talks about her grandfather. (L2CD-S-13)

Additionally, in (3), the adverb *too* functions as a booster to amplify the student's attitude toward the statement, while in (4) it means *also*:

(3) S: oh. too cold i don't want to do anything. (L2CD-S-7)

(4) T: okay today we're gonna spend time re- um preparing for the test too okay? so, does, anyone have their keyword cards with them? (L2CD-T-19)

Items such as (2) and (4), which did not function as a hedging or boosting device, were excluded from our final analysis. Examining each instance in context permitted us to determine the specific function of each item and to discount those items not serving as a hedge or booster.

Upon identifying all instances ofboosters andhedges in both sub-corpora, these items were normalized to occurrences per 1000 words (ptw). Differences in distribution between the two sub-corpora were calculated usinglog-likelihood. Similar to a Chi-square test, alog-likelihood is a common statistical measure used in corpus analyses to compare differences in two corpora (Baker 2010), as it determines whether the differences in occurrences are statistically significant. Rayson's (n.d.) Log-likelihood Calculator was used to perform the log-likelihood analysis. Any value of 3.84 or higher is significant at the $p < 0.05$ level.

Results and Discussion

Table 4.1 shows the pervasiveness of hedges and boosters in both the L2CD-S and 2CD-T. However, these stance elements, as the table shows, are more frequent in the L2CD-T at a significant level. This is not surprising since teachers contribute more to classroom discourse than L2 students and have better control over these stance features. As indicated in Table 3.2 (Chap. 3), the L2CD-S sub-corpora accounts for slightly over 15% of the entire L2CD corpus.

Nonetheless, both teachers and learners used these interpersonal resources very frequently, with greater than one hedging or boosting device occurring every 50 words in the L2CD-T and nearly one device occurring every 50 words in the L2CD-S. While the "common sense" view of language in the classroom is that it is a vehicle to impart and receive knowledge, the findings show that both teachers and students are heavily involved in evaluating the propositional content and each other in the classroom. In their analysis of EAP lessons and university lectures,

Table 4.1 Comparison of hedges and boosters in the two sub-corpora

	L2CD-S		L2CD-T		
	Tokens	Per 1000 words	Tokens	Per 1000 words	Log-likelihood
Hedges	239	9.46	2294	16.31	74.36*
Boosters	224	8.87	1162	8.26	0.93
Total	480	18.33	3456	24.57	34.04*

*A log-likelihood greater than 3.84 indicates a p-value less than 0.05

Lee and Subtirelu (2015) found that instructors in both educational contexts draw heavily on these interpersonal resources to mark their stance toward content and students. According to Hyland (2009), "evaluative language helps to create and negotiate interpersonal relations" between teachers and learners (p. 104), and thus contributes to the "high levels of involvement and interactivity" distinctively found in classroom discourse (p. 102). Although Hyland (2009) and Lee and Subtirelu (2015) focus on the stance features of teachers, the results show that learners are also highly involved in contributing to the establishment of rapport in the classroom.

Patterns of Hedges in Learner Talk and Teacher Talk

As shown in Table 4.1, both learners and teachers used hedges more frequently than boosters. In the L2CD-S, nearly 52% were hedges, while in the L2CD-T, the number was over 66%. The table also shows that the L2CD-T (16.31 ptw) comprised significantly greater instances of hedges than the L2CD-S (9.46 ptw), thus demonstrating that learners are less tentative in their assertions than are teachers. This finding supports previous research on instructor discourse. Lee and Subtirelu (2015) also found that both EAP and university teachers used hedges at a highly frequent level. As Hyland (2009) explains, hedges are highly common in instructor discourse, as such resources are used to display caution toward information presented as well as to demonstrate modesty and politeness in an effort to reduce the inherent teacher-student power asymmetry in the classroom.

Upon examining the specific linguistic resources used to qualify statements in the L2CD-S, we found that six expressions (*bit, just, maybe, sometimes, think, would/'d*) constituted nearly 87% of all hedging devices, and the students only used 20 out of the 102 potential devices examined. The teachers, conversely, utilized about half of all hedging devices investigated, and 18 items (e.g., *could, might, pretty*) made up nearly 88% of all hedging devices in the L2CD-T. The restricted variety of hedging devices found in the L2CD-S suggests that these students' linguistic repertories for marking uncertainty were quite limited. Considering that these ESL learners were still in the process of developing both linguistic and communicative competence, this finding is not surprising. The narrow range of hedging devices used and the relative infrequency of hedges overall might also be suggestive of the rather limited contribution learners make to classroom discourse as a whole. As Walsh (2002) reports, most student contributions to classroom discourse are short in both length and quantity. Therefore, perhaps, it is not only their restricted language abilities but also the lack of overall contribution to the classroom discourse that might have affected their use of hedges, particularly since a great majority of students' contributions in the L2 classroom are often short responses to teachers' display questions.

However, as shown in Table 4.2, similarities exist among the top five most frequently utilized hedging devices in the two sub-copora. The two groups share three common devices: *just*, *maybe*, and *think*. Expectedly, *just* is among the most frequently used devices, as illustrated in (5) and (6).

Text Samples 4.2 (5–17) Patterns of Hedges in Learner and Teacher Talk

(5) S1: yes. but, i i i talk about but <u>just</u> a little bit. i don't think that i can. explain (L2CD-S-11)

(6) T: this is the same as number one it's <u>just</u> a different way to say it. (L2CD-T-6)

Similar to *just* being highly frequent in both EAP teacher and student speech, it is the most common mitigator in academic spoken discourse (Lee and Subtirelu 2015; Lindemann and Mauranen 2001). While *just*

Table 4.2 Top five most frequent hedging devices in the two sub-corpora

	L2CD-S				L2CD-T		
	Hedging device	Tokens	Per 1000 words		Hedging device	Tokens	Per 1000 words
1	**think**	100	3.96	1	**just**	361	2.57
2	**maybe**	40	1.58	2	could	231	1.64
3	**just**	35	1.39	3	would/'d	228	1.62
4	sometimes	19	0.75	4	**think**	210	1.49
5	bit	7	0.28	5	**maybe**	206	1.47

is the most preferred hedging device in the L2CD-T, the most frequent hedging word in the L2CD-S is the mental verb *think*:

(7) S9: i think the Church of England is better than Church of (L2CD-S-22)

Nearly 42% of hedges identified in the L2CD-S consist of *think.* Biber (2006b) also found that *I (don't) think* is a highly common stance marker in classroom discourse to express uncertainty. In fact, *I think* has been found to be highly frequent across various university speech events (Poos and Simpson 2002) as well as in learner-learner interactions (O'Boyle 2014). The student's uncertainty in (7) is confirmed by the teacher (8), who responds by repeating twice that the statement is merely the student's opinion:

(8) T: there comes Binh's opinion okay very good that's your opinion right? (L2CD-T-22)

However, the relative overuse of *think*, as opposed to the range of other hedging options available, is suggested of learners' limited linguistic repertories for conveying uncertainty.

Furthermore, Poos and Simpson (2002) found that *kind of* and *sort of* (and their reduced forms) were two of the most frequent hedges in academic spoken English. While both of these phrases appear in the L2CD-T to varying degrees, neither of them occur in the L2CD-S. The learners did not use *sort of* at all, and *kind of* was used only in the literal sense (i.e., *a type of*):

(9) S5: people make this kind of gesture when they pass an acquaintance or stranger along the street (L2CD-S4)

It is also important to note that the modals *could* and *would* are among the top five most frequently used hedges in the L2CD-T, as shown in Table 4.2. Slightly over 57% of all hedges in the L2CD-T are modals. Lee and Subtirelu (2015) found that modals are highly frequent in both EAP teacher and university instructor discourse. In the L2CD-S, however, only approximately 5% are hedging modals. In fact, there are only 61 total instances of modals, and those used as hedging devices account for about 28% of all modals. The remaining roughly 72% are dynamic (10) or deontic (11) modals:

(10) S6: honestly. they could not agree on how to set up each branch of the new government. (L2CD-S-24)
(11) S7: would you pronounce this? (L2CD-S-7)

In (10), the student uses *could* to discuss the lack of ability of the U.S. government to come to an agreement on how to establish the branches of its government, while, in (11), *would* is utilized to request for the teacher to pronounce a word.

Now, we turn to examining the sub-functions of hedges in the L2CD-S and L2CD-T sub-corpora. As Table 4.3 shows, both students and teachers used content-oriented more than audience-oriented hedges. Specifically, both teachers and students made greater use of accuracy-oriented hedges than speaker-oriented hedges to mitigate the certainty of the propositional content, but the L2CD-T included more than twice as many of these hedges as the L2CD-S.

The learners primarily used *just* and *maybe*, which comprised over 57% of all such speaker-oriented hedges:

(12) S5: we're just we're just mixing because we want uh we were we were one colon- from Spain (L2CD-S-2)
(13) S2: for example we'll write this, the title maybe use we know every time we use the and then, yesterday you use just a use one letter to, word. (L2CD-S-21)

Table 4.3 Comparison of hedge sub-functions in the two sub-corpora

	L2CD-S		L2CD-T		
Sub-functions	Tokens	Per 1000 words	Tokens	Per 1000 words	Log-likelihood
Content-oriented	131	5.19	1804	12.82	130.65*
Accuracy-oriented	131	5.19	1769	12.58	124.04*
Speaker-oriented	0	0.00	35	0.25	11.56*
Audience-oriented	108	4.28	490	3.48	3.55

*A log-likelihood greater than 3.84 indicates a p-value less than 0.05

Including these two items, the other main accuracy-oriented device that students employed (i.e., *sometimes*) is among the top five most frequent hedges in the L2CD-S, as shown in Table 4.2. This suggests that the majority of learner hedges are those used to express uncertainty of the accuracy, reliability, or precision of statements made. The accuracy-oriented hedges in the L2CD-T are more diverse. Besides *just, could*, and *maybe* listed in Table 4.2, the teachers also frequently used of a host of other devices including *might* (14) and *little*, often expressed as lexical phrases *a little* and *a little bit* (15):

(14) T: okay some of you might need to practice them again this weekend okay? all right? because these are gonna show up on, the note-taking, and some of them will be on our test, all right? yeah? (L2CD-T-19)

(15) T: okay, all right yeah, so, um sometimes people say what they believe but they don't do what they believe, okay? i would s- well i'm not saying that you let's let's change this a little a little bit okay? (L2CD-T-13)

Although very few speaker-oriented hedges (e.g., *seem, suggest*) are present in the L2CD-T, it is interesting to note that the students did not employ any of this hedge type. As mentioned previously, speaker-oriented hedges moderate a speaker's categorical commitment to assertions as a way to protect the speaker from criticisms, and thus reduce the speaker's discourse presence (Hyland 1996). Perhaps, due to the nature of L2 classroom interactions, there may be less of a need for learners and teachers to guard against threats of criticism. Lee (2016) contends that EAP teachers use various means to encourage student participation in order to enhance interaction in the classroom and to demonstrate that students' contributions are important in the negotiation of knowledge. Although teachers may correct learners' linguistic mistakes or challenge their ideas, L2 teachers would need to be much more open to and less critical of learners' errors or ideas in order to increase participation. Walsh (2002) observes that some aspects of teacher talk unintentionally obstruct learner involvement and can impede learning potential. Therefore, it is possible that the L2CD-S's lack of speaker-oriented hedges is indicative of classrooms where students feel encouraged to participate in classroom dialogues without having the need to protect themselves from being overly criticized. Another possibility is that, as these learners were still in the process of learning English, they had yet to develop sophisticated language to inject face-saving hedges. More likely, however, participants in L2 classrooms make very little use of such hedging devices, as evidenced by the lack of this hedge type even in the L2CD-T. Therefore, this hedge type might be less reflective of classroom discourse, while such strategies might occur more commonly in academic writing where writers need to reduce their propositional commitment in order to protect them against threats of contradiction (Hyland 1996).

However, as shown in Table 4.3, no significant difference was found for audience-oriented hedges between the two sub-corpora. While the students used this type nearly as much as they did content-oriented hedges, the teachers made little use of audience-oriented hedges. Audience-oriented hedges function to moderate potential interlocutor disagreement, thus potentially permitting greater listener acceptance. In the L2CD-S, such hedges were primarily realized through the modal *think* (92.6% of audience-oriented hedges), while *think* (42.9%) and *would/'d* (46.5%) are most frequent in the L2CD-T (totaling 89.4%):

(16) S10: i think religion is part of belief. (L2CD-S-2)
(17) T: so. i think, organization wise. i would suggest you move this sentence. you'll make it. it, it, it's better. (L2CD-T-1)

In these examples, the learner and teacher employ these audience-oriented hedges to reduce the force of the proposals made in their efforts to anticipate the interlocutor's potential objections and to demonstrate deference. In so doing, they avoid forcing the listener, who may hold different perspectives, to comply with their insistence.

The two groups utilized hedges quantitatively and qualitatively in different ways. The EAP teachers displayed greater uncertainty than students in their endeavor to show modesty and politeness as a way to reduce the power distance between themselves and their learners. As learners are still in the process of developing their linguistic and communicative repertoire, it is not surprising that the linguistic representations of their hedging strategies were limited in variety and quantity. The varied amounts of hedges used by teachers are not only indicative of their better command over these interpersonal resources, but they also may be one way of providing L2 learners with linguistic models of how to interact meaningfully and appropriately in communicative situations, although students at this point in their development may only notice a few at a time. As shown in Table 4.2, the L2CD-S and L2CD-T share three of the top five most frequent hedging devices. This may be suggestive of the impact of teachers' classroom discourse practices, though limited, on learners' speech in the classroom.

Patterns of Boosters in Learner Talk and Teacher Talk

Unlike hedges, no significant difference was found for boosters in the two sub-corpora, as shown in Table 4.1. Similar to Lee and Subtirelu (2015), boosters were less frequently utilized than hedges in both sub-corpora. Both teachers and learners employed boosters in roughly the same amount. However, as also shown in Table 4.1, there are only slightly fewer boosters than hedges in the L2CD-S, unlike the L2CD-T where hedges are considerably greater than boosters. Actually, over 48% of all stance markers examined are boosters in the L2CD-S, while the L2CD-T consist of only a third. Even in written genres, such as argumentative essays (Lee and Deakin 2016), master's theses and PhD dissertations (Hyland 2004), and research articles (Hyland 2005), boosters are much less frequently utilized than hedges. Thus, it seems as though EAP teachers' use of hedges and boosters match the conventions of Anglophone culture in general. Given that there are no comparable studies of students' use of boosters in the classroom, we are unable to determine to what extent these L2 learners compare with other student populations. Nevertheless, relative to the teachers, these learners expressed much more certainty in their statements, perhaps, partly due to their limited linguistic abilities.

This limitation in the students' linguistic repertories is reflected in the types of boosting devices used. Similar to their restricted range of hedges,

Table 4.4 Top five most frequent boosting devices in the two sub-corpora

	L2CD-S				L2CD-T		
	Boosting device	Tokens	Per 1000 words		Boosting device	Tokens	Per 1000 words
1	**know**	117	4.63	1	**very**	312	2.22
2	so	26	1.03	2	**know**	157	1.12
3	**very**	23	0.91	3	**a lot/lots**	130	0.92
4	always	12	0.48	4	actually	92	0.65
5	**a lot/lots**	11	0.44	5	really	86	0.61

the learners were confined to only 12 expressions out of the 61 possible booster resources examined. Among these 12, over 88% consisted of only six devices. In contrast, the teachers used 30 of the total booster expressions analyzed, although they mainly relied on 13 (over 94% of all boosters).

Table 4.4 presents the top five most frequent boosters found in the two sub-corpora. For the students, these five devices account for nearly 85% of all boosters in the L2CD-S, while for teachers, the top five items comprise about two-thirds of all boosters. As can be seen, the stative verb *know* is the most preferred boosting item in the L2CD-S (over 52% of all boosters).

Text Samples 4.3 (18–27) Patterns of Boosters in Learner and Teacher Talk

(18) S6: i have problems. i know this doesn't look good, but doesn't sounds good or bad. (L2CD-S-2)

The learner in (18) informs the teacher that he is aware that something does not appear to be "good" in his essay. The learners used this verb over four times more frequently than the second booster on the top five list. While the EAP teachers also utilized *know* quite frequently, the most commonly employed booster in the L2CD-T is *very*, as in:

(19) T: excellent and very nice sentence stress did you hear that? that sounded wonderful. (L2CD-T-22)

This may be expected, as it is one of the most widely used boosters in the English language. Research has revealed that *very* is not only highly frequent in conversations (Kennedy 2003), but is also more commonly used in university classrooms than academic writing (Swales and Burke 2003). In (19), notice the use of the collocation *very nice*. Another common collocate occurring with *very* in the L2CD-T is *very good:*

(20) T: different words are okay as long as it's the same idea i like that. that's actually a <u>very good</u> thing to do Rosalie. (L2CD-T-10)

Unsurprisingly, the phrases *very good* and *very nice* are frequent in the L2CD-T sub-corpora. It has been found that *good* and *nice* are some of the most frequent collocates with *very* in English conversations (Biber et al. 1999). *Very* is also among the top five most frequently utilized boosters in the L2CD-S. Interestingly, however, *very good* and *very nice* appear only once each in the learner sub-corpora. This may be due to the fact that teachers are the ones responsible for assessing students' performances while learners are not expected to evaluate their teachers directly. In the L2CD-S, no collocational patterns were found with *very*; the learners used *very* with a host of other adjectives (e.g., *gentle, different, cold, fast*).

Before examining the booster sub-functions in the two sub-corpora, we highlight the fact that three of the top five boosters in the L2CD-T also appear among the top five in the L2CD-S. As we reported earlier, learners and teachers share three of the top five hedges (Table 4.2). We suggested that learners might be incidentally acquiring, to varying degrees, the types of language used to mark stance that teachers tend to use most frequently. The similarities in the most frequently used boosters in the two sub-corpora seem to further support our claim.

Among the booster sub-categories analyzed, the learners and teachers used both types of boosters in significantly different ways. The learners employed emphatics significantly more frequently than the teachers, but the L2CD-T includes significantly more amplifiers (Table 4.5).

The learners used three other emphatics (e.g., *of course, true*), but the principal means by which the learners asserted their conviction was

Table 4.5 Comparison of booster sub-functions in the two sub-corpora

	L2CD-S		L2CD-T		
Sub-functions	Tokens	Per 1000 words	Tokens	Per 1000 words	Log-likelihood
Emphatics	134	5.30	519	3.69	13.05*
Amplifiers	90	3.56	643	4.57	5.22*

*A log-likelihood greater than 3.84 indicates a p-value less than 0.05

through the mental verb *know*, as explained above. This was also true for teachers, who overwhelmingly preferred *know* over other emphatic boosters (30.3% of all emphatics), as in:

(21) T: you had a chance to talk a little bit about, um the ideas as well as some using some of the content words, and i <u>know</u> some people are still struggling with what exactly one point five means, uh let's talk about this again … (L2CD-T-17)

In addition to this verb, the teachers used 15 other boosting devices in varying degrees, including *clear, sure, of course*, and *true*. Nonetheless, compared to the learners, the teachers did not make much use of emphatics. Unlike learners, EAP teachers may be mindful of the need to moderate one's assertions in an effort to open up the dialogic space.

Amplifiers, however, are more frequent in the L2CD-T. The primary amplifying adverb the teachers used was *very*, as reported above. They also used 11 other amplifying adverbs, although, including *very*, the teachers mainly used four other amplifiers: *a lot/lots, always, so*, and *too*. Together, these five adverbs accounted for over 92% of all amplifiers the teachers employed. *A lot/lots*, the second ranked amplifier in the L2CD-T, most frequently collocated with *of*, as in *a lot of/lots of*:

(22) T: we have <u>a lot of</u> things to look at actually for grammar. let's look at. let's look at verbs, because i left i left you with hanging … (L2CD-T-3)

(23) T: i can give you <u>lots of</u> homework because we have a long weekend. (L2CD-T-9)

Dissimilar to the teachers, the students were quite restricted in the range of amplifying adverbs used, primarily limiting themselves to those four amplifiers listed in Table 4.4: *a lot/lots*, *always*, *so* and *very*; for example:

(24) S4: on Friday we have a lot of homework (L2CD-S-10)
(25) S1: i always put many information. (L2CD-S-21)
(26) S3: chocolate make you so happy (L2CD-S-7)
(27) S7: how about the words in the is very different. (L2CD-T-16)

These four items account for 80% of all amplifying adverbs found in the L2CD-S. Remarkably, the four adverbs that the learners most commonly used are among those five that teachers also most frequently used. While these amplifying adverbs are obviously frequent English words, it is striking that all of the ones that the learners used most often are those that the teachers also commonly employed. This finding appears to provide additional support to our contention that learners implicitly may be adopting the hedging and boosting strategies of their teachers, at least the most frequent ones. Due to their high frequency of use by teachers, they might be much more salient for learners, and thus they may be easier to notice and use for learners, as reflected in their high frequency in the L2CD-S.

Related to issues of interaction in the classroom, the next chapter further focuses on interpersonal resources in the classroom discourse practices of EAP learners and teachers by examining their uses of personal pronouns.

Note

1. In Hyland (1996), audience-oriented hedges are referred to as reader-oriented hedges, and speaker-oriented hedges are called writer-oriented hedges because his focus was on written rather than spoken language.

5

You, I, and *We*: Personal Pronouns in EAP Classroom Discourse

Personal pronouns are important markers of teacher-student relationships, as they permit both parties to locate themselves and each other in the varying conversational spaces in classroom settings. They also serve as critical indicators of degrees of personal involvement and interaction in the classroom. While a growing number of studies have examined instructors' use of personal pronouns in university classrooms, very little is known of L2 learners' and teachers' use of the same. This chapter explores personal pronouns, specifically *you*, *I*, and *we* and their variants in learner and teacher speech in the EAP classrooms. We not only examine the distribution of these pronouns in the L2CD-S and L2CD-T, we also report on the comparative analysis of their sub-functions in the two sub-corpora.

Personal Pronouns in the Classroom

Personal pronouns play important roles in the classroom, as these markers reflect levels of learner and teacher involvement, engagement, and interaction in classroom events. From the perspective of politeness theory (Brown and Levinson 1987), the use of inclusive-*we*, including both

E. Friginal et al., *Exploring Spoken English Learner Language Using Corpora*,
DOI 10.1007/978-3-319-59900-7_5

speaker and hearer, has a rapport-maintenance effect, leading to positive politeness. However, *you* and *I* have a distancing effect, resulting in negative politeness. According to Brown and Levinson, positive politeness strategies are oriented toward a hearer's positive face and are employed to attend to the hearer's desires to be liked and respected. In contrast, negative politeness strategies aim to minimize threats to the hearer's negative face and seek to avoid imposing on the hearer. Similarly, personal pronouns, in Kamio's (2001) theory of information territory, mark a speaker's conceptualization of the proximal and distal conversational spaces of the speaker and hearer. The use of *I* and *we* indicates the proximal space of the speaker's territory while *you* is used to position the hearer in the hearer's territory. The positioning of the speaker and hearer in a continuum of domains in the conversational space references how a speaker conceptualizes his/her degree of closeness with a hearer.

Due to their importance in classroom interactions, a growing number of studies have examined the distributions, forms, and functions of personal pronouns in university classrooms. In her analysis of L1 and L2 English-speaking mathematics teaching assistants (TAs), Rounds (1987a, b) reported that *we* was the most frequently used pronoun in successful TAs' classroom discourse practices. Using MICASE, Fortanet (2004) examined personal pronouns in university lectures, colloquia, and study groups, and compared her findings with that of Rounds. Contradicting Rounds, Fortanet found that *you*, as opposed to *we*, is the preferred pronoun in these academic speech events. In fact, *we* was found to be the least represented pronoun. Fortanet attributes these differences to the changing nature of academic spoken discourse. Specifically focusing on different phases of academic lectures (i.e., introduction and closing) in MICASE, Cheng (2012) and Lee (2009) explored personal pronouns in university lecturers of small and large classes. Similar to Fortanet (2004), they both found that *we* is less frequently used than *you* and *I*. Yet, while Lee (2009) found greater use of *you* in large-class and *I* in small-class lecture introductions, Cheng (2012) reported that all pronouns are much more common in small-class lecture closings. The differences may be attributed to the fact that Lee (2009) only examined *you*, *I*, and *we* while Cheng (2012) analyzed all pronoun forms, including possessive determiners and pronouns; and their respective corpora consisted of different phases of university lectures. Yeo and Ting (2014) also investigated the use of personal pronouns in large-class lecture introductions delivered in English at a Malaysian university. Supporting previous studies, they found that *we* is the least frequent while *you* is the most frequent in these lecture introductions. Yeo and Ting further analyzed their data to examine different pronoun functions; for example, *you* for audience (or audience-*you*) and *you* for an indefinite reference (generalized-*you*). Like Cheng (2012), they found that university instructors made greater use of the audience-*you* than the generalized-*you* across disciplines and class sizes. These studies suggest that the greater use of the audience-*you* indicates lecturers' desires to establish rapport and maintain high levels of student interaction and participation.

Within Hyland's (2005) interpersonal model of metadiscourse, Lee and Subtirelu (2015) examined the use of personal pronouns in university lecturer (in MICASE) and EAP teachers' talk. They found that *you* occurs significantly more frequently than *I* and *we* combined in both EAP and university instructors' discourse, and that EAP teachers use significantly more *you* than university lecturers. Concentrating specifically on EAP teachers, Lee (2016) analyzed the most frequently occurring clusters (e.g., *we're going to/gonna, I want you to*) in different phases of classroom lessons (i.e., opening, activity-cycle, closing). He found that *we're going to/gonna* and *I'm going to/gonna* were the most common cluster in the opening phase, but *you're going to/gonna* were more common in the other two phases. Lee suggests that these pronoun choices reflect EAP teachers' conceptualization of students' and their own roles in classroom events.

Although these studies have made important contributions to our understanding of university and EAP instructors' use of pronouns in the classroom, little is known of EAP learners' use of these interpersonal resources and how they compare with their teachers. Recently, a few studies have examined students' personal pronoun usage in the classroom. Cheng (2012) investigated university students' pronoun choices in MICASE lecture closings. Unlike lecturers, students most commonly used *I*. In fact, *I* occurred more frequently than *you* and *we* combined. When they did use *we*, it was used primarily to refer to the speaking student and classmates, but excluding the teacher. O'Boyle (2014) compared students' use of *you* and *I* and their cluster patterns (including pronoun repetitions) in two corpora: various L1 university classroom genres (i.e., lectures, seminars, workshops, group work) and L2 learner-learner interactions in EAP classroom group tasks. Dissimilar to Cheng (2012), O'Boyle (2014) found that *you* is more frequently used than *I* by both student groups and university instructors. In fact, she reports that *you* is significantly higher in L2 than L1 students' discourse, but it is most frequent in teacher talk. L2 learners also used *I* more frequently than both L1 students and lecturers. Furthermore, the stance marker *I think* was found to be the most frequent 2-word cluster in both L1 and L2 learner talk, but it occurred nearly three times as frequently in the L2 learner corpus.

Although O'Boyle's study provides important insight into L2 learners' use of personal pronouns, only examining L2 learner-learner interactions limits our understanding of how EAP learners use these interpersonal features in relation to their teachers. As she acknowledges, investigations into how learners and teachers use personal pronouns in the context of typical classroom lessons are needed. Such studies would allow us to better understand how learners and teachers conceptualize and position each other in the unfolding discourse of the classroom as well as how interactions between class participants are realized through these interactional markers.

Analytical Procedure

Using the L2CD-S and L2CD-T sub-corpora introduced in Chap. 3, this section describes the procedures used to analyze personal pronouns in both sub-corpora. Based on previous analyses of personal pronouns in classroom discourse, particularly university settings, Table 5.1 presents the framework we adopted in analyzing first and second person pronouns in the two sub-corpora. The subject, object, and possessive determiner forms of the first person singular (*I, me, my*), first person plural (*we, us, our*), and second person pronouns (*you, your*) were analyzed. However, reflexive and possessive pronouns (e.g., *myself, mine*) were excluded in our analysis because these forms were highly infrequent in both sub-corpora, as also found in previous studies (e.g., Crawford Camiciottoli 2005; Yeo and Ting 2014).

Table 5.1 Framework for personal pronoun classification

Pronoun	Referent	Example
First person		
I, me, my	The speaker only	*Okay. All right so I wanna talk a little bit about what's going to happen today is Monday*
Inclusive *we, us, let's, our*	The speaker and audience	*Can we use our vocabulary cards?*
Exclusive *we, us, our*	The speaker and other people	*All right can I I need to collect the tests after you ... You know we switch them out we use them again so...*
Second person		
Audience *you* (sub & obj), *your*	The audience only	*Okay you tell me about your notes?*
Generalized *you* (sub & obj), *your*	Indefinite or impersonal subject	*So, to balance means that, you keep track of all the money ... your checks...*

The variants of the first person singular pronoun are used to make reference to the speaker only, or in our case a student (1) or teacher (2).

Text Samples 5.1 (1–10) Pronoun Variants

(1) S: <u>i</u> don't know about this. (L2CD-S-1)
(2) T: <u>i</u> want you to look and see if they are correct. (L2CD-T-1)

Following Crawford Camiciottoli (2005), *you* and its variants can denote two different referents: audience-*you* or generalized-*you*. Audience-*you* is used to refer to only a student, a teacher, a group of students, or the entire class:

(3) S: Burt can <u>you</u> come for a minute? (L2CD-S-7)
(4) T: what i need <u>you</u> to do now is please take out a piece of paper. (L2CD-T-7)

In (3), the student directly addresses the teacher (Burt) to ask for assistance, while, in (4), the teacher addresses the entire class. In contrast, generalized-*you* makes reference to an indefinite referent:

(5) S: it's important to learn about values because, you can understand why people act the way they do, and it's easy for you to mingle with them. (L2CD-S-13)

(6) T: it's kind hard to pay a thousand dollars a month when you don't have a job, okay that's, problem number one (L2CD-T-13)

In both examples, the referent is a generic, non-specific *you*, which can be substituted by an indefinite subject (*people*) or *we*. Generalized-*you* is used when an alliance with others is not previously established, and thus it, pragmatically speaking, is nearly equivalent to *we* (Kamio 2001). However, it should be acknowledged that, in a few instances, it is not always clear whether the referent is audience-*you* or generalized-*you* (Yeo and Ting 2014). Therefore, a significant effort was made to recover the intended meaning by closely examining each example in its context.

Lastly, the first person plural pronoun was categorized into two types: inclusive-*we* and exclusive-*we* and their variants. In previous studies (e.g., Cheng 2012; Fortanet 2004; Rounds 1987b; Yeo and Ting 2014), other functional types of *we* were analyzed (i.e., *we* for *I*, *we* for *you*, and *we* for indefinite). However, as Yeo and Ting (2014) points out, "[i]t may suffice to analyze the use of *we* using the dichotomy of inclusive-*we* and exclusive-*we* to study use of personal pronouns" in the classroom, as such fine-grained distinction of *we* was not very revealing. Therefore, we chose to only analyze inclusive- and exclusive-*we* and their object and possessive determiner forms. Inclusive-*we* includes both the speaker and audience (e.g., student(s) and teacher or teacher and student(s)):

(7) S: what we gonna do today. (L2CD-S-11)

(8) T: Yosibell i'll talk to you after class okay? we'll talk about it because now Bill's gonna come up and talk, so i'll talk to you right after class today. okay? (L2CD-T-11)

In contrast, exclusive-*we* includes the speaker but excludes the addressee. When a teacher uses the exclusive-*we*, he or she excludes the student(s):

(9) T: we call it arranged marriages. in the US, that doesn't occur very hardly ever unless it's a not for American, family. not very often. so that's a value or a belief. (L2CD-T-3)

In this example, *we* does not mean the teacher and students; instead, it refers to the English-speaking community, of which the teacher is a part. However, in this study, when a student uses the exclusive-*we*, he or she excludes the teacher:

(10) S: what do we give you for today. (L2CD-S-19)

In (10), *we* refers to the student and other classmates but not the teacher. We, however, excluded the expression *here we go*, as this idiom does not necessarily denote the speaker, audience, or some other referent, and was exclusively used by one teacher.

To analyze personal pronouns in the L2CD-S and L2CD-T, we again used *AntConc* (Anthony 2014) to search electronically for every instance of the various forms of first person and second person pronouns. After identifying all examples of these pronouns in both sub-corpora, we manually examined each pronoun in its context and categorized it according to its sub-functions, based on the analytical framework presented in Table 5.1. We then counted the occurrences of these pronouns, and the items were normalized to occurrences per 1000 words (ptw) in both sub-corpora. To determine whether the differences in occurrences were statistically significant, we conducted a log-likelihood analysis using Rayson's (n.d.) Log-likelihood Calculator. Any value of 3.84 or higher is significant at the $p < 0.05$ level.

Results and Discussion

Table 5.2 shows that personal pronouns were widely used by both students and teachers. A total of 2205 instances of personal pronouns were identified in the L2CD-S (87.29 ptw), and 13,373 occurrences were found in the L2CD-T (95.07 ptw). This translates into nearly one in every 10 words uttered being a first or second person pronoun in the L2CD-T, and almost one in every 11 words being one of these pronouns in the L2CD-S. In fact, these pronouns are some of the most frequently used words in both sub-corpora. In the L2CD-S, *I* is the most frequently used word, *you* is ranked fourth, and *we* is ranked

Table 5.2 Comparison of personal pronouns in the two sub-corpora

	L2CD-S		L2CD-T		
Pronouns	Tokens	Per 1000 words	Tokens	Per 1000 words	Log-likelihood
First person					
I	1008	39.90	2961	21.05	274.69*
me	105	4.16	487	3.46	2.78
my	119	4.71	216	1.54	83.42*
Total	1232	48.77	3664	26.05	324.36*
we	225	8.91	1545	10.98	9.08*
us	3	0.12	90	0.64	14.52*
let's	2	0.08	374	2.66	106.13*
our	12	0.48	126	0.90	5.25*
Total	242	9.58	2135	15.18	52.00*
Second person					
you (sub & obj)	692	27.39	6449	45.85	190.35*
your	39	1.54	1125	8.00	178.85*
Total	731	28.94	7574	53.84	305.09*
Grand Total	2205	87.29	13,373	95.07	14.08*

*A log-likelihood value greater than 3.84 indicates a p-value less than 0.05

seventeenth.[1] In the L2CD-T, *you* is ranked first, *I* is ranked fourth, and *we* is ranked sixteenth. The pronouns account for nearly 9% of all words in the learner and 9.5% of the teacher sub-corpora. As the table shows, *I* exceeds the use of *you* and *we* combined in the L2CD-S, while *you* occurs much more frequently than both *I* and *we* combined in the L2CD-T. Interestingly, while the teachers used *we* significantly more frequently than the learners, *we* is the least frequently used pronoun among all pronouns investigated in both sub-corpora.

Fortanet (2004) explains that personal pronouns are important indicators of conceptualizing teacher-student relationships, used either to establish rapport or create distance. Lee (2009) found that small-class lecture introductions include more *I* and *you* than large classes, as such classes engender favorable conditions for establishing friendlier teacher-student relationships, and thus maintaining positive politeness is found to be less necessary. He argues that one of the principal ways of maintaining high levels of student involvement and engagement is through the use of *we* and *you*. However, Lee (2016) found that EAP teachers' decision to use *we* or *you* may be more dependent on whether teachers actually participate in classroom tasks. In addition, even though inclusive-*we* is thought of as the primary pronoun in university classrooms (Round 1987b), our findings of the L2CD-T support recent studies that have found *you* to be the most frequently used pronoun in both university lectures and EAP classrooms (Lee and Subtirelu 2015; Yeo and Ting 2014). Similarly, confirming recent research (e.g., O'Boyle 2014), *I* and *you* are highly frequent in the L2CD-S. However, unlike O'Boyle, our findings show that *I* occurs much more frequently than *you* in learner discourse. This difference may be due to the L2CD-S consisting of L2 learner speech in teacher-student interactions while O'Boyle's data consist of L1 speakers in university lectures and L2 peer-peer interactions.

O'Boyle (2014) also found that L2 learners use *I* more frequently than both L1 students and lecturers, which in some ways supports our finding. She argues that L2 speakers in language-focused classrooms "may rely more on a personal perspective to engage with content" (p. 47). In classroom interactions, (over-)reliance on *I* locates L2 students in the center of the conversational space, or a speaker's territorial domain (Kamio 2001). The L2CD-S includes significantly more *I* than the L2CD-T. This finding may not be surprising, as students in EAP classrooms are tasked to complete various academic and language-focused tasks by their teachers, who explicitly position learners within that space.

As shown in Table 5.2, *you* occurs significantly more frequently in the L2CD-T. By locating the addressee in the hearer's informational territory (Kamio 2001), this pronoun functions "to orient listeners to the discourse and focus students' attention on the topic" (Hyland 2009, p. 107), but in EAP classrooms, teachers often use it in order to set up pedagogical tasks that learners are instructed to perform (Lee 2016). By addressing students directly, EAP teachers adhere to a task-based approach and "maintain students' engagement and ensure their participation in performing various pedagogical tasks" (Lee and Subtirelu 2015, p. 60). Since the primary charge of EAP teachers is to facilitate academic tasks and activities and EAP learners' responsibility is to perform them (Basturkmen 2009), it is not surprising that learners' primary pronoun is *I* and teachers' main pronoun is *you* in the classroom. This may suggest that EAP classroom interaction consists of teachers primarily placing students and students locating themselves within their conversational space. The high frequency of *I* and *you* also suggests that the EAP classroom is a highly interactive and involved communicative site.

First Person Plural Pronouns in Learner and Teacher Talk

We explained previously that *we* was categorized into inclusive- and exclusive-*we*, and that it is the least represented pronoun in both sub-corpora. As shown in Table 5.2, *we* occurs approximately once in every 100 words in the L2CD-S (9.58 ptw) and about 1.5 times in every 100 words in the L2CD-T (15.18 ptw). In fact, *we* only accounts for slightly more than 10% of the pronouns in the L2CD-S and approximately 15% in the L2CD-T.

As can also be seen in Table 5.2, significant differences were found for each variant of the first person plural between the two sub-corpora. The teachers used all variants in greater amounts than the learners. Supporting our findings on EAP teachers, recent research on university instructors also shows that *we* is less frequently used than *I* and *you* across disciplines, class sizes, and lecture phases (Cheng 2012; Lee 2009; Lee and Subtirelu 2015; Yeo and Ting 2014). Lee (2016) found that in EAP lessons, specifically the opening phase, teachers commonly used *we* to inform students of upcoming lessons and to set up the lesson agenda (e.g., *so <u>we</u>'re gonna prepare for the second test, <u>we</u>'re gonna do some note-taking, and <u>we</u>'re also going to find out about our presentations that are coming up next week okay?*). Examining students' pronoun usage, Cheng (2012) found that *we* was the least represented pronoun in university student discourse, which confirms our findings.

In the gradation of closeness, *we* is considered to represent a greater psychological closeness with respect to the speaker's and hearer's territories (Kamio 2001). However, this degree of closeness can vary depending on the context. The inclusive-*we* includes both the speaker and hearer in the conversational space. Therefore, in the classroom, the use of inclusive-*we* marks both the teacher and learners as members of the same classroom group. In contrast, the exclusive-*we* excludes the hearer from the center

Table 5.3 Comparison of 'we' in the two sub-corpora

	L2CD-S		L2CD-T		
Pronouns	Tokens	Per 1000 words	Tokens	Per 1000 words	Log-likelihood
Inclusive					
we	9	0.36	1453	10.33	404.26*
us	0	0.00	88	0.63	29.07*
let's	2	0.08	374	2.66	106.13*
our	12	0.48	124	0.88	4.96*
Total	23	0.91	2039	14.50	507.54*
Exclusive					
we	216	8.55	92	0.65	467.93*
us	0	0.00	2	0.01	0.66
our	3	0.12	2	0.01	5.22*
Total	219	8.67	96	0.68	468.88*

*A log-likelihood greater than 3.84 indicates a p-value less than 0.05

of the information territory, and thus it "refers to a more or less delimited group of people of which *I* is the central member" (Kamio 2001, p. 1116).

Table 5.3 shows the frequencies of inclusive- and exclusive-*we* in both sub-corpora. The learners used the exclusive-*we* significantly more frequently than the teachers; however, the inclusive-*we* is significantly more common in the L2CD-T. In fact, the learners rarely used the inclusive-*we* while the teachers seldom used the exclusive-*we*. Previous studies found that university instructors preferred the inclusive-*we* to the exclusive-*we* (e.g., Cheng 2012; Crawford Camiciottoli 2005; Fortanet 2004; Lee 2009, 2016). Likewise, the EAP teachers primarily used the inclusive-*we*, as it helps to "establish and maintain high levels of student involvement" and interactivity (Lee and Subtirelu 2015, p. 60); for example, see below (11):

Text Samples 5.2 (11–12) Use of Inclusive-*we*

(11) T: okay these were about chapter three. the reading questions, you guys remember what i'm talking about here. this one? it looks like this. we started it in class on Monday, okay? if you would take this

out what i'm going to have you do just, quick as a warm-up is discuss your answers, with a partner okay? and then we'll we'll check them as a whole class, before i do the lecture today okay? (L2CD-T-24)

In this example, the teacher uses the first inclusive-*we* to remind students of an experience in the previous class while the second (and third) inclusive-*we* is used to inform students that the whole class, including the students, will review the answers together. As Lee (2009) suggests, the frequent use of *we* "may engender an illusory feeling of inclusion, creating a feeling of a joint endeavor" between teachers and students (p. 51).

Similar to this study's L2 learners, Cheng (2012) found that when university students use *we*, they almost never include the teacher; that is, they primarily use the exclusive-*we* to refer to the student and classmates:

(12) S: can we use our vocabulary cards? (L2CD-S-7)

As can be seen, the student positions other students in the center of the conversational space but locates the teacher outside the domain of the student's territory (Kamio 2001).

Fortanet (2004) argues that the inclusive-*we* is more common than the exclusive-*we* in instructor speech. She proposes that teachers use *we* more as a "co-operative than as a distancing device" (p. 63). While this may be true for both academic content and academic language-oriented teachers, our findings suggest that it is not an accurate reflection of learners' classroom discourse. Like the university students in Cheng's (2012) study, the learners in our data primarily used the exclusive-*we* to distance themselves from the teacher. Rather than creating a group-consciousness between the student(s) and teacher, the students' use of *we* indicates their endeavor to establish group solidarity among themselves. As mentioned previously, however, *we* is relatively infrequent in both learner and teacher discourses. Instead, both groups preferred to use *you* and *I*, the focus of the sections to follow.

Second Person Pronouns in Learner and Teacher Talk

This section examines second person pronouns, with a particular focus on the two sub-functions. In the classroom, *you* can function to express speakers' attitudes, assist in organizing their talk, or create distance between class participants. In Kamio's (2001) terms, "*you* is located in the distal domain of the conversational space, which corresponds to the hearer's territory" (p. 1118). This pronoun, according to Kamio, implies a greater distance between the speaker and hearer. Supporting Lee and Subtirelu (2015) and Yeo and Ting (2014), *you* is more frequent than *we* in both sub-corpora. The high frequency of *you* is indicative of highly interactive classrooms (Hyland 2009). As shown in Table 5.2, *you* constitutes about a third of all pronouns in the L2CD-S and approximately 57% of all pronouns in the L2CD-T. Similar to other studies (e.g., Lee and Subtirelu 2015), our findings show that *you* is the most frequently used pronoun in EAP teacher discourse. However, it does not support Cheng (2012) or Lee (2009), who found that, at least in academic lecture introductions and closings, *you* is less preferred than *I* by small class instructors. One possible reason for these differences may be that, unlike our study, Cheng (2012) and Lee (2009) focused on different phases of academic lectures (i.e., closing and opening). Additionally, our finding of *you* in the L2CD-S diverges from O'Boyle (2014), who found that *you* is more frequent than *I* in learner talk. This difference may be due to O'Boyle's corpora containing L1 students engaged in a range of classroom genres (e.g., lectures, seminars) and L2 learners in group interactions, while the L2CD consists of primarily whole-class, teacher-student interactions.

Table 5.4 presents the frequency of audience- and generalized-*you* in the two sub-corpora. Both the learners and teachers used the audience-*you* more frequently than the generalized-*you*. In the L2CD-S, audience-*you* constitutes 83.4% of all second person pronouns, and, in the L2CD-T, 93.6% is comprised of audience-*you*. These findings mirror the use of *you* by students and instructors in small class lecture closings (Cheng 2012).

In academic lectures, the highly frequent use of audience-*you* is considered to mark instructors' attempts "to establish a relationship

Table 5.4 Comparison of 'you' in the two sub-corpora

	L2CD-S		L2CD-T		
Pronouns	Tokens	Per 1000 words	Tokens	Per 1000 words	Log-likelihood
Audience					
you	586	23.20	6067	43.13	243.90*
your	24	0.95	1022	7.27	199.30*
Total	610	24.15	7089	50.40	374.50*
Generalized					
you	106	4.20	382	2.72	14.43*
your	15	0.59	103	0.73	0.61
Total	121	4.79	485	3.45	9.79*

*A log-likelihood greater than 3.84 indicates a p-value less than 0.05

with their students ... and to solicit audience participation and to orient students to the lecture" (Yeo and Ting 2014, p. 30). Lee (2009) offers an explanation for the high use of *you* in teachers' discourse in small classes from the perspective of politeness theory (Brown and Levinson 1987). As explained earlier, *you* and *I* have a distancing effect, resulting in negative politeness, while *we* has a rapport-maintenance effect, leading to positive politeness. In small classes, the affective and physical distance between instructors and students is generally closer. Therefore, teachers' high use of audience-*you* may be indicative of a lesser need to maintain positive politeness, due to teachers' and students' familiarity with one another. In EAP classes, learners' greater use of audience-*you* also seems to reflect the lesser necessity to mitigate the distancing effect that *you* engenders, as EAP teachers place great effort in increasing student involvement and participation.

As shown in Table 5.4, the learners used audience-*you* significantly less frequently than the teachers. As mentioned previously, EAP learners' main task is to engage in a range of academic and linguistic tasks, while EAP teachers' primary responsibility is to establish conditions for learning by setting up these pedagogic tasks, and teachers use audience-*you* as the principal pronoun for achieving this goal (Lee and Subtirelu 2015). In fact, Lee (2016) found that *you're going to/gonna* is EAP teachers' most preferred lexical phrase to outline an activity's procedures; for example:

Text Sample 5.3 (13) Preferred Lexical Phrases

(13) T: okay, uh so you're gonna read, and i'm going to count the time for you. when you finish reading. you're going to look up you're going to find out, the the time that has not been crossed out. and write that down. all right? (L2CD-T-14)

The teacher in (13) provides detailed instruction on how the learners will complete the timed-reading task. Lee (2016) further reports that teachers primarily use *you* when giving instructions since they usually do not participate in most classroom tasks. Referencing students directly not only allows a teacher to maintain learner engagement, but also distances the teacher from the students, and thus places the responsibility of task completion on the students.

The learners' use of audience-*you* was primarily focused on seeking clarification (14) or assistance (15):

Text Samples 5.4 (14–18) Patterns of Audience-*you*

(14) S: teacher i i still don't understand what, you had just given to me. (L2CD-S-15)

(15) S: how do you pronounce this word. formed … .formed or form/ Id/. (L2CD=S-21)

As these examples illustrate, the learners position teachers distally from their conversational center in order to direct teachers' attention to their specific needs.

One of the most common discourse markers in L1 speech is *you know*, which is used to maintain discourse flow in conversational interactions. O'Boyle (2014) found that L1 university students use *you know* in greater frequency than L2 learners. In the L2CD-S, *you know* appears 59 times, and slightly more than half of these (1.19 ptw) are interpersonal discourse marker:

(16) S: we couldn't talk, yester- or after class on Wednesday. because. you know it's like, Hyunh had to go because, her aunt. (L2CD-S-11).

Our finding seems to support O'Boyle that *you know* as a discourse marker is infrequent in learner speech. However, due to the fact that her learner corpus consists of peer-peer interaction, it is unclear whether the frequency of *you know* in our data is representative of learners' general use of this discourse marker in teacher-student interaction.

In contrast to audience-*you*, the L2CD-S consists of a significantly greater number of generalized-*you* than the L2CD-T, although no significant difference was found for generalized-*your*. This does not support previous studies (e.g., Cheng 2012), which found that academic lecturers use the indefinite *you* more frequently than students. It should be noted that Cheng only investigated lecture closings. In such closings, students' contributions to the classroom discourse are mainly responses to their instructors, while teachers' discourse primarily involves indicating end of the class, previewing future lectures, and dismissing the students.

Kamio (2001) suggests that when it comes to the indefinite, generic use of *you*, "the boundary which divides WE and YOU is very weak … so that the territories of the speaker and of the hearer can almost merge" (p. 1119). In other words, unlike the audience-*you*, the generalized-*you* and *we* are not contrastive, and speakers use the generalized-*you* to indicate a lack of previously established alignment. In the L2CD-T, the teachers mainly used the generalized-*you* when they were either explaining or clarifying something:

Text Samples 5.5 (19–20) Patterns of Generalized-*you*

(17) T: we use balance, balance is used kind of like these terms, and balance mean you make things equal zero. so, to balance it means that, you keep track of all the money y- th- your checks have written. and you make sure that, the number you have is the right number that the bank has. (L2CD-T-8)

In (17), the teacher explains what balance and balancing a checkbook mean. As can be seen, all instances of *you* can be substituted with *we*. It seems to be a strategy used by teachers to blur the speaker and hearer boundaries in an effort to involve students in a shared experience.

As one might imagine, students are often asked by teachers to answer their questions in order to check their understanding or knowledge. In the L2CD-S, most uses of generalized-*you* are in response to these questions:

(18) S: indentured servant, is you had to pay them right?

In this example, the indefinite *you* is used in response to the teacher's question about the meaning of indentured servant. Similar to teachers, learners' use of the generalized-*you* evokes a sense of closeness and solidarity with their teachers.

First Person Singular Pronouns in Learner and Teacher Talk

In this section, our attention shifts to the first person singular pronoun. Obviously, this pronoun refers to the speaker only, and it marks a clear distinction between the speaker and the hearer. As shown in Table 5.2, the first person singular is the preferred pronoun in learner talk (48.77 ptw), and is the second most commonly used pronoun in the L2CD-T (26.05 ptw). The learners used *I* (39.90 ptw) and *my* (4.71 ptw) significantly more frequently than teachers (*I*: 21.05 ptw; *my*: 1.54 ptw), though no difference was found for *me*. These findings contrast with previous findings of students' and instructors' use of *I* in the classroom. Cheng (2012) found that university students use *I* less frequently than lecturers in lecture closings, and O'Boyle (2014) reports that *I* is less frequent than *you* in both L1 and L2 learner speech. As noted earlier, these differences may be due to the fact that this study's sub-corpora are based on full EAP lessons, while Cheng's (2012) corpus includes only lecture closings, and O'Boyle's (2014) corpora consist of L2 learner group interactions and various L1 university classroom genres.

One possible reason for the greater use of *I* in the L2CD-S than the L2CD-T might be attributed to students' focus on communicating content and moderating their own subjective position than establishing and maintaining "interpersonal, intersubjective positions and connecting with the informational space of others" (O'Boyle 2014, p. 43). As O'Boyle explains, L2 learners may attend more to achieving their communicative goals than aligning with positions of other classroom participants. Compared to L1 students, L2 learners have been found to over-rely on *I* due to the nature of L2 classrooms. In language-focused classrooms, this positioning of the learner in the domain of the speaker's territory may be needed to engage with classroom content and tasks and to express stance. As reported in Chap. 4, the two most frequent stance verbs in the L2CD-S are *think* and *know*, which are almost always preceded by *I*:

Text Sample 5.6 (21) *I + think/know* Sequence

(19) S: because loan and borrow is a i think is a different. (L2CD-S-8)
S: can. can you okay, i know that you're gonna put the recording and recordings with that no? but can you read again? (L2CD-S-20)

Using the clusters function in *AntConc*, we found that *I think* and *I know* account for over 12% of all instances of *I* in the L2CD-S, and they occur 3.33 ptw and 1.50 ptw, respectively. O'Boyle also reports that the L2 learners in her study used *I think* three times more frequently than the L1 students. She suggests that, in learner speech, *I think* may serve as a discourse marker, particularly in turn-initial points, to first locate the learners' propositions clearly within their own territory. However, it is more likely due to learners' limited linguistic repertoire to express stance, as discussed in Chap. 4.

Although less frequent than *you*, the high frequency of *I* in the L2CD-T is representative of small classes in general (Cheng 2012; Lee 2009). In such contexts, it is less necessary for teachers to mitigate the distancing effect that the use of *I* engenders since the physical and emotional distance between teachers and students is closer. Therefore, as Lee (2009) notes, it may be advantageous for teachers to use *I* frequently to create a certain distance from the learners in the intimate teacher-learner relationship of small classrooms.

This chapter analyzed one dimension of deixis (personal deixis), with a focus on first and second person pronouns. In Chap. 6, we explore spatial deixis in EAP learner and teacher talk, one of the most fundamental elements of face-to-face interaction.

Note

1. For convenience, we refer to all variants of the personal pronouns investigated as *I*, *you*, or *we*, unless we focus on specific variants.

6

This/That, Here/There: Spatial Deixis in EAP Classroom Discourse

In Chap. 5, we examined person deixis in the form of first and second person pronouns. In this chapter, we concentrate on spatial deixis, a highly common feature in face-to-face interactions but one that is under-researched in classroom settings. Specifically, we explore the use of demonstratives and adverbs of locations in the L2CD-S and L2CD-T, and we compare learners' and teachers' use of these spatial deictics in the EAP classroom. By examining their use of spatial deictics, important insights can be gained on how each group conceptualizes objects and one another in the physical space of the classroom and connects with one another's informational space.

Spatial Deixis

Deictic markers are essentially pointing words, whose meanings derive from the situational context of utterance. As an important marker showing the relationship between language and context, the use of spatial deictics is one way in which speakers use language to encode and interpret dimensions of spontaneous, face-to-face interaction. Despite variations in the ways spatial deixis is realized in different languages, it is a feature of

E. Friginal et al., *Exploring Spoken English Learner Language Using Corpora*,
DOI 10.1007/978-3-319-59900-7_6

all languages because of its significance in connecting the interaction to its context (Cairns 1991). In English, spatial deixis is primarily expressed through devices such as demonstratives *this/these* and *that/those* and locative adverbs *here/there*. These deictic expressions mark locations with reference to the speaker's position on the spatial axis, and the center shifts as conversational turns change from one speaker to the next; therefore, the referent also changes each time it is used (Cairns 1991).

English speakers divide space in binary ways, with *here*, *this*, and *these* marking something proximal (or close) while *there, that, and those* indicate entities distal (or distant) in relation to the speaker's orientation (Levinson 1983). This "proximal/distal continuum," according to Cairns (1991), is considered to be "the basic criterion for spatial deixis" (p. 26). Interpretation of these deictic markers depends on the speaker and hearer sharing a common context. Spatial deictics allow the speaker to direct the hearer's attention in line with the speaker's point of reference, whether the referent is physically or psychologically close or distant. Similarly, using the ecological metaphor of territory, Kamio (2001) proposes that spatial deixis can be understood in terms of "general perceived space," whereby the conversational space is split into "proximal and distal subareas" (p. 1113), and "the speaker's territory…is proximal to the speaker, whereas the hearer's territory…is distal to the speaker, but proximal to the hearer" (p. 1114).

Furthermore, these proximal and distal deictic markers are further categorized into gestural or symbolic deixis (Levinson 1983). Gestural deixis are often accompanied by a non-verbal gesture (e.g., pointing or showing), as illustrated in (1), while symbolic deixis are those expressions that refer to commonly shared knowledge between the speaker and hearer or an entity not visible within the context of utterance, as shown in (2):

Text Samples 6.1 (1–2) Commonly Shared Knowledge

(1) S: okay, my friend, <u>thi- this</u> chair is for you. (L2CD-S-3)
(2) T: the London Company was <u>here</u> to make money. (L2CD-T-21)

In (1), it is easy to imagine the student pulling up or pointing to the chair as he says *this chair*. In (2), *here* is not the immediate context of the classroom, but it can be easily interpreted due to the teacher's and students' shared knowledge of the London Company having been in the United States at some point.

Biber et al. (1999) found that the demonstrative determiner and pronoun *that* is exceedingly more common in conversations than written registers, but *this*, *these*, and *those* are relatively more frequent in academic writing. They also observe that both *here* and *there* are more frequent in conversations, and *there* is preferred to *here* when referencing places. Furthermore, singular forms of these spatial deictic markers are more frequent than their plural forms in conversations. In their analysis of a corpus of casual conversations, O'Keeffe et al. (2011) also report that *that* is the most frequently used spatial deixis, and *that* and *there* are among the top 20 most frequent words in their corpus of conversations. These findings clearly show the importance of examining spatial deixis, as they play a crucial role in real-time, face-to-face interactions (O'Keeffe et al. 2011).

Despite their importance in face-to-face interactions, we are aware of only one study that has specifically examined spatial deixis in classroom discourse. In a study of university lectures across disciplines, Bamford (2004) explored the use of *here* in MICASE and another corpus of guest lectures (Siena corpus), and compared these lectures with casual conversations. In both lecture corpora, instructors made greater use of gestural *here* to make reference to visuals and to highlight "the common spatial context" of the lecturer and students (p. 135). In addition, she observes that *here*, in academic lectures and conversations, is used in different ways and that the use of deixis is one way lecturers tailor their talk to students' linguistic needs. Biber et al. (2004) found that certain lexical bundles include spatial deictics (e.g., *that's one of the, and this is a*), and these bundles occur only in classroom teaching. These bundles, as they report, serve as referential bundles used to identify an entity. Furthermore, although focused on discourse markers (e.g., *and, okay*), Yang (2014) shows that *that* and *this* are among the top 20 most frequent words in Chinese college EFL teachers' discourse and in MICASE lectures, which supports both Biber et al.'s (1999) and O'Keeffe et al.'s (2011) findings of *that* in casual conversations. Likewise, *that* was reported to be among the top 10 most frequent words in L1 and L2 students' speech (O'Boyle 2014).

Bamford (2004) proposes that much more research on spatial deixis in the classroom is needed, as very little is known of how students and teachers use these markers of spatial orientation, which when used successfully "can be a demonstration of social proximity—an informational enactment of intimacy" (Sidnell and Enfield 2016, p. 237). The remainder of this chapter focuses on our analytical procedure and reports our findings of spatial deixis, specifically demonstratives (both pronouns and determiners) and adverbs of location, in learner and teacher talk.

Analytical Procedure

To examine spatial deixis in the EAP classroom, we once again use the L2CD-S and L2CD-T introduced in Chap. 3 to compare how learners and teachers conceptualize spatial orientation in the classroom relative to each other. We limited our analysis to demonstrative determiners (*this chair/these chairs, that book/those books*), demonstrative pronouns (*this/these, that/those*), and adverbs of location (*here/there*), as these are considered the most common ways of expressing locations of entity in relation to a speaker's information territory. Using *AntConc* (Anthony 2014), we searched electronically for each instance of these deictic markers. Upon identifying all examples in the L2CD-S and L2CD-T, each potential item was examined manually in its context in order to determine whether it was functioning as a spatial deictic, non-deictic, or another deictic.

Demonstrative pronouns and determiners can function as spatial deictics, discourse deictics to point to anaphoric (previous) or cataphoric (subsequent) references, or non-deictics. In (3), *this* functions as spatial deixis, whereas in (4), it serves as a discourse deictic marker:

Text Samples 6.2 (3–13) Examining Spatial Deixis

(3) S: i have <u>this</u> paper teacher. (L2CD-S-4)

(4) T: the main idea should be bigger than the one sentence. for example, when we look at the paragraph with writing, the main idea, personal communication in Turkey. <u>this</u> is the main idea sentence. (L2CD-T-3)

As can be seen, the student in (3) uses *this* to indicate that the location of the paper is proximal to his territory. However, in (4), *this* points anaphorically to *personal communication in Turkey*. The non-deictic use of *this* is illustrated in (5):

(5) T: so in general, that's the big difference, okay? but there might be some occasions where they make some money or some you know, it's not. a hundred percent this way or that way but in general that's the big difference, okay? (L2CD-T-22)

This in (5) is categorized as non-deictic use because it is part of a somewhat fixed idiomatic expression, *this way or that way*, used to convey a lack of complete certainty.

Biber et al. (1999) explains that *that* is one of the most flexible English words. In addition to its spatial (6) and discourse (7) functions, it can function as a complementizer (8), relative pronoun (9), and stance adverbial (10):

(6) S: who need use that paper. (L2CD-S-1)

(7) T: and you know sometimes, even there's two examples, broke and he has broken. simple past or present perfect. so the reason for this, is because, he broke it, which is a simple past action, but you could say, in a five year period, he's, the breaking is still happening. so that's why th- there's sometimes two choices. (L2CD-T-4).

(8) S: yes. but i i i talk about but just a little bit. i don't think that i can. explain. (L2CD-S-11)

(9) S: Kohls say that to make sense of another culture, we must understand that basic belief assumption and values of cult- in a group (L2CD-S-3)

(10) T: you're right if you got that much money. you need to share it. (L2CD-T-8)

Therefore, demonstratives that did not function as spatial deixis were excluded from the analysis.

Here and *there* are also multifunctional. They can serve as a spatial (11) or temporal deictic (12), but *there* can also function non-deictically as a dummy subject (13).

(11) S: you can stay there. (L2CD-S-10)

(12) T: well guys i think we're gonna have to stop here for right now we're not finished, we're gonna continue this on Monday because i wanna give you back your, voice recording two results okay so, let's just hold on that okay? (L2CD-T-21)

(13) S: there are thirteen value for example competition many American are competitive. (L2CD-S-13)

Items such as (12) and (13) were also omitted from our analysis, as they are not used in a spatial deictic sense.

After identifying those demonstratives and locative adverbs that only functioned as spatial deictics, the tokens were normalized to occurrences per 1000 words (ptw). Additionally, using *AntConc*'s clusters function, the two sub-corpora were analyzed for the most common recurring two- to five-word lexicogrammatical phrases, and the concordances were examined to determine whether these clusters were used in a spatial deictic sense. The search resulted in very few four- and five-word clusters, but many two- and three-word lexical phrases. Because of the size of the L2CD corpus, we established the following criteria to minimize the impact of individual speaking styles: the cluster appears in each teacher's lesson in at least four lessons, and at a normalized frequency of 0.5 ptw. We then used Rayson's (n.d.) Log-likelihood Calculator to determine whether the differences in occurrences of the demonstratives and place adverbs, and their associated clusters, between the two sub-corpora were statistically significant; a log-likelihood value of 3.84 or higher is significant at the $p<0.05$ level.

Results and Discussion

The results show that, while less frequent than personal pronouns (see Chap. 5), spatial deixis is very common in both learner and teacher classroom talk. As they are also highly common in casual conversations (Biber et al. 1999), the findings suggest that the EAP classroom is reflective of a highly conversational speech event. Table 6.1 shows the distribution and

Table 6.1 Comparison of proximal and distal deixis in the two sub-corpora

	L2CD-S		L2CD-T		
	Tokens	Per 1000 words	Tokens	Per 1000 words	Log-likelihood
Proximal deixis	323	12.79	2612	18.57	44.08*
Distal deixis	197	7.80	2422	17.22	143.44*
Total	520	20.59	3456	35.79	167.49*

*A log-likelihood greater than 3.84 indicates a p-value less than 0.05

normalized frequencies of proximal, distal, and total deictics used in the two sub-corpora.

As can be seen, one spatial deictic is used every 50 words in the L2CD-S and nearly twice per 50 words in the L2CD-T. Furthermore, as shown in Table 6.1, the learners overwhelmingly preferred proximal to distal deictics. Similar to their use of personal pronouns (Chap. 5), the learners' preference for perceiving space within the speaker's territory is indicative of a highly egocentric positioning (Kamio 2001). In contrast, the teachers seemed to shift the center of location from the territory of the teacher to that of the learners more or less equally. Although the constant movement of the referential location of entities is considered to cause some confusion (O'Keeffe et al. 2011), it is reflective of interactive and contextualized classrooms in which teachers coordinate people and objects spatially to assign different types of associated meanings. It can be argued that while EAP learners tend to conceptualize classroom space closer to themselves, teachers seem to view the classroom space, including classroom participants and objects, more widely in their attempts to direct learners' attention to entities proximally and distally from the teachers' speaker territory.

However, Table 6.1 shows that not only is spatial deixis exceedingly more frequent in the L2CD-T, but that teachers used significantly more proximal and distal deictics than the learners. This may be partially explained by the fact that the L2CD consists primarily of whole class talk where the teachers do most of the talking and their conversational turns are much longer in length. Csomay (2007) found that students take more turns than lecturers in university classrooms. However, slightly over 20% of student turns consists of one-word utterance, but only 1.5% of teacher turns contained one word. Therefore, the difference between learner and teacher use of spatial deixis is probably due to learners' contributions to the L2CD being comprised mostly of shorter utterances that are mainly responses to teacher questions, as discussed in Chap. 3.

Demonstratives in Learner and Teacher Talk

In both sub-corpora, demonstratives are the principal spatial deixis used, as Table 6.2 shows. In fact, nearly 86% of spatial deixis employed in the L2CD-S are demonstratives, and over 81% are demonstratives in the L2CD-T. As the table also shows, although teachers frequently used *this*, they preferred to use distal spatial deictic *that* more, which supports previous findings of university lecturers (O'Boyle 2014) and casual conversations (Biber et al. 1999). In the L2CD-T, the demonstrative *that* is ranked 10th, and *this* is 15th. The L2CD-S, on the other hand, contains a greater number of *this* than *that*, which diverges from O'Boyle (2014), in which *that*, but not *this*, is among the top 10 most frequently used words in both L1 and L2 learner talk. In the L2CD-S, *this* is the 13th most frequent word, and *that* is ranked 27th. As discussed in Chap. 5, however, it is important to note that O'Boyle's corpus of L2 learner talk consists of only learner-learner interactions. When it comes to demonstratives, our findings again demonstrate that learners tend to locate entities more in their own territory. The teachers, however, are inclined to use demonstratives to position classroom participants and objects both distally from and proximally within their speaker territory.

Identical to our findings of overall proximal and distal deixis used, the L2CD-T contains significantly more proximal and distal demonstratives than the L2CD-S, as shown in Table 6.2 However, no significant difference was found for *this*. Furthermore, the singular forms of demonstratives are much more common than the plural forms in both sub-corpora, which supports Biber et al.'s (1999) analysis of conversations. Actually, the learners rarely used the plural forms.

Turning to the most frequent lexical phrases in the two corpora, only two-word clusters occurred at a minimum of 0.5 ptw. In the L2CD-S,

Table 6.2 Comparison of demonstratives in the two sub-corpora

	L2CD-S		L2CD-T		
	Tokens	Per 1000 words	Tokens	Per 1000 words	Log-likelihood
this	261	10.33	1603	11.40	2.21
these	6	0.24	315	2.24	66.99*
Total	267	10.57	1918	13.63	16.20*
that	177	7.01	1966	13.98	93.96*
those	3	0.12	207	1.47	48.22*
Total	180	7.13	2173	15.45	124.16*

*A log-likelihood greater than 3.84 indicates a p-value less than 0.05

only six two-word clusters (three distal and three proximal) met the established criteria. The most frequent demonstrative clusters in the learner sub-corpora are the proximal deictics: *this one* (1.58 ptw) and *this is* (1.31 ptw):

Text Samples 6.3 (14–20) Demonstratives in Learner and Teacher Talk

(14) S: this one or this one? (L2CD-S-10)
(15) S: this is a crown, yeah. (L2CD-S-3)

In (14), the learner uses *this one* to ask the teacher which assignment is for homework, while the learner uses *this is* in (15) to name the entity within the student's spatial territory.

In the teacher sub-corpora, 11 two-word clusters were identified, of which six were singular distal demonstratives and five, proximal. Among the most frequent distal deictics, *that's a* and *is that* occur 0.71 ptw and 0.70 ptw, respectively:

(16) T: okay that's a transition word. what's the correct punctuation. (L2CD-T-6)
(17) T: hi Carlos how are you. is that your pen? (L2CD-T-M)

The teacher in (16) uses the distal demonstrative to identify the transition word used by a student, and locates the referent in the proximal space of the student. In (17), the teacher inquires about whether a specific pen belongs to the student. Regarding two-word clusters with proximal demonstratives, the most frequent are *this is* (2.34 ptw), a shared cluster with the learners, and *in this* (0.74 ptw):

(18) T: yeah, oh that is wrong, yeah it's wrong you were right it is wrong. yeah, i have to, now this is correct actually that's a good thing you pointed that out Diep now see Diep, was a, a teacher. (L2CD-T-13)

(19) T: folks i wanna point something out out to you about using can and can't don't do anything with this paper yet don't fill in this paper yet. leave this blank, don't do anything with this yet. (L2CD-T-9)

In (18), the teacher points to a typo that a student identified in a handout the teacher distributed to the students. Notice that when the teacher points out the mistake, she uses *that,* but uses *this* when indicating what is correct. As Cairns (1991) points out, spatial deixis can be used to create a psychological distance from a proposition in order to express attitude. The teacher appears to use *this is* to establish a mental closeness to the correction while distancing herself from the error with *that is*. In (19), it is clear that the teacher uses the combination of a locative preposition and demonstrative determiner to direct the learners' attention to the paper in his hand. Though less frequent, teachers also used the two-word cluster *this one* (0.65 ptw), the second most frequent lexical phrase in the L2CD-S:

(20) T: let's look at this one over here. this is a fact. and she's gonna talk about the bird, as a symbol. so, she's given us a fact about, the national bird is called Turpial. (L2CD-T-5)

In this example, *this one* is preceded by the prepositional verb *look at* to draw the learners' focus to a symbol, in this case the national bird of Venezuela, which is listed in another student's essay.

Although *that* is more common in teacher talk than *this*, teachers utilize both these demonstratives to draw students' attention into and away from their proximal space to expand the perceived classroom space. In contrast, learners tend to bring the teacher into their speaker territory rather than shift the focus away from them as the center to a much lesser degree, and thus seem to contract the classroom space. This notion of space contraction and expansion is further realized in EAP learners' and teachers' employment of locative adverbs, *here* and *there*.

Locative Adverbs "here" and "there" in Learner and Teacher Talk

Table 6.3 shows that both the learners and teachers favored *here* over *there*. In the L2CD-S, nearly 77% of the adverbs are *here*, while, in the L2CD-T, approximately 74% are *here*. Biber et al. (1999) states that these place adverbs are common in casual conversations, and that *there* is preferred over *here* when referencing locations. It seems that in classroom interactions, however, not only are they less frequent in both learner and teacher talk, at least in comparison to demonstrative spatial deictics, *there* is much less common than *here*. As Bamford (2004) points out, different registers and genres use spatial deixis in different ways.

In her study, Bamford (2004) also found that the relative frequency of *here* is rather low in university lectures. Although she only provided the raw totals of *here*, we were able to establish normalized frequencies because the sizes of the two corpora used were reported. In her data, *here* on average only occurred 3.33 ptw in MICASE lectures, while it appeared even less frequently in the Siena corpus (2.35 ptw). The difference in frequency between the EAP teachers and university lecturers may be attributed to the greater need to physically contextualize lesson content and activities in EAP classrooms than university lectures, in which the lecturers cover a large amount of dense subject concepts and ideas. Therefore, academic lecturers may rely more on other linguistic means to

Table 6.3 Comparison of "here" and "there" in the two sub-corpora

	L2CD-S		L2CD-T		
	Tokens	Per 1000 words	Tokens	Per 1000 words	Log-likelihood
here	56	2.22	694	4.93	41.74*
there	17	0.67	249	1.77	19.58*

*A log-likelihood greater than 3.84 indicates a p-value less than 0.05

direct and guide learners' focus through the cognitively challenging task of listening to lectures over a lengthy period of time (Lee and Subtirelu 2015). Upon examining potential clusters, no lexical phrases with *here* or *there* that met our criteria were found, and therefore we do not discuss this any further.

The disproportionally greater use of *here* in the L2CD-S also points to learners' confining the classroom space primarily within their speaker territory and anchoring the point of reference in egocentric ways, mainly focused on their individual interest. With the greater use of *here*, EAP learners appear to reduce the spatial context of the classroom to the vicinity nearest to them.

Text Samples 6.4 (21–27) Locative Adverbs in Learner and Teacher Talk

(21) S: <u>here</u>. I have it <u>here</u>. (L2CD-S-5)
(22) S: oh you put <u>here</u> you put <u>here</u>. (L2CD-S-9)

In (21), the student responds to the teacher's query about the outline of her essay, and in (22), the learner attempts to draw the teacher's attention to something on her mid-semester evaluation report, a report given to students at this IEP to show their progress. Locating the referent close to them may not, to a certain extent, be surprising as learners in many ways are restricted to their speaker territory, as teachers regulate learners' positioning within the classroom. However, as discussed below, they made very little use of *there*, thus suggesting that greater emphasis is placed on their individual, proximal interest than that of the class.

As mentioned above, the teachers also favored *here* to *there*. Not only is *here* much more frequent than *there* in the L2CD-T, but the teachers also used the proximal deictic significantly more frequently than learners, as shown in Table 6.3. In fact, it appears two times more frequently in the teacher sub-corpora than the learner sub-corpora.

(23) T: this is a document. so let's take a look at, some of the abbreviations. you have categories, so, we have verb mistakes <u>here</u>, and there're abbreviations like this, V T, you might be familiar with these from other teachers.

In (23), the teacher draws all learners' attention to the verb mistake, which is accompanied by her pointing to the document displayed on the screen. Through their use of *here*, EAP teachers are able to not only cater to the linguistic needs of L2 learners, but also "to create rapport with student listeners" (Bamford 2004, p. 136), as the use of *here* can help to establish a sense of shared contextual and cognitive referents. Thus, unlike EAP learners, teachers' use of *here* seems to be focused more on viewing the classroom as a shared space.

This notion of sharing the classroom space is further suggested by teachers' significantly greater use of *there* than learners, as shown in Table 6.3. The learners rarely used *there*, and when they did, the referent was mostly a location outside of the immediate context of the classroom:

(24) S: i don't know where is there. (L2CD-S-3)
(25) S: yeah, because i know how to go there and the end if i go (L2CD-S-22)

In both examples, the learners refer to places unrelated to the immediate situation of the classroom. This may suggest that learners restrict their use of locative adverbs to referents closest to them, thus contracting the classroom space. The teachers, on the other hand, used *there* primarily to locate entities within the classroom:

(26) T: i want you to take a look at the little vocabulary list there, just see if you can match, those, definitions to the words that are in those sentences. so take a minute, and do that. (L2CD-T-8)
(27) T: yeah just write on there and i and i'll put it up there and i'll give it back to you. (L2CD-T-13)

In (26), *there* is used to point to the vocabulary list on the sheet that the teacher distributed to the students. This use of *there* locates the referent in the teacher's distal territory but the students' proximal territory. The teacher in (27) uses *there* first to indicate that the student should write the sentence on her paper, thus distancing the teacher from the referent. However, in the second use of *there*, the referent is the document camera used in the classroom to display images, including papers, on the screen.

The referent in this case is not proximal to the student, but distal to both teacher and student. While *there*, as a distal deictic, is considered to locate the referent to the hearer's proximal territory, EAP teachers commonly use *there* to refer to a space distant to both the teachers and learners. In doing so, they expand the perceived classroom space in their effort to create a context that is shared by all participants. Nonetheless, compared to *this* and *that*, both learners and teachers did not make much use of locative adverbs in their conceptualization of classroom space and each other.

Part III

Learner Talk in Language Experience Interviews

7

Exploring Learner Talk in English Interviews

The guiding question behind this section is straightforward: what can we learn about the L2 learning experience by asking L2 learners to discuss their own L2 learning? In order to answer this question, we use specialized software to analyze the semantic content of L2 learner talk as advanced English learners reflect on their learning experience in a structured interview. By using three different analytical techniques, we approach the question from different angles, distinguishing both general patterns in the experience of learning a L2 as well as individual differences in learning experience. The purpose of this and the following chapters in Part III, therefore, is threefold: (1) to discover the words and themes used by highly proficient L2 English learners as they describe their learning experience; (2) to discern what these words can tell us about the learning process; and (3) to determine what these words can tell us about individual learners.

All the chapters in this section rely on the L2 Experience Interview Corpus (Polat 2013a), described below. The chapters also use the same innovative mixed-methods approach (Riazi 2016), which combines qualitative interview data, quantifiable semantic content analysis, quantitative multi-dimensional or cluster analysis, and qualitative interpretations of these quantitative findings. General aspects of the corpus

E. Friginal et al., *Exploring Spoken English Learner Language Using Corpora*,
DOI 10.1007/978-3-319-59900-7_7

and methodology are discussed in Chap. 7, while analytical techniques specific to only one chapter are addressed in that particular chapter. Together, the findings of these separate studies offer a coherent picture of the lived experience of L2 learning, tapping into learners' psychosocial understanding of how and why they have learned a L2.

L2 Experience Interview Corpus

The L2 Experience Interview Corpus was developed by Polat (2013a) to address important methodological gaps in the study of advanced L2 learning. A persistent methodological issue in L2 research, which has been discussed at length elsewhere (e.g., Larsen-Freeman and Long 2014), is the division between small-*n*, qualitative, non-generalizable studies and large-*n*, quantitative, generalizable studies. The small-scale studies provide thick description and an understanding of complex phenomena in specific situations, but findings from these studies are usually not representative and cannot be applied outside of the specific research situation. The large-scale studies may be more representative and reliable, but they often do not offer satisfactory in-depth explanations of the complexity of L2 learning. While many researchers now combine qualitative and quantitative analyses at various stages of the research process, it is quite difficult to blend the true strengths of each of type of study to conduct a large, reliable, in-depth, richly descriptive format that captures the nuances of the L2 learning process.

The L2 Experience Interview Corpus aims to do just that, by providing transcriptions of detailed interviews with a large number of advanced learners on the topic of their own learning experience. One hundred twenty three interview texts are included in the corpus, for a total word count of 143,115. (Texts range in length from 379 words to 3334 words, with an average length of 1164 words.) Each participant was interviewed by the same researcher and received exactly the same questions in the same order, so that any differences in the interview text are the result of differences in the participant's speech rather than feedback from the interviewer. The resulting corpus, therefore, combines the best of quantitative and qualitative data collection: it is richly descriptive and detailed, but also relatively large-scale and directly comparable across all texts. Details about the participants and data collection process are presented below.

Participant Information

Participants were all currently enrolled graduate or undergraduate students and had lived in the USA (or any other English-speaking country) for no more than one year. Participants came from 23 countries, spoke 27 native languages (see Table 7.1), and represented 43 academic majors (see Table 7.2). This diversity ensures a representative sample of university-level English language learners. Sixty-five (52.85%) of the participants were female and 58 (47.15%) were male. Ninety-five (77.23%) participants were graduate students and 28 (22.76%) were undergraduate students. The average age of participants was 26.

Data Collection

Data were collected in 2013 at a large American research university in a diverse metropolitan area. Structured interviews were held with each student in a study room on campus and were all conducted by one of

Table 7.1 Native languages represented by participants

Language	Number	Language	Number	Language	Number
Mandarin	33	Spanish	3	Catalan	1
French	18	Hindi	2	Crimean Tatar	1
Indonesian	17	Japanese	2	Dari	1
Korean	12	Pashto	2	Georgian	1
Italian	11	Portuguese	2	Haitian Creole	1
Telugu	5	Turkish	2	Hungarian	1
Dutch	3	Arabic	1	Kyrgyz	1
Farsi	3	Armenian	1	Malayalam	1
Russian	3	Bengali	1	Romanian	1
Total languages:	27				

Note: When participants listed multiple native languages, each language was listed separately in this table, resulting in a higher number of languages than participants

Table 7.2 Academic disciplines of participants

Major	Number	Major	Number
Economics	26	Epidemiology	1
Biology	11	Financial Engineering	1
Business Administration	8	Information Systems	1
Computer Science	8	International Business	1
Chemistry	7	Law	1
Public Health	7	Management of Technology	1
Education	6	Materials Engineering	1
Political Science	6	Math	1
Actuarial Science	5	Mechanical Engineering	1
English	4	Philosophy	1
Finance	4	Piano Performance	1
Applied Linguistics	3	Prosthesis and Orthosis	1
Industrial Engineering	3	Public Administration	1
Risk Management	3	Public Financial Policy	1
Communication	2	Public Policy	1
Marketing	2	Screenwriting	1
Anthropology	1	Social Work	1
Biochemistry	1	Spanish	1
Biomedical Engineering	1	Statistics	1
Biomolecular Engineering	1	Taxation	1
Chemical Engineering	1	Undeclared	1
Criminal Justice	1		
		Total	43 majors

Note: When participants listed multiple majors, each major was listed separately in the table above, resulting in a higher number of majors than participants

the authors. Interviews ranged in duration from five to 27 minutes. Each interview strictly followed the interview protocol shown in Table 7.3, which was developed from previous L2 experience interviews (e.g., Polat 2013b). Students were allowed to speak for up to 4 minutes in response to each question. The interviewer did not ask follow-up questions or interrupt students, except to enforce the time limit. Limited backchanneling cues, such as "Oh" or "I see," were provided to set students more at ease and more closely resemble authentic conversation. This procedure ensured that all students received the same input before answering questions and were not inadvertently primed to produce different types of language.

Table 7.3 Interview protocol

1. Tell me about your experience learning English.
2. Do you like learning English? Why or why not?
3. Why do you want to learn English?
4. What are the most important things you do to help you learn English?
5. What do you do to improve your speaking and listening ability?
6. What do you to improve your reading and writing ability?
7. How do you learn grammar?
8. How do you learn vocabulary?
9. Do you feel that most people learn in the same way that you do, or in a different way?
10. How do you feel when you use English?
11. Is there anything you want to change about your English learning experience?
12. Is there anything else you want to discuss about your English learning experience?

Transcription

Interviews were transcribed by the interviewer and one paid research assistant (whose work was checked by the interviewer). Because all students received the exact same questions from the interviewer, there was no need to include her words in the corpus. Therefore, only L2 learner responses are included, making it completely the interview speech of L2 English speakers.

Content Analysis Programs

Even though a corpus may be both large and richly detailed, it does not follow that an analysis of that corpus will be able to make use of all the information the corpus can offer. This is where the particular analytical framework used in these studies, semantic content analysis, becomes valuable. Semantic content analysis is similar to traditional corpus research in that it uses computer programs to examine the properties of many texts from many speakers. However, it differs from traditional corpus studies in one important way. In most corpus research, the ultimate goal is to understand language itself, so texts are considered to be one large corpus for what they can tell us about language use. In contrast, in semantic content analysis, the object is to investigate the people behind the text. This means that texts are considered for what language use can tell us about the specific speakers or writers using the language, both as a group and as individuals. Researchers in this area often use participants' own words to learn more about their psychological state, personal characteristics, beliefs, intentions, or other psychological information.

The value of using such a semantic approach to analyze the meaning behind texts lies in its ability to capture authentic psychological experience, in contrast to the rehearsed, inauthentic answers that participants might provide on a questionnaire. As Tausczik and Pennebaker (2010) point out:

> Language is the most common and reliable way for people to translate their internal thoughts and emotions into a form that others can understand… The words we use in daily life reflect what we are paying attention to, what we are thinking about, what we are trying to avoid, how we are feeling, and how we are organizing and analyzing our worlds. (p. 25, 30)

Because words reflect the speaker's "cognitive schema," semantic content analysis "provides a replicable methodology to access deep individual or collective structures such as values, intentions, attitudes, and cognitions" (Duriau et al. 2007, p. 6). By detecting meaningful semantic patterns in naturally occurring language, researchers can probe the psychological content of communication.

The goal of using text to learn about psychological content can be achieved through content-neutral programs or psychology-oriented programs, and in the following chapters we use one of each type. The content-neutral program used in Chap. 8, T-Lab (Lancia 2004), is similar to many corpus analysis programs in that it provides basic co-occurrence information on frequency, context, and co-variance of lemmas in a corpus. However, it has several additional features that are useful in understanding how learners use particular words. T-Lab can identify the themes and "elementary contexts" within a corpus and then perform a cluster analysis of these themes to show their relationship to each other and the larger corpus (Lancia 2016).

The psychology-based program used in Chaps. 9 and 10 is Linguistic Inquiry and Word Count (LIWC; Pennebaker et al. 2007), which has been extensively used by experimental psychologists "to identify a group of words that tapped basic emotional and cognitive dimensions often studied in social, health, and personality psychology" (p. 6). LIWC is quite different from the neutral text-processing programs most often found in corpus linguistics research. It operates by analyzing the individual texts within a corpus and producing quantitative output with information about the specific words used in each text. For each of its dictionary categories, LIWC provides a percentage describing how much of each text falls into that category. For example, in the category Positive Emotion, Text 1 might contain 1.57% and Text 2 might contain 3.20%. These percentages indicate that 1.57% of the total words in Text 1 fall within the Positive Emotion category and 3.20% in Text 2 are contained in that category. This can be interpreted to mean that the speaker in Text 2 used more positive emotion words than the speaker in Text 1 during the interview. LIWC provides this type of information in all 80 linguistic and psychological categories for each speaker. The result is a complete list of how big or small a portion of each text is related to each psychological category, which in turn provides important information on the psychological orientation of the speaker.

Although LIWC contains 80 dictionary categories, Chaps. 9 and 10 use only those most relevant to L2 learning. (See Pennebaker et al. 2007, for a complete list of LIWC categories and input words.) These include social process categories (Family, Friends, Humans); affective processes (Positive Emotion, Negative Emotion, Anxiety, Anger, Sadness); cognitive processes (Insight, Causation, Discrepancy, Tentativeness, Certainty, Inhibition, Inclusivity, Exclusivity); perceptual processes (Seeing, Hearing, Feeling); and relativity processes (Motion, Space, Time). The categories that were excluded include LIWC's overtly grammatical processes, which refer mostly to function words and fillers. While function word analysis has proven very informative with native speakers, we judged this category to be too unreliable an indicator with L2 English speakers. In addition, the categories called Personal Concerns (e.g., Home, Money, Religion, and Death) were deemed less relevant to understanding the L2 experience and, therefore, not included in Chaps. 9 and 10.

Analyzing L2 experience interviews with content analysis software, therefore, answers not only a methodological need—providing feasible quantitative analysis for richly detailed qualitative data—but also allows for a different type of psychosocial analysis of L2 learning. Starting from the premise that learners themselves can tell us a great deal about their own experience, this technique goes behind the scenes (so to speak) of the learning process and gleans as much information as possible from the particular words that learners select to describe their L2 experience. Although this methodology certainly has limitations, it can provide new insights that have not previously been available to researchers. In other words, even as new technologies and techniques come along, we may find that learner talk is more valuable to the study of L2 learning than ever before.

Data Analysis

Because the L2 Experience Interview Corpus is both new and novel, it is worth considering the data from several points of analysis. Referring back to our question at the opening of this section, our main goal is to learn as much as we can about the L2 learning experience. So what exactly can the corpus tell us about this experience, and what types of analysis are needed to find it? Table 7.4 provides a summary of the three analyses that follow.

Table 7.4 Summary of research analyses using L2 Experience Interview Corpus (Polat 2013a)

Chapter	Analysis	Conducted with	Performed on	Identifies
8	Hierarchical cluster analysis	T-Lab	Keywords (identified from entire corpus)	General themes of the L2 learning experience common to all learners
9	Multi-dimensional analysis	SPSS	LIWC scores (only psychosocial features)	Psychosocial dimensions of the L2 learning experience common to all learners
10	Hierarchical cluster analysis	SPSS	LIWC scores (only psychosocial features)	Groups of learners who share a similar L2 learning experience

First, we seek to identify general themes that emerge in learners' discussion of their L2 learning experience. Of the many text analysis tools available in T-Lab, a cluster analysis offers one of the more interesting ways of organizing themes based on keywords. From the results of this cluster analysis (which is based on a correspondence analysis of key contexts in the corpus), we can see which lemmas tend to cluster together in learners' descriptions of their L2 experience. This analysis reveals not just which words are important, but also which words tend to be discussed together, perhaps reflecting the aspects of the L2 experience that are most salient for L2 learners. Chapter 8, therefore, is devoted to exploring the strongest general (i.e., non-psychosocial and psychosocial) themes that emerge across all texts in the corpus.

In Chaps. 9 and 10, we turn to the psychological expertise provided by LIWC to analyze the psychosocial content of the L2 experience interviews. A psychosocial exploration is an important complement to the general thematic exploration of the corpus because the L2 learning process is, essentially, a psychological undertaking. As described above, semantic content analysis has been frequently used by experimental psychologists to understand the cognition and affect underlying a person's statements. By analyzing the corpus through the lens of LIWC's specialized dictionaries, we can extract latent psychosocial information that would be missed in a standard thematic analysis.

Chapter 9 analyzes the frequency information provided by LIWC to discern psychosocial dimensions across all texts of the corpus. Specifically, a multi-dimensional analysis is performed using LIWC output, which reveals four distinct psychosocial dimensions that are somewhat different from those found in the general thematic analysis. This process yields a different and complementary way of viewing the L2 learning experience, one that perhaps offers a deeper look into the learning process itself.

Chapter 10 also uses LIWC output, but as a means of studying individual learners rather than the group as a whole. While Chaps. 8 and 9 seek to understand the collective experience of all learners in this corpus, Chap. 10 groups these learners into clusters based on the types of words each learner uses to describe her or his experience. A cluster analysis is conducted using the quantitative psychosocial output of LIWC, resulting in three clusters of L2 learners. We then analyze differences in L2 performance (represented by TOEFL scores) between the three clusters, suggesting a possible relationship between cluster membership and L2 learning.

Together, these three different analyses offer a nuanced and triangulated view of the experience of learning ESL. Instead of relying on questionnaires administered to many participants, or in-depth interviews conducted with a few participants, the three studies in Chaps. 8, 9, and 10 take advantage of a novel methodology to mine the interviews of 123 learners. In the following three chapters, we consider what learner talk can tell us about the L2 learning experience, as well as the ways in which this methodology can lead to future research.

8

Thematic Cluster Analysis of the L2 Experience Interview Corpus

This chapter addresses two research questions. First, what semantic clusters are identifiable in the L2 Experience Interview Corpus (Polat 2013a), and second, what can these clusters tell us about the participants' L2 learning experience? Starting with our transcribed sentences (called "elementary contexts") as the basic unit of analysis, the T-Lab software identifies keywords from the corpus, performs a correspondence analysis, and then conducts a cluster analysis based on parameters entered by the user. (See Lancia 2016, for a complete description of T-Lab operations.) In this case, a three-cluster option was selected as the most explanatory model, representing 37.73% of shared variance, with $p = 0.027$. This means that T-Lab (Lancia 2004) recognized three distinct groups of words that tend to co-occur with each other (internal homogeneity) and tend not to occur with words in the other two clusters (external heterogeneity). The three thematic clusters, which we have named *Classroom*, *Communication*, and *Studying*, are discussed in turn below.

E. Friginal et al., *Exploring Spoken English Learner Language Using Corpora*,
DOI 10.1007/978-3-319-59900-7_8

Cluster 1: Classroom

The first cluster, Classroom, contains lemmas strongly linked to the external classroom experience of L2 English learning: (*primary*, *elementary*, *middle*, and *high*) *school*, *study*, *year*, *learn* (v.), *learning* (n.), *teach*, *grammar*, *teacher*, *class*, *old*, *young*, *exam*, *university*, *course*, *score*, *college*, *grade*, *education*, *age*, *junior*, and *senior*. The frequencies of the 30 most representative words in Cluster 1 are shown in Table 8.1, along with the X^2 score showing how representative each word is of this cluster.

Table 8.1 Most representative lemmas in Classroom cluster

Lemma	X^2	Freq. in Cluster	Freq. in Corpus
school	855.066	634	685
high	420.127	280	288
study	265.016	345	457
year	264.618	234	270
start	225.2	233	285
learn	207.694	929	1677
learning	170.931	299	433
middle	150.247	105	110
English	134.237	1527	3165
teach	121.398	139	176
grammar	106.759	336	563
experience	101.764	129	169
junior	87.168	57	58
teacher	83.315	106	139
class	62.065	212	361
old	54.54	46	52
interest	54.298	116	177
elementary	54.062	34	34
young	53.007	50	59
senior	52.471	33	33
exam	48.231	79	112
university	47.504	76	107
course	47.403	120	191
score	46.891	41	47
decide	42.656	29	30
college	41.988	41	49
grade	39.47	29	31
education	38.814	34	39
age	38.393	32	36
primary	38.152	24	24

Given the subject matter of the L2 experience interview, the frequency and co-occurrence of these words are entirely unsurprising. Students tended to discuss the concrete biographical details of their learning experience by explaining how and when they studied English in school and at university, with an emphasis on grades, exams, and grammar. Perhaps the most interesting feature of this category is the strong connection between *grammar* (which is only rarely used in this corpus to mean primary or elementary school) and the classroom experience. Although the interview included separate questions devoted to grammar, vocabulary, speaking/listening, and reading/writing, only *grammar* clustered together with biographical descriptions of academic learning. For example, one student says, "I learned grammar in my middle school and high school, but I'm not good at grammar part…So I didn't do any specific things, just learn my grammar part in middle school and high school." Another explains: "I think the grammar is from middle school and high school, because in Asia, I think Asian people they really concerned about their grammar for the writing. So I think most of the grammar things I learned from middle school and high school."

In other words, one strong focus of the L2 learners in this corpus is simply being in the English classroom. At least for those students who ultimately came to study in the USA, L2 English learning is strongly connected to studying at school, particularly to studying grammar and taking exams.

Cluster 2: Communicating

The second cluster identified by T-Lab has a focus on speaking, listening, and interacting with other speakers. Here, the most representative words include those directly involved in meeting and talking with native English speakers in the U.S. context: *speak*, *people*, *talk*, *American*, *friend*, *accent*, *native*, *language*, *communicate*, *speaker*, *each other*, *listen*, *meet*, *lab*, *travel*, *English speaking*. The experience of communicating with English speakers (particularly native English speakers) also seems to draw heavily on emotions (*feel*, *confident*, *comfortable*) and cognition (*understand*, *mean*, *know*), as well as judgments of ability during the communication process (*able to*, *better*, *fast*). Another strand within this cluster (*watch*, *movie*, *subtitle*, *TV*) appears to refer to consuming media in order to improve listening skills. Other similar words, although not among the 30 most representative, further confirm the theme of communication: *opportunity* (X^2 = 22.852), *culture* (X^2 = 21.245), *nervous* (X^2 = 17.59), *try* (X^2 = 17.183), and *embarrass* (X^2 = 15.24), among others. Table 8.2 provides a list of the 30 most representative lemmas in this cluster.

The semantic content of Cluster 2 is perhaps encouraging for L2 English teachers, as it indicates that another prominent theme of the

Table 8.2 Most representative lemmas in Communicating cluster

Lemma	X^2	Freq. in Cluster	Freq. in Corpus
speak	393.092	701	1232
feel	217.998	225	327
people	210.033	401	716
talk	209.965	250	383
American	202.463	166	220
friend	169.825	173	250
accent	142.415	91	108
native	138.097	151	224
watch	131.604	164	255
understand	113.724	212	375
language	93.28	312	641
communicate	88.633	101	152
movie	84.417	126	208
speaker	79.478	77	109
confident	63.708	34	37
subtitle	60.483	37	43
each other	59.345	32	35
different	57.208	158	310
TV	54.206	77	125
listen	54.059	212	450
comfortable	44.258	41	57
able to	41.056	50	77
better	39.084	99	190
mean	35.703	188	422
lab	33.636	17	18
meet	31.801	36	54
travel	31.801	36	54
fast	28.707	36	56
know	26.303	297	747
English speaking	25.888	36	58

learning experience for these students is using English for authentic communication. While this may not be surprising given that the interview participants are all matriculated into academic programs in the USA, we cannot take for granted that students will spend much time practicing their speaking skills, especially with native English speakers. Students from countries such as China and Korea, particularly those in math and science departments, may spend much of their time with students and even professors from their own L1 background. Several students allude to this scenario: "But I find some new ways of learning English and other people should try to do, talk more to American people and try to speak English between Chinese people," or "But from the speaking, I think other people also do the same way they want to speak particularly with the native speaker, but if they cannot find it they speak to people from their friend, try to practice their speaking."

In general, students indicate that they want to interact with native English speakers while they are in the USA, but are often unsure of their skills or have difficulty with the interaction. For example, one student reports, "For speaking I always try to speak because you know sometimes when you are not familiar to this language you feel a little bit scary I mean nervous to use it to communicate with people. I guess the best way to improve the speaking ability is just try to speak it, don't set a limit to yourself." Another says, "Actually I think my listening skills are improved enough…I can understand all people who are speaking in front of me. But there are some bad things with my speaking and yeah I should improve it. What I can't do is I can't speak with people, with American people."

Comments like these confirm the distinctive role of affect in this dimension of the L2 learning experience. It seems that many L2 learners at American universities are positively oriented toward interacting with native speakers and see it as an important part of their experience, but such interactions may be difficult, uncomfortable, and infrequent. Again, this is not necessarily a new finding regarding communication between native speakers and non-native speakers, but what is interesting is how closely intertwined these communication and affect words are in the L2 Experience Interview Corpus. The data and our analysis are able to empirically confirm that these are salient and closely related aspects of the L2 learning experience.

Cluster 3: Studying

The studying cluster has very strong links to reading and writing, including lemmas such as *word*, *paper*, *vocabulary*, *book*, *dictionary*, *sentence*, *article*, *novel*, *textbook*, *newspaper*, *magazine*, and *list*. There are many references to self-study, as students mention *improve*, *remember*, *try*, *google*, *look*, *help*, *guess*, *check*, *memorize*, and *look up*. Clearly, this strand of the L2 learning experience involves independent learning through written, rather than spoken, media. See Table 8.3 for a list of the 30 most representative lemmas in this cluster.

Table 8.3 Most representative lemmas in Studying cluster

Lemmas	X^2	Freq. in Cluster	Freq. in Corpus
read	980.598	708	918
write	563.932	503	711
reading	406.307	325	438
word	338.788	383	592
paper	187.442	112	132
vocabulary	179.333	202	311
book	139.115	195	324
dictionary	110.795	73	90
sentence	92.485	93	137
improve	76.551	196	388
article	76.037	48	58
novel	46.03	29	35
textbook	43.357	44	65
remember	41.032	68	119
try	40.518	227	530
newspaper	39.881	32	43
day	37.06	77	144
google	36.962	16	16
look	35.551	50	83
help	34.471	113	237
expression	31.066	22	28
guess	30.706	62	115
check	28.981	21	27
online	28.346	14	15
memorize	28.212	65	125
GRE	25.877	42	73
look up	24.906	14	16
magazine	24.092	15	18
news	22.97	26	40
list	22.548	22	32

In contrast to the Communication cluster, which had lower X^2 values for its top lemmas, the Studying cluster contains much higher X^2 values for its most representative lemmas. This means reading and writing are very strongly related to this cluster and quite distant from the other two clusters. They are undisputedly the dominant themes of this strand of experience, but are well complemented by the other, surrounding lemmas. Several examples explain this tight relationship:

Text Sample 8.1 Reading and Writing in Studying Cluster

> *That's mostly because I like to read books and the books I read are mostly English. So when I read them in Dutch the sequel is not translated yet, so I just really really want to read that book so I will order it online and I will get the English version and I will read that, and that helps a lot to read. Just to keep on reading, to practice your reading.*
>
> *Reading is closely related to writing, so when I read, I try to read various materials, which is not focused on my research area. For example I try to read newspaper or through the internet, so. It doesn't take long time to read one page or two page, I just read.*
>
> *So if you don't read then you won't have a rich vocabulary. So reading for me is quite essential, because through reading I am developing my vocabulary, my analysis skills, so for me reading has an essential role.*

These results show that for this group of students at least, reading and writing, while closely connected to each other, are quite separate from other aspects of the L2 learning experience. Regarding the learning process, this finding seems to confirm that written skills and vocabulary may not be easily integrated into oral communication skills, or at least that learners view them as two very different subsets of the L2 experience.

Discussion

As a starting point for our investigation of the L2 Experience Interview Corpus, this analysis deepens our understanding of salient themes within the L2 learning experience. First, these learners strongly equate L2 English learning with classroom learning, since the majority of their time spent learning English is at school. The classroom is in turn strongly connected to grammar and exams, indicating that the grammar-translation method of teaching is frequently used in these participants' home countries. In fact, the majority of students interviewed for this study reported that their English learning experience in middle and high school was filled with pencil-and-paper exercises and limited authentic communication. This was true for learners from all parts of the world. Some students suggested that this focus on grammar exercises resulted in part from their teachers' lack of English proficiency, and many also felt that their national education systems were to blame for favoring poor teaching methods or for simply allowing apathetic teaching. Chinese and Korean students frequently complained about the grammar- and test-focused nature of their educational systems. Many students from Europe, Asia, the Middle East, and Latin America felt that their secondary education had not prepared them well for speaking and listening in authentic communicative interactions. Table 8.4 contains representative comments on students' experiences with grammar.

The second theme identified in the L2 experience interviews was the process of communicating with other speakers, including both positive and negative aspects. The Communicating cluster is especially interesting in light of the classroom and grammatical emphasis of Cluster 1, as it reflects a very different understanding of the purpose of L2 learning. Here, the widespread poor opinion of secondary-school English classes often gives way to a positive impression of the L2 experience when learners begin to use English for authentic communication. While not every student reported this pattern, it seems to represent a distinct strand of the L2 learning experience. Because their school instruction tended to be grammar-translation, this group of students (as high-schoolers) found English rather meaningless and boring; yet as young adults, many realized that English would help them to study abroad, travel, attend graduate school, or reach career goals, and they became newly devoted to studying or seeking opportunities to practice. Table 8.5 contains statements from some of these students that capture their changing experience as they discovered the language as a means of authentic communication.

Table 8.4 Comments on grammar-translation teaching methods

Nationality	Comments
French	That's pretty much all how our classes were; we just had grammar and only grammar. That's why I think we can be ok at grammar but we're really bad at talking. Because we just don't practice a lot, so it was just practice about grammatical things and everything so it could be really boring, but that's how we got our bachelor's, so
Chinese	I learn grammar because in China the English teacher they teach a lot of grammar. That's how I learn grammar, especially in the high school. I believe the major part of the English exam is about the grammar, about how you write your sentence, your vocabulary, all grammar. It's only about 20 percent about the listening, and there's no speaking test in china in English exam. Yeah all about grammar I think, at least 60 percent in my opinion
Korean	I saw many problems in Korea, when it comes to learning English. Because we only focus on the reading and grammar, and sometimes listening, but students cannot actually write in English and speak in English... Because many Korean students actually hate learning English, because it's really stressful, and it's not fun, because they always focus, memorize the vocabulary and memorize the grammar rule and those kind of things that makes students hate English
Italian	Then I actually started to learn English in my lower high school... And it was kind of strange because actually the professor that taught us English was a French professor and he had to learn English for teaching us English. So you can imagine that it was something very very related to the book and really basic things like what's your name, where are you from, and basic stuff like that. So it was not kind of very expanded or very interesting experience actually. In the high school as well because my English professor had a dialectal accent from the southern part of Italy so her English was not so good basically

The third theme identified by the T-Lab analysis is that of self-study, particularly of reading and writing. This is evidently an important aspect of L2 learning that is complementary to the first two themes of classroom learning and oral communication. While learners (consciously or unconsciously) appear to describe speaking and interacting as a fairly emotional process, reading and writing seem strongly linked to cognition with words such as *memorize*, *try*, *remember*, *improve*, and *guess*. In contrast

Table 8.5 Comments reflecting changing L2 learning experience

Participant	Comments
French	I used not to like it because it was all very theoretical and everything. But now I'm just learning by speaking with people, it's very interesting, and you learn a lot from them, so pretty much it's very good. It's very good
Italian	Actually when I was young I totally hated it because it was my parents' choice and I couldn't really find out why it was so important to know English. Then when I enrolled in the university I realized it was the most important language to know, even if it is not the most spoken, it is the most important and probably widely understood. So I actually like it
Chinese	Actually before I came here I think learning English like agh, it's horrible. Because nobody speak English around me, and we don't write stuff in English, we don't write article in English, so learning English kind of suffering, torturing like that. But after I planned my plan to come here I kind of enjoyed it, because I have to improve…I think I kind of figure out the amazing part of the English. Because I think also my PI think, also he used to be a Chinese and now he's a citizen of here, we discuss this a lot, so we think that the language of English is more precise than Chinese, especially for scientific area. It's like there are specific words, just this words can describe your feeling or your project or what you're doing. But no such kind of very precise English in Chinese… And also people here all speak English so I enjoy speaking English
Chinese	When I was young I hate English. Because just like said you usually practice for the test. You not really for your regular usage. And when I was a high school student my teachers say the goal for us you have to pass, you have to get point over 90 degree. If you didn't achieve the goal you will be punished. So at that moment I just want to get a goal the teacher gave us. But maybe after when I was 22, 23 years old, I enjoyed traveling so I went to a lot of countries and English is the useful language no matter where you go. And I like to talk and I like to share my experience, my stories with other people, so I like to use English from then. And I think that point to change my attitude to learning English. So I like English right now because I'm here
Korean	Learning English wasn't really a pleasure for me back in Korea, but while I was studying abroad with foreign student and teachers speaking English, it was kind of survival skill to have. So that was big motivation for me to learn English. After that I enjoy watching movie and cartoon in English and that kind of helps me to be motivated in learning English. So I think that's more like exploring culture through the language, that is my motivation

to the external/biographical dimension of the Classroom cluster or the relational/communicative dimension of the Communicating cluster, the Studying cluster represents much of the hard work students put in to reach and flourish in their academic programs in the USA.

In sum, then, the three clusters provide empirical support for three distinct and important strands within the L2 learning experience. In Chap. 9, we will turn to the primarily psychological dimensions of the L2 experience, which add depth to our understanding of the L2 experience described in this chapter.

Methodological Limitations

Because this is an exploratory methodology, we should consider some important potential limitations. One of these, regarding the reliability of using L2 learners' words with a technique developed for L1 speakers, will be considered in Chaps. 9 and 10. Another important consideration is whether there is a minimum number of words necessary for the accuracy of this method. In order to be as inclusive as possible, the present study analyzed interviews from all participants, regardless of interview length. The very wide range of text lengths (379 words to over 3000 words) may have impacted the results in some way. Of particular concern is very short texts, which may not provide a long enough sample of the learner's experience to be truly representative or informative on her or his views. On the other hand, some learners are naturally more talkative than others, and it may be inappropriate (even detrimental to the representativeness of the sample population) to eliminate interviews simply because they are short. This is an issue that should be investigated in future studies.

9

Psychosocial Dimensions of Learner Language

While the preceding chapter looked at general semantic themes in the L2 Experience Interview Corpus, the present chapter turns to the psychological (learner-internal) and social (learner-external) themes in learner interviews. Specifically, we want to know how 22 psychosocial categories within the Linguistic Inquiry and Word Count program (LIWC; Pennebaker et al. 2007) relate to the language experience interviews of 123 advanced English language learners, and whether this relationship indicates larger dimensions of co-occurring features within the L2 learning experience. To address this question, we use exploratory principal component analysis to examine co-occurrence patterns among semantic variation across the interview texts.

Exploratory principal component analysis was used to identify potential psychosocial dimensions of language learning experience, as expressed through the language learning interviews. Procedures followed the analysis pioneered in Biber (1988) and frequently used to examine linguistic patterns (e.g., Grieve et al. 2010; Hardy and Friginal 2012). The 22 indices from LIWC were used as grouping factors and were entered into a principal component analysis in SPSS 20, using Varimax rotation with Kaiser normalization. This analysis indicated which semantic features

E. Friginal et al., *Exploring Spoken English Learner Language Using Corpora*,
DOI 10.1007/978-3-319-59900-7_9

Table 9.1 Rotated component matrix of psychosocial features

	Component			
Feature	1	2	3	4
family	−0.045	0.046	0.121	0.606
friend	−0.062	−0.018	0.351	−0.461
humans	0.342	0.040	0.006	−0.024
posemo	0.378	−0.133	0.219	−0.037
negemo	0.024	0.873	−0.061	0.063
anxiety	0.005	0.806	−0.042	−0.044
anger	0.060	0.097	0.025	0.645
sadness	0.023	0.340	−0.404	−0.327
insight	0.511	0.112	−0.150	−0.120
cause	−0.141	−0.028	−0.033	0.459
discrepancy	0.239	0.215	−0.479	−0.191
tentative	0.579	−0.355	−0.147	−0.110
certainty	0.387	−0.104	−0.032	0.388
inhibition	−0.241	−0.054	−0.362	0.000
inclusive	−0.023	0.140	0.669	0.047
exclusive	0.497	−0.064	−0.010	−0.092
see	0.171	−0.153	0.482	−0.054
hear	−0.119	0.013	0.631	−0.088
feel	0.481	0.331	0.121	0.038
motion	−0.143	−0.227	0.037	0.316
space	−0.505	−0.153	−0.132	−0.042
time	−0.293	−0.011	0.176	−0.181

co-occur frequently within interview texts, and these groups were then interpreted as experiential dimensions of language learning.

The analysis resulted in four components, which together represent 34.64% of the shared variance in interview texts. Bartlett's Test of Sphericity revealed the analysis to be significant at $p < 0.000$. The rotated component matrix is shown in Table 9.1. Features with positive or negative loadings over 0.30 are grouped in Table 9.2.

In order to interpret the four components into dimensions of language learning experience, the psychosocial content and potential significance of each feature was considered in the context of language learning interviews. *AntConc* (Anthony 2014) was used to find and explore each word within the interview context.

Table 9.2 Component features

Component	Loading	Features
1	Positive	Tentative, Insight, Exclusive, Feel, Certainty, Positive Emotion, Humans
	Negative	Space
2	Positive	Negative Emotion, Anxiety, Sadness, Feel
	Negative	Tentative
3	Positive	Inclusive, Hear, See, Friend
	Negative	Discrepancy, Sadness, Inhibition
4	Positive	Anger, Family, Cause, Certainty, Motion
	Negative	Friend, Sadness

Note: Features for each component are listed from highest loading to lowest

Dimension 1: Positive-Learning

The features that loaded positively in Dimension 1 come primarily from the Cognitive Mechanisms categories of LIWC (Tentative, Insight, Exclusive, Certainty), which suggests that this dimension is focused on the cognitive processes behind language learning. Many of the most frequent words are contained in the Insight index, including *learn* (1684 words), *think* (1430 words), *know* (839 words), and *understand* (363 words), thus highlighting the salient thinking aspects of language learning. (Throughout the chapter, word frequencies will be listed in parentheses following the introduction of a word.) Many other very frequent words come from the Exclusive index: *but* (1690), *just* (1073), *not* (1007), *or* (885) and *really* (707).

The fact that these are function words helps to explain their frequency, but it is important to note that these words did not load in any other dimensions, suggesting that they are particularly important in explaining the processes behind language learning. For example, *but* is used to describe past learning events ("I had some basic English course there but basically I learned English before that by listening music"), learning strategies ("when I use my laptop or my computer I use Merriam-Webster and Dictionary.com but most of the time I use Google translate"), affect ("I get kind of shy because I want to express myself but when I can't find the specific word I'm kind of stuck"), and many other aspects of the learning process. *Just* is similarly descriptive of learning ("we had other classes in which we just practiced language with native speakers"), as are *not* ("I always think I should have learned English first with conversation, not grammar or vocabulary") and *really* ("it's important to me really to understand the structure of the sentence"). See Table 9.3 for a list of the most frequent words in these positive indices for Dimension 1.

Interestingly, the seemingly contradictory indices Tentative and Certainty both loaded positively in Dimension 1, although Tentative loaded more strongly and contains many more frequent words. The words in this index include *or* (885), *some* (700), *a lot* and *lots* (665), *if* (630), *maybe* (495), *most* and *mostly* (408), *something* (319), *sometimes* (319), and *kind of* (318). In other words, these are terms used to describe habits, procedures, or processes in the past or present that relate to learning. Typical examples of the Tentative category are "what is most important or most efficient way to improve my English, I am considering that

Table 9.3 Positive psychosocial features of Dimension 1

Tentative	Insight	Exclusive	Feel	Certainty	Posemo	Humans
or (885)	learn (1684)	but (1690)	feel* (345)	all (401)	good (474)	people (715)
some (700)	think* (1430)	just (1073)	hard (152)	every (207)	like* (453)	
lot* (665)	know* (839)	not (1007)		always (154)	improv* (404)	
if (630)	understand* (363)	or (885)		everything (109)	friend* (254)	
maybe (495)	feel* (345)	really (707)			important (194)	
most* (408)	find* (166)	if (630)			better (191)	
something (397)	memor* (142)	something (397)			well (190)	
sometimes (319)	remember* (119)					
kind of (318)						
guess* (116)						
usually (101)						

Note: Asterisks indicate that all lemmas were included in the frequency count

question now," "sometimes I will watch some soap opera on internet," "I really improve my English by reading a lot of the textbooks," and "I see that that would be better if I started learning earlier." Certainty words, such as *all* (401) and *every* (207), are used in a very similar way, mostly to explain learning events or processes: "I have the possibility to talk English all day long if I want," "first I make a list of every step in every test I have to take," and "so I'm applying all the strategies." In this light, Tentative and Certainty words are actually very complementary and are logically connected as the descriptors of L2 learning.

Three features that loaded positively in Dimension 1 are not Cognitive Mechanisms: Feel, Positive Emotion, and Humans. Feel is the only perceptual process in this dimension, and its main representatives are *feel** (345) and *hard* (152). The lemma *feel* itself is duplicated in the Insight category, making it doubly influential in connection with learning English: "I feel that my English knowledge was based on grammatical knowledge," or "I feel confident that people can understand me." Unsurprisingly, *hard* is frequently associated with language learning, as in "it's sometimes hard to understand but I really pay attention," or "the first days are very hard and then as time goes by I become more fluent." Humans is the only social category of Dimension 1, and its only major representative is *people* (715). *People* is often used to describe communication and speaking ("you feel a little bit scary I mean nervous to use it to communicate with people"), but it is also used to explain beliefs about learning ("different people learn it in a different way") or learning methods ("a lot of people learn English by listening to the tv").

It is especially noteworthy that Positive Emotion—the only affective category in Dimension 1—occurs alongside the cognitive and perceptual categories that are descriptive of the learning process. The co-occurrence of words such as *good* (474), *like** (453), *improve** (404), and *friend** (254) with *learn*, *think*, and *understand* suggests that the learning process engenders positive feelings: "this is also a good way of learning it," "definitely I like learning English," "I think that I improved a lot in the past two years," "to improve my speaking I try to speak English with my friends most of the time," or "I like learning English because it is exciting to learn a new thing, especially a new language." Although negated versions of these words also occur, most instances are indeed positive; for example, *not good* appears only 37 times (out of 474 *goods*), and *don't/ doesn't like* occurs only 10 times (out of 453 *likes*). Therefore, it seems that there is a clear current of positive affect underlying this dimension.

The only feature to load negatively in Dimension 1 is Space, which includes words such as *at, in, international, little*, and *on*. The fact that these location words tend not to co-occur with cognition and positive affect suggests that in speaking about learning, students focus on processes, actions, and internal experience rather than places and external events. This seems quite logical, but it is perhaps noteworthy that Space is the only index to have a strongly negative loading in relation to cognition and positive emotion.

Taken together, the features of Dimension 1 seem to imply that one very prominent aspect of the language learning experience combines the cognitive processes of learning with positive feelings about learning. While it is hardly surprising that Insight and other cognitive words should be used to describe learning, it is interesting—and perhaps very gratifying to applied linguists—to see these processes accompanied by positive affect. Of course, this connection shows only correlation and not causality, without providing clues as to whether positive affect enables learning, or whether successful learning produces positive feelings. What the Positive-Learning dimension does reveal is that the potent combination of cognitive processes and positive emotion is one of the most salient aspects of the language learning experience for the English language learners who participated in this study.

Dimension 2: Negative-Anxious

In contrast to the Positive-Learning dimension, Dimension 2 loads strongly on negative affect: three of its four positive loadings involve negative feelings (Negative Emotion, Anxiety, Sadness), and the fourth positively loaded index, Feel, is closely related. (See Table 9.4 for frequently occurring words.) On the other hand, while this dimension is statistically very strong, words in the Negative-Anxious dimension are much less frequent than the learning and positive affect words of Dimension 1. Only *difficult* occurred more than 100 times (116 instances), and many

Table 9.4 Positive psychosocial features of Dimension 2

Negemo	Anxiety	Sadness	Feel
difficult (116)	nervous (26)	fail* (8)	feel* (343)
problem (86)	shy (24)	alone (7)	hard (152)
bad (57)	afraid (21)	lose* (6)	
wrong (43)	stress* (18)	useless (5)	
	confus* (16)		
	embarrass* (12)		
	uncomfortable (10)		
	awkward (9)		
	pressure (8)		

Note: Asterisks indicate that all lemmas were included in the frequency count

of the words are actually infrequent. For example, just a few words in the Sadness index (fail*, 8, alone, 7, lose*, 6, and useless, 5) were enough to make it a feature of this dimension. In addition, some words are used in a rather neutral context that somewhat mitigates their negative impact: "I think that is the biggest failure at Chinese education actually," "it gives me more incentive not to be shy," or "for me learning English was not that difficult." On the other hand, anxiety and negative emotions are an undeniable component of the language learning experience, and it is hardly surprising that they form an underlying dimension within the language experience interviews.

Negative emotion was expressed most frequently through *difficult*, as in "I feel it's a little difficult when somebody speaks too fast," "the most difficult part for me is pronunciation," "writing is sometimes difficult, you make some mistakes," and "in the beginning of this year it was quite difficult." Interestingly, as these examples show, in most cases *difficult* was used to describe a specific situation or skill rather than English learning as a whole. Similarly, *problem* (86), *bad* (57), and *wrong* (43) usually refer to particular times or circumstances: "maybe the main problem is that I cannot understand all the words," "I like learning English, my main problem probably is a lack of time," "if you have a bad professor you don't learn it," "I think my grammar was pretty bad," or "even though you are using wrong grammar they may just pretend they get it."

Anxiety and Sadness words are used with varying degrees of intensity, sometimes expressing mild emotion and sometimes acute disappointment. *Nervous* (26) or *embarrass** (12), for example, are often used in a mild sense ("I feel a little nervous from time to time," "English still makes me kind of nervous because that's not my native language," "sometimes I will feel embarrassed because I can't fully express my thoughts"), whereas *fail* can sound shattering ("I had a year off before university because I failed the first time," "I hope I can practice my English one or two hours every day, but I fail to do so. I'm a little lazy I think"). Many words in these categories, such as *shy* (24), *confus** (16), *uncomfortable* (10), and *awkward* (9), imply transient feelings or responses to situations that were temporary and have improved over time.

Nevertheless, the Negative-Anxiety dimension of language learning seems self-evident and has been well documented in studies on language learning anxiety (e.g., Horwitz 2010). The fact that it emerges as a distinct dimension in the present study appears to confirm the important, if limited, role it plays in the language learning experience. The only negatively loaded feature of this dimension, Tentative, was the feature with the strongest positive loading in the Positive-Learning dimension, further indicating that negative emotions may be diametrically opposed to facilitative learning processes.

Dimension 3: Social-Participatory

Dimension 3 loads positively on one cognitive category (Inclusive), two perceptual categories (Hear and See), and one social category (Friend; See Table 9.5 for word frequencies for each feature). Of these, the Inclusive words *and* (4347), *we* (952) and *with* (821) are by far the most frequent, probably because they are function words and are frequent in most corpora. However, these words loaded strongly in

Table 9.5 Positive psychosocial features of Dimension 3

Inclusive	Hear	See	Friend
and (4347)	listen* (452)	watch* (255)	friend* (254)
we (952)	hear* (82)	see* (178)	roommate* (28)
with (821)		look* (104)	boyfriend (8)

Note: Asterisks indicate that all lemmas were included in the frequency count

only one dimension, suggesting that they have a specific role to play in co-occurring with Hear, See, and Friend. Hear has only two primary words, *listen** (452) and *hear** (82), while See has three main words (*watch**, 255, *see**, 178, and *look**, 104). The Friend index is comprised mainly of *friend** itself (254), but *roommate** (28) and *boyfriend* (8) also occur.

Together, these categories suggest a dimension of language learning in which students talk with other people, meet friends, and are generally participatory in social and communicative activities. Students explain, "I try to listen to as many people with different accents as I can," "going to see the professors, speaking English with the professors, this was helpful," "I have another American friend, so when we talk actually I'm learning some new things from them," and "I think when you really want know it you have to speak to people and just read and watch movies and listen to songs so you understand it." Many students view speaking and listening as important aspects of their L2 learning process, and by participating in conversations and activities, they make friends and improve their English skills.

The negative loadings of this dimension (Sadness, Discrepancy, and Inhibition) seem to complement its four positive features. Sadness, as described in Dimension 2 above, disappears when students are actively engaged in communicating and interacting with people. Discrepancy, which includes words such as *if*, *need*, *want*, and *would*, implies a dissonance between reality and desire, and this also seems to ebb when students discuss their social and participatory activities. Inhibition words (*avoid*, *careful*, *discipline*, *forget*, *ignore*, *keep*, *limit*) also tend not to occur in Dimension 3, suggesting that students check their inhibitions when speaking, listening, and interacting.

The Social-Participatory dimension of language learning may be particularly salient for students who are studying in the USA for the first time, as the participants in this study were. Many students described having to speak and interact in English for the first time, and while this led to some degree of anxiety, in general this appears to be a positive and important aspect of the learning experience.

Dimension 4: Education

The positively loaded indices of Dimension 4 (Anger, Family, Cause, Certainty, and Motion) seem, at first glance, to be quite disparate psychosocial features. They are, however, linked by common referents (such as *grammar*, *school*, or *class*) which are not part of LIWC's psychosocial dictionaries, and many of these categories are actually connected to biographical discussions of English learning through education and study. Descriptions of language learning events and habits—in school, at home, at university, or while studying in the USA—form the basis of the Education dimension. See Table 9.6 for the frequently occurring words in each of these positive dimensions.

Perhaps the most striking feature of this dimension is Anger, which loads very strongly at 0.645, but which consists primarily of one word, *hate**. With only 14 occurrences in the corpus, *hate* is a rare but powerful lemma, often used to describe particular aspects of L2 English learning ("I really hate to write papers," "I hate grammar") or feelings from the past ("when I was young I hate English"). In a few instances, hate was ascribed to other people ("because many Korean students…memorize the vocabulary and memorize the grammar rule and those kind of things, that makes students hate English," "I think they hate me, really now I am going there all the time, I ask them strange question"). One student used it to explain her love-hate relationship with English ("I have two very different feeling at the same time towards English. Sometimes I really hate English, but sometimes I really love English"). In general, *hate* was used

Table 9.6 Positive psychosocial features of Dimension 4

Anger	Family	Cause	Certainty	Motion
hate* (14)	parent* (41)	because (1345)	all (401)	go* (425)
	family* (26)	use* (619)	every (207)	take (248)
	father* (14)	how* (395)	always (154)	come* (238)
	mom* (12)	make* (221)	everything (109)	change* (113)
	mother* (10)	why (149)		
	sister* (8)	since (120)		
	brother* (5)	change* (113)		
	relative* (5)			

Note: Asterisks indicate that all lemmas were included in the frequency count

within very limited boundaries, but it was often implicated in grammar- and school-related activities.

The second very strongly loaded feature of Dimension 4 is Family, which primarily consists of *parent** (41), *famil** (26), *father** (14), *mom** (12), *mother** (10), *sister** (8), *brother** (5), and *relative** (5). Participants talked about their parents in terms of how parents made them study English ("I took English in school but my parents also wanted me to have a tutor," "I'm just learning because my parents want me to"), opportunities that their parents gave them ("I'm really thankful to my parents for giving me the chance to live even for a few weeks in an English speaking country, and that made all the difference"), or having parents for role models or even fellow participants in language learning ("my parents talk English at home," "my parents are really good examples for people who want to learn a language"). *Father*, *mom*, and *mother* were also used to describe parental activities, encouragement, or enforcement in learning English at home: "my father introduced me to English books," "it was influenced by my father because my father has a strong interest in learning English," "my father made me change all the compound sentences to simple sentences and all the simple sentences to complex sentences from the newspaper," "when I was young my mom began to teach me about some words," "English was my mom's passion actually," and "my mom would give me topics and I would write essays on it." As might be expected, participants discussed brothers and sisters in terms of speaking or learning together as children ("my sister and I would speak English between us when we were back home").

The two Cognitive Mechanisms categories of this dimension, Cause and Certainty, contain many terms that are useful in describing what happened, how it happened, and why; these words include *because* (1345), *use** (619), *all* (401), *how** (395), *make** (221), *every* (207), *always* (154), *why* (149), and *since* (120). While such words can certainly be used in many different senses, they clearly play a role in talking about habits or procedures related to learning: "we are very used to study because at the very end we are graded on all the program," "back in middle school we use tapes," "they use various method to make you feel you're happy about learning," and "that's how I learned listening." Certainty words, in particular, often describe what was done at school ("the teacher will ask us to recite all vocabularies and we will have small quizzes," "I don't think we talked at all in class," "so every day I spend about half an hour for listening news," "in high school it was six years and every day we have at least one English classes").

The last positive feature of the Education dimension, Motion, seems logically to relate to describing events and activities with words such as *go** (425), *take** (248), *come** (238), and *change** (113). Again, students often use these lemmas to talk about past experiences ("I went to the courses and I did all the homeworks and the assignments and I came to the USA," "after I went to middle school I started to study the grammar part"), requirements ("I want to study at United States so I need to take TOEFL, take GMAT"), or decisions ("that's why I decide to come here," "I have no plan to come America before I come here").

Friend and Sadness are the only two negatively loaded categories of Dimension 4, suggesting that the dimension indeed focuses on the procedural, work-related aspects of language learning rather than the social side reflected in Dimension 3. It is certainly interesting that Friend and Family—two categories often linked in social processes—are inversely related in this dimension of language experience. Upon closer inspection, however, it makes sense that the family would be instrumental in encouraging, supporting, or requiring language learning, since parents are often key influencers or decision makers in a child's life. Friends, on the other hand, are important in the Social-Participatory aspect of learning, but may not necessarily contribute to the sustained motivation or values that support successful language acquisition. When students mention the more routine events or studious habits in their English experience, their friends and acquaintances are conspicuously absent.

In summary, then, the Education dimension seems mainly descriptive of external events or study habits, in contrast to the first three dimensions, which tend to focus on the internalized aspects of the language learning experience. This does not imply that it is any less important, since formal education, family encouragement, and consistent learning routines are doubtless essential to the language acquisition process.

Discussion

While we have just looked at four potentially separate and salient dimensions within the L2 learning experience, it is important to remember that students probably do not perceive their learning process in such a fragmented way. All learners are likely to experience various dimensions at various times throughout their L2 experience, perhaps simultaneously or perhaps in quick succession. The purpose of this model is simply to provide a new heuristic for learners to understand their own psychology during the learning process, and for instructors to dynamically understand and interpret learner challenges.

Thus, the experiential approach explored in this study suggests that learners and teachers will benefit from considering L2 learning as a whole that is influenced by many aspects of the learner's life. Even factors that teachers may not know about or may not have considered important could play a vital role in the learning process. Both students and teachers should be ready to address factors from any of the four dimensions that could impact a learner's experience and attainment. By maintaining this level of awareness and seeing learning as a long-term investment, teachers and learners may be able to enhance both L2 proficiency and enjoyment of the learning process.

Methodological Limitations

The quantitative methodology presented here, while innovative, does have certain limitations. The analysis was based on a computer program developed by psychologists for purposes other than studying L2 learning. Twenty-two LIWC categories were used here to identify psychosocial elements of L2 learning, but it is possible that the selected categories are not the most informative for L2 experience interviews. One very promising route for future inquiry is to develop a semantic content analysis application specific to L2 learning. This could be applied both to the psychosocial aspects of the L2 experience, as well as to other aspects of the L2 experience not explicitly covered in this study.

10

Profiles of Experience in Learner Talk

In contrast to the previous two chapters, which analyzed the themes and dimensions horizontally across the entire L2 Experience Interview Corpus, this chapter vertically analyzes and compares the psychosocial traits of each interview participant. We apply the methodological advantages offered by semantic content analysis and the L2 Experience Interview Corpus to study holistic patterns of individual differences among advanced L2 learners. In order to do this, we use Linguistic Inquiry and Word Count (LIWC; Pennebaker et al. 2007) to detect clusters of psychosocial traits that might suggest distinctive profiles among L2 learners. In other words, are there discernable clusters of psychosocial traits present in the interviews, and do these clusters of traits correspond to larger patterns that could be considered learner profiles? These questions are addressed using cluster analysis to identify clusters of learners who describe their L2 learning experience in similar ways. We then use an additional dataset—self-reported TOEFL scores of 96 of the interview participants—to examine the relationship of the newly identified profiles to differential outcomes on the TOEFL.

E. Friginal et al., *Exploring Spoken English Learner Language Using Corpora*,
DOI 10.1007/978-3-319-59900-7_10

Cluster Analysis

In this analysis, interviews that share similar LIWC category scores are considered to be more alike and are, therefore, grouped into a cluster. The first step in this procedure was to normalize frequency counts for all 22 psychosocial features in each text, which involved converting the LIWC percentages into z-scores. These normalized counts were then entered into an agglomerative hierarchical cluster analysis in SPSS 20 that used furthest neighbor clustering. The distance measure selected was squared Euclidean distance, which frequently is used with hierarchical clustering (Burns and Burns 2008).

A group of three clusters was found to be optimal for this dataset after a series of test runs involving three to five groups. The following criteria were taken into account when determining the appropriate number of clusters. First, the clusters should contain enough students to be representative and relatively proportional; the five-cluster solution was eliminated because only a few of the 123 students were classified in some clusters while others had many students. Second, the clusters should provide information about the psychosocial features, so correlations were compared for both the three- and four-cluster solutions and the LIWC features. The three-cluster solution was found to correlate more highly with LIWC features, which meant that it was more informative. To explore which experiential features were most important across the three clusters, we considered two types of information: mean Z scores per cluster and a qualitative analysis of psychosocial words as they appeared in the interview context.

Because clusters are based on the tendency of certain categories to occur together in some texts but not in others, the interviews which have similar category patterns cluster together. In order to analyze which psychosocial categories were frequent and infrequent in each cluster, z-scores were averaged for the interviews from each cluster. By averaging the z-scores (e.g., Friginal et al. 2014), patterns of category use can be more clearly revealed. For instance, for all interview texts shown to be in Cluster 1, the z-scores for Family were averaged, resulting in an overall Family score of 0.926. This was done for all psychosocial features of all three clusters (see Fig. 10.1 for total scores). The resulting mean z-scores for some features were strongly or moderately positive, while z-scores for

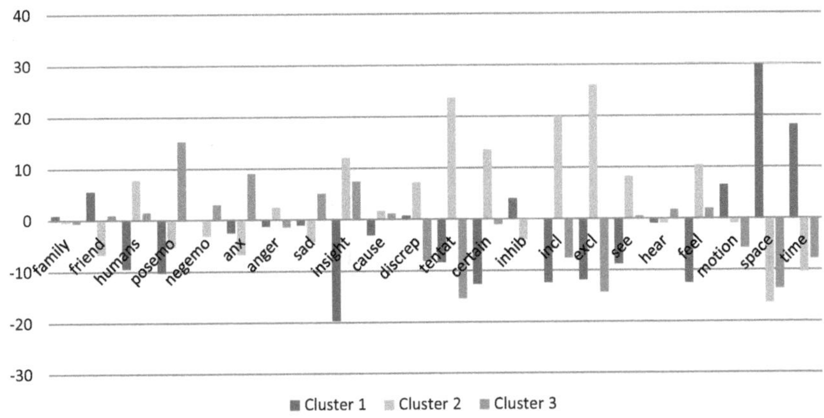

Fig. 10.1 Comparison of psychosocial features in all clusters

other features were strongly or moderately negative. These mean z-scores ranged from a high of 29.949 to a low of −19.635. For the purposes of this analysis, +5 or −5 is considered the threshold at which features show significant loadings. This decision was made based on the degree of differentiation that occurred in the data, and it allows us to focus on the features most strongly represented in each cluster. Therefore, all features that had combined z-scores of higher than +5 or lower than −5 were included in the interpretation of word usage for that cluster.

In order to interpret how psychosocial features varied across the three clusters, *AntConc* was used to examine word use in context. This was done simply by looking at the words from each LIWC category as they were used by students in the cluster. For example, one of Cluster 1's high z-score categories was Space, which contains 220 words such as *down*, *anywhere*, and *little*. *AntConc* was used to find every instance of all 220 of these words in Cluster 1 interview texts. This procedure was repeated for each strongly represented category in all three clusters. This resulted in word frequency counts for these strongly represented semantic categories, as well as contextual information about the use of each word. Based on this analysis, each cluster was considered to represent a certain way of experiencing L2 English learning, with underlying patterns of word use that present a cohesive psychosocial picture of the L2 learning experience of those students.

Table 10.1 Comparison of clusters by nationality

Country	Cluster 1	Cluster 2	Cluster 3
Afghanistan	1	1	0
Armenia	1	0	0
Brazil	0	1	0
China	5	16	12
Colombia	0	1	1
France	3	6	6
Georgia	0	1	0
Haiti	1	0	1
Hungary	0	1	0
India	2	4	3
Indonesia	8	3	5
Iran	1	1	1
Italy	5	4	2
Ivory Coast	1	0	0
Japan	1	1	0
Korea	5	3	5
Kyrgyzstan	1	0	0
Moldova	0	1	0
Netherlands	1	1	1
Romania	0	1	0
Spain	0	1	0
Turkey	2	0	0
Uzbekistan	0	1	0
Total	38	48	37

The clusters were somewhat evenly distributed, with 38 students (30.89%) in Cluster 1, 48 students (39.02%) in Cluster 2, and 37 students (30.08%) in Cluster 3. To determine whether the clusters were disproportionate based on nationality, the nationalities of students in each cluster were compared. As Tables 10.1 and 10.2 show, nationality is well distributed across the three clusters. For example, Iran and the Netherlands, which both have three students, have one student in each cluster; India has two, four, and three, respectively; Korea has five, three, and five. Indonesia appears somewhat unbalanced, with eight students in Cluster 1, three students in Cluster 2, and five students in Cluster 3. However, the only country which appears very unbalanced is China, which had the most participants of any country. This could be a chance occurrence, or it could be a result from the types of majors that Chinese students pursuing higher education in the USA tend to have.

Table 10.2 Comparison of clusters by geographic region

Country or region	Cluster 1	Cluster 2	Cluster 3
South Asia	10	7	8
Central Asia and Middle East	7	3	1
Western Europe	9	12	9
Latin America and Caribbean	1	2	2
Eastern Europe	0	3	0
East Asia	11	20	17
Africa	1	0	0
Total	38	48	37

To further explore this possibility, academic discipline was also compared across clusters (see Table 10.3). Two majors, Economics and Public Health, appear to be disproportionately represented in Cluster 1, and two majors, Biology and Computer Science, are disproportionately underrepresented in this cluster. The fact that Chinese students are heavily concentrated in Biology and Computer Science helps explain why there are more Chinese students in Clusters 2 and 3. In addition, Indonesian students in this sample were heavily concentrated in Economics, which relates to the large number of Indonesian students in Cluster 1.

Cluster 1: Narrative

As shown in Fig. 10.2, Cluster 1 contains four psychosocial categories that have positive loadings higher than 5 and eight categories that load negatively higher than 5. The positively loaded features (shown in Table 10.4) are Space, Time, Motion, and Friend, and the negatively loaded features are Insight, Certainty, Feeling, Inclusivity, Exclusivity, Positive Emotion, Seeing, and Tentativeness. Given the types of words these students favor, and the contexts in which they are used, students in Cluster 1 seem to focus on action and description, making their L2 experience interviews flow like a narrative of events. (Throughout the chapter, word frequencies will be listed in parentheses following the introduction of a word.) The particularly high loadings on Space and Time (with words such as *in*, 1192, *when*, 368, *time*, 206, and *then*, 181) often occur in descriptive accounts of the past ("I remember *when* I decided to really be good

Table 10.3 Comparison of clusters by academic discipline

Discipline	Cluster 1	Cluster 2	Cluster 3
Actuarial Science	0	2	2
Anthropology	0	0	1
Applied Linguistics	1	2	0
Biochemistry	1	0	0
Biology	1	5	5
Biomedical Engineering	0	0	1
Business Administration	3	3	3
Chemical Engineering	1	0	0
Chemistry	1	3	3
Communication	1	0	0
Computer Science	1	5	2
Criminal Justice	0	0	1
Economics	14	8	4
Education	1	3	2
English	0	2	0
Finance	1	1	2
Financial Engineering	0	0	1
Industrial Engineering	0	2	1
Information Systems	1	0	0
International Business	1	0	0
Law	0	1	0
Management of Technology	0	0	1
Marketing	0	0	1
Materials Science	0	1	0
Math & Statistics	0	2	0
Mechanical Engineering	1	0	0
Philosophy	0	0	1
Piano Performance	0	1	0
Political Science	1	2	3
Prosthesis and Orthosis	1	0	0
Public Administration	0	1	0
Public Financial Policy	1	0	0
Public Health	5	1	1
Risk Management	0	0	1
Screenwriting	0	1	0
Social Work	1	0	0
Spanish	0	1	0
Taxation	0	1	0
Undeclared	0	0	1
Total	38	48	37

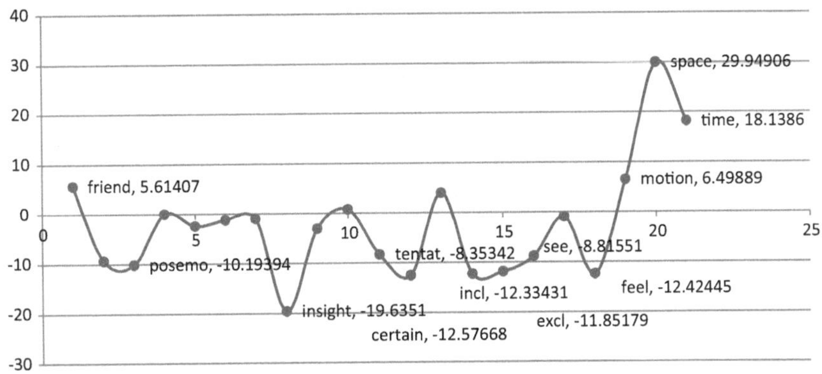

Fig. 10.2 Significant features of Narrative cluster

Table 10.4 Positive psychosocial features of Narrative cluster

Motion	Space	Time	Friend
go* (177)	in (1192)	when (368)	friend* (82)
take* (93)	at (159)	time* (206)	roommate* (12)
come* (77)	on (144)	then (181)	colleague* (5)
change* (33)	high* (112)	year* (130)	
travel* (21)	countr* (94)	now (119)	
put* (19)	up (52)	first (103)	
front (16)	international (42)	start* (100)	
catch* (12)	middle (40)	sometimes (95)	
attend* (11)	little (38)	after (74)	
leave* (11)	point* (33)	back (57)	
step* (10)	where (35)	still (51)	
	out (30)	before (49)	
	world (28)	day (46)	
	levels (23)	new* (45)	
	big* (21)	always (44)	
	around (20)	usually (37)	
	environment (15)	month* (35)	
	outside (15)	begin* (33)	
	over (15)	already (31)	

Note: Asterisks indicate that all lemmas were included in the frequency count. Numbers in parentheses represent word or lemma frequency in English," "I developed my writing *when* I started prepare the TOEFL test," "within that period of *time* since 2003, I was gradually studying," "*then when* I was in my college, *then* we are learning more in reading"). They also occur in explanations of study habits ("*when* I found a difficult vocabulary *then* I stopped the movie and tried to write down the words," "here I put eighty hours per week *in* using English"). The L2 learning experience for Narrative students emphasizes action, activities, and classes; that is, what they have done in the past and what they do in the present to improve their English abilities.

This action- and event-oriented experience of language learning seems to include social activities with friends and acquaintances. Within the Friend category, *friend** (81) is by far the most frequent lemma, but *roommate** (12) and *colleague** (5) also occur several times. *Friend* was used both in the context of what interviewees do with their friends ("I text to my *friends* in English," "I have another American *friend*, so when we talk actually I'm learning some new things"), and also to describe what friends do to learn English ("I rely on English course to improve my English but my *friends* he only watch movies and listen to music to study English," "I have some *friends* who their parents they paid them one year during the high school to just leave the school during one year and study in America or Australia"). *Roommate** and *colleague** were used in a similar way: "I live in a apartment with three *roommates* and two of them are American," "one of the best way to learn English I think is to have a native *roommate*," or "I always use online dictionaries, or I ask my *colleagues*."

Interestingly, the Narrative cluster has many more negative than positive features. While three of the four positively loaded features (Motion, Space, and Time) come from the Relativity group and describe time-bound activities, many of the negatively loaded features belong to Cognitive Mechanisms (Insight, Tentativeness, Certainty, Inclusivity, Exclusivity), which is associated with thought processes. This lack of cognitive words suggests that Narrative students are indeed focused on actions and events related to L2 English learning rather than thinking about or analyzing it. The perceptual processes, Seeing and Feeling (which normally include words such as *see*, *watch*, and *feel*), are also negatively loaded in this cluster, suggesting that Narrative students are more concerned with actions than with observing or translating those actions into internal experience. In addition, the negative loading for Positive Emotion indicates that, while these students do not display strong negative emotion or anxiety, they may not view L2 English learning as a positive or enjoyable experience.

Cluster 2: Cognitive

Cluster 2, tellingly, is opposite to Cluster 1 in many of its categories, and it loads overwhelmingly positively in one particular group of features: Cognitive Mechanisms. (See Fig. 10.3 for a visual display of loadings and Table 10.5 for key words used in positively loaded features.) While two cognitive features, Causation and Inhibition, have slightly negative loadings, the six positively loaded cognitive categories (Insight, Discrepancy, Tentativeness, Certainty, Inclusivity, Exclusivity) seem to dominate the L2 learning experience of Cognitive students. Two other positive features, See and Feel, are perceptual categories indicative of observation or of the student's internal response to the world. Only one positively loaded category, Humans, relates to the non-cognitive aspects of language learning.

Though it is not the most strongly loaded category, Insight contains some of the most functionally important words in the Cognitive cluster. *Learn** (727), *think** (576), *know** (417), and *understand** (152) all

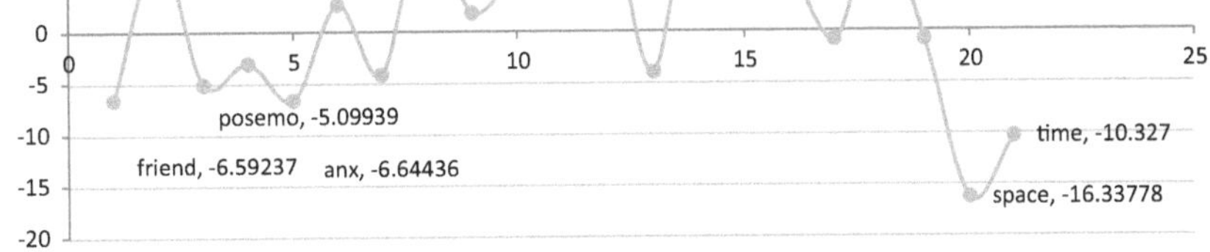

Fig. 10.3 Significant features of Cognitive cluster

Table 10.5 Positive psychosocial features of Cognitive cluster

Humans	Insight	Discrepancy	Tentativeness	Certainty
people (328)	learn* (727)	if (296)	or (428)	all (183)
person (31)	think* (576)	need* (151)	some (306)	every (76)
girl* (10)	know* (417)	would* (117)	if (296)	always (74)
kid* (14)	feel* (157)	should (57)	lot (287)	everything (65)
child* (9)	understand* (152)	mistake* (45)	maybe (255)	correct* (45)
	memor* (72)	problem* (37)	something (172)	sure (35)
	find* (57)	could* (34)	sometimes (166)	never (32)
	remember* (45)	normal (18)	most* (152)	definitely (21)
	question* (40)	hope* (9)	kind of (139)	everybody (20)
	meaning (30)	must (7)	guess* (71)	confiden* (18)
	realiz* (27)	rather (8)	pretty (52)	perfect* (15)
	idea* (23)		any (42)	totally (13)
	reason* (23)		anything (40)	everyone (11)
	explain* (22)		question* (40)	certain (10)
	knowledge (19)		depend* (39)	
	decide* (18)		usually (34)	
	become* (16)		probably (31)	
	concentrate* (13)		might (25)	
	answer* (12)		possib* (23)	
			almost (24)	
Inclusivity	**Exclusivity**	**Seeing**	**Feeling**	
and (2016)	but (706)	watch* (100)	feel* (157)	
we (426)	just (558)	see* (91)	hard (73)	
with (348)	not (470)	look* (40)	hand (6)	
each (30)	or (428)	beaut* (9)	touch* (6)	
around (24)	really (396)	view* (5)		
out (22)	if (296)	picture* (4)		
into (21)	something (172)			
plus (12)	without (18)			

Note: Asterisks indicate that all lemmas were included in the frequency count. Numbers in parentheses represent word or lemma frequency describe the cognitive processes behind L2 learning and are used in many ways by students in this cluster. Students discuss L2 English learning in general terms ("we cannot choose to *learn* English, it's mandatory," "it's very good to *learn* English," "for me just *learning* English is really tough") or describe learning methods and approaches ("you're *learning* grammar by speaking to other people," "I tried some other ways to *learn* English," "I'm kind of visual *learning* so I have to write down and see," "I *learn* English automatically with my major materials"). While *learn** most often accompanies general preferences, approaches, or beliefs about language learning rather than specific strategies, *know** is sometimes used with more detailed descriptions: "if there's a word I don't *know* I usually look it up in the dictionary," "the main problem that I *know* is hard to control is just accent and the intonation of the sentences," and "so when you hear you *know* that sounds bad or that sounds wrong." In general, however, students using these Insight words tend to focus less on specific activities and more on a broader view of L2 English learning.

The word *think** is somewhat different from the other major Insight words in that it almost always occurs in the phrase *I think*. Rather than describing mental processes per se, *I think* usually presents the speaker's opinion on a wide range of topics: "I *think* the most important thing is communicating to other people," "I *think* reading and writing is inseparable," "I *think* my study process is not that bad," "I *think* that's the beauty of English," or "language I *think* is like a sport, so the more you use it the better." *Think** thus provides an interesting connection to the other Cognitive Mechanism categories that are strongly represented in the Cognitive cluster, most of which relate to the speaker's degree of certainty, desires, opinions, and hypothetical subjects.

Tentativeness and Certainty both appear in this cluster, but as we saw above in Dimension 1, these two seemingly opposite categories are actually natural partners. Major words in these categories include *or* (428), *some* (306), *if* (296), *maybe* (255), *all* (183), *sometimes* (166), *most** (152), *kind of* (139), and *every* (76). Mainly function words and adverbs, these terms often modify thoughts and opinions about language learning, which are rarely absolute and may need to be hedged or further explained in some way ("that's pretty much how I learned *some* things," "they use very basic languages and sentence structure so it's *kind of* easier," "it's *kind of* nice to discover a culture by using its language," "with vocabulary it's better to do it *maybe* the old-fashioned way"). Although often used alongside thought processes, these words also accompany explanations of approaches or strategies ("I *sometimes* will read *some* English novel," "I was trying to memorize *some* words").

Inclusivity and Exclusivity words serve a similar function, that of hedging, elaborating, or somehow extending descriptions of language learning processes. *And* (2016), *but* (706), *just* (558), *not* (470), *or* (428), *we* (426), *really* (396), and *with* (348) appear in utterances such as "I think the key factor is the amount of time *and* effort to use English," "before it was *just* theory and I didn't *really* practice English," "you have time to see what you did wrong *but* it's hard to improve," and "I tried remembering each with a new word *or* something like that, *just* something to sort of remember everything."

Discrepancy words, while not as frequent as the other Cognitive Mechanisms categories, add an interesting layer to the opinions, explanations, and analysis in Cognitive learner interviews. As the category name implies, these words relate to hypothetical situations that might or could happen but are at odds with what has actually happened: *if* (296), *need** (151), *would** (117), *should** (57), *mistake** (45), and *problem** (37). *If* is often used to describe things that need to be done or changed ("*if* I want to survive here I *need* to speak with people," "*if* I were to relearn English again I *would* really skip that area," "*if* I don't want to learn English I will not try hard," "*if* I keep doing like this, I'll eventually get better and better"), while *need** obviously expresses needs related to language learning ("I *need* take some exam in English," "I *need* to do some grammar thing," "I *need* time"). *Would** typically describes what the student would like ("*if* I had an American roommate I think it *would* be better," "definitely I *would* change my writing pattern," "I *would* like to do an internship here next year"). *Mistake** and *problem** are often framed in terms of confession, avoidance, or correction ("I know I make a lot of *mistakes*," "maybe the main *problem* is that I cannot understand all the words," "this method will help me to avoid the grammar *mistakes*"). Taken together, these words seem to indicate a tendency to analyze what could be done differently, or what could happen differently, to make the L2 learning experience more closely match the learner's expectations.

The two perceptual categories of the Cognitive cluster, Seeing and Feeling, contain just a few frequently occurring words (*feel**, 157, *watch**, 100, *see**, 91, *hard*, 73, *look**, 40). Among these learners, *feel** is often used in a way similar to Discrepancy words, describing a frustration or mismatch between desire and reality: "sometimes I will *feel* embarrassed because I can't fully express my thoughts," "it's not that I *feel* bad, but sometimes I get this *feeling* that I'm kind of limited," "I *feel* I have a lot to learn," or "using English makes me *feel* like getting in trouble because… I cannot express myself by English very appropriately." Similarly, *hard* typically refers to difficulties and challenges ("sometimes it's very *hard* to talk to people in English"). While *watch** appears almost exclusively in the context of watching television or movies and *look** almost always occurs in the phrase *look it up*, *see** relates to the learner's interaction with the language and its speakers ("by *seeing* what other people do, you kind of absorb what they are doing to start doing the same way," "I try to converse to native speakers to *see* how they speak," "I could *see* how the words are put together in the English language").

The only social category to receive a positive loading in this cluster, Humans, owes its position to one word: *people*. In contrast to Narrative students, who talked about friends and acquaintances, Cognitive students prefer the more impersonal *people*. This corresponds to the more abstract content of their interviews, and *people* is typically used to discuss beliefs or opinions about L2 English learning in general: "many *people* are just shy to say something," "such *people* can't come forward and express their views," "*people* won't understand what I'm saying," or "there is some *people* who speak very good English with a little accent." As a result, even the Humans category is connected to an analytical perspective for students in this cluster.

Three of the negatively loaded categories in the Cognitive cluster (Friend, Space, Time) suggest that these students did not frequently discuss events and social activities as part of their L2 learning experience in the same way that Narrative students did. The two other negatively loaded categories (Positive Emotion, Anxiety) indicate that they also did not focus on affective aspects of language learning, either positive or negative. Instead, these students kept their attention on the cognitive and perceptual aspects of the L2 experience, seemingly regarding it as a thinking, analytical process rather than an activity-related or emotional experience. However, the fact that Discrepancy words, such as *if*, *need*, *would*, and *mistake*, occur frequently in these interviews hints at an underlying dissatisfaction or frustration with L2 English learning, one that is expressed in wistful hypotheticals rather than outright negative emotion.

Cluster 3: Affective

In contrast to Cluster 1, which highlights action, and Cluster 2, which highlights cognition, Cluster 3's positively loaded features are primarily affective (Positive Emotion, Anxiety, Sadness, Insight), with Positive Emotion by far the most strongly loaded (see Fig. 10.4 for significant features). Negatively loaded categories in this cluster are Discrepancy, Tentativeness, Inclusivity, Exclusivity, Motion, Space, and Time. In other words, apart from the single cognitive category Insight, the action and thinking words that characterized the first two clusters occur infrequently in the Affective cluster, while emotion takes center stage in these interviews.

In the positive emotion category, the most common words are *good* (136), *like** (135), and *improve** (133) (see Table 10.6 for frequent words in the positively loaded categories). *Good* is sometimes used to refer to

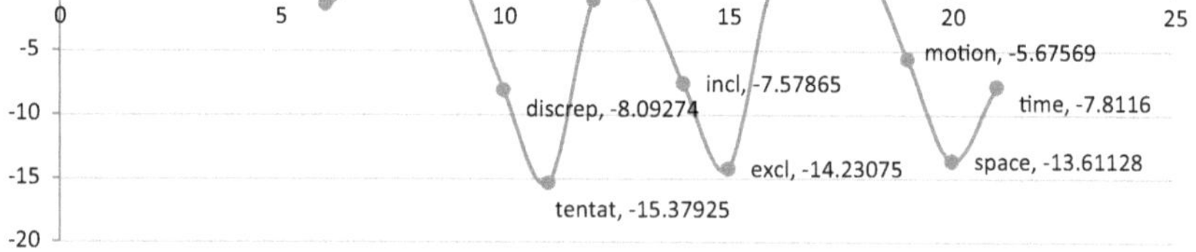

Fig. 10.4 Significant features of Affective cluster

Table 10.6 Positive psychosocial features of Affective cluster

Positive Emotion	Anxiety	Sadness	Insight
good (136)	confus* (9)	fail* (5)	learn* (493)
like* (135)	nervous (9)	alone (4)	think* (481)
improv* (133)	shy (6)	useless (3)	know* (230)
friend* (82)	afraid (5)	disappoint* (2)	feel* (91)
well (63)	ashamed (5)	lose* (2)	understand* (91)
better (60)	uncomfortable (4)	suffer* (2)	remember* (40)
ok (60)	awkward (3)		find* (38)
important (55)	crazy (3)		memor* (28)
interest* (33)	scar* (3)		mean* (20)
love* (24)	pressur* (2)		explain* (19)
comfort* (23)	stress* (2)		reason* (18)
easy (23)	worried (2)		question* (17)
confiden* (22)	avoid (1)		sense* (13)
helpful (19)	embarrassed (1)		prefer* (12)
sure (19)	fear* (1)		become* (11)
useful (19)	miserable (1)		relat* (11)
best (14)			choose* (9)
helps (13)			idea* (9)
hope* (12)			figur* (7)
enjoy* (12)			believe* (5)

Note: Asterisks indicate that all lemmas were included in the frequency count. Numbers in parentheses represent word or lemma frequency

English proficiency or specific English skills ("I think I'm quite *good* at it," "actually I was pretty *good* at grammar because of my background," "I do actually get *good* at reading because I build very large vocabulary") or is used to describe feelings about English speaking ("I feel pretty *good* about my experience," "I know you understand me that's a *good* feeling," "I'm feeling *good* to use English"). Students also describe a variety of circumstances and beliefs about L2 English learning with *good*: "I think if you want to be *good* at a language you have to keep practicing it," "music was a *good* way to help us learn," and "this is *good* for you to find a job." *Like** is used both to discuss aspects of English learning that students like ("I *like* languages so I think I *like* English," "I *like* learning English because I could watch Hollywood movie or drama without subtitles," "I *like* to learning English because I *like* to talk with people," "I do *like* writing, I'm writing a blog as well") as well as actions they would like to take ("I would *like* to speak in English on campus," "I would *like* to be able to talk in a more correct way"). *Improv** can refer to past, present, or future improvements: "I think I really really *improved* the first weeks," "you see you are *improving* and that's nice to see," "I try to *improve* my writing skill also," "reading novels good idea to *improve* my reading skills," or "I'd like to *improve* my intonation."

While Positive Emotion has many frequently occurring words, the Anxiety and Sadness categories have just a few words in total; where these words occur, therefore, they must be considered significant. The Anxiety words *confus** (9), *nervous* (9), *shy* (6), and *afraid* (5) mainly describe occasional or temporary negative feelings about English learning: "I get *confused* sometimes," "many times I feel *confused* about what they are talking about," "I feel a little *nervous* from time to time especially when I give presentations in English," "I'm quite a *shy* person so I don't speak a lot unless I'm forced to," and "in the beginning I'm a little *afraid* of speaking with others." Interestingly, of *asham**'s five occurrences, four were produced by one student, meaning that it was quite infrequent among most Affective students. Sadness words (including *fail**, 5, *alone*, 4, and *useless*, 3) occur at a very low frequency and are often explained in some impersonal or specific circumstances ("I think grammar education is really a big *failure*," "I try to speak when I'm *alone*, I try to make sentences," "people like me might prefer just study *alone*," "in Korea I spent a lot of time, I felt it was *useless* because we are so focusing on grammar").

The Insight words of the Affective cluster are quite similar (though proportionally less frequent) to those used by students in the Cognitive cluster: *learn** (493), *think** (481), and *know** (230) are the most common, followed by *feel** (91) and *understand** (91). These words are used to describe the general process or experience of language learning, as well as students' opinions about language learning through *I think*: "I *think* we only *learn* about this very very superficial English in middle school," "I didn't do anything specific to *learn* grammar," "before I came here I *think learning* English is like agh, it's horrible," "I love English so much so I can *learn* it by myself," or "I *think* I didn't waste much time in *learning* English."

Although Affective students attend to the cognitive processes of learning and knowing, they score low in the Cognitive Mechanisms categories that signal hedging, demurring, or dissonance (Discrepancy, Tentativeness, Inclusivity, Exclusivity). This relative lack of Insight features, which were used frequently among Cognitive students to elaborate their thoughts or provide alternative explanations, suggests that these students feel less need to explain circumstances or expand on hypothetical situations. Their L2 learning experience is presented as more straightforward, with fewer appearances of *but*, *just*, *not*, *or*, *if*, *maybe*, *need*, and *kind of* to clarify or expound (or perhaps excuse). Affective students also score low in the motion, space, and time categories so important in the Narrative cluster; they dwell instead on their positive feelings toward English and their beliefs about the learning process.

Overall, the Affective cluster is differentiated from other clusters by its emphasis on affect and insight. It seems quite significant that Positive Emotion occurs together with Anxiety and Sadness (but *not* Negative Emotion), since these features do not appear at first to be complementary or cooperative. These students seem to simply focus more on emotion in general than other students, since neither Narrative nor Cognitive students scored strongly on any kind of emotion (and both scored low on Positive Emotion). Also, the appearance of Sadness and Anxiety words does not necessarily imply negativity, since we saw above that in many cases such words describe specific situations or do not refer to the learner herself. This co-occurrence suggests that Affective students attend to both positive and negative emotions in the language learning process, but the much greater prevalence of Positive Emotion words points to a generally positive relationship with English learning.

The prominence of affective categories in the Affective cluster, paired with attention to thinking and learning, suggests that these students' L2 learning experience is based on an ability to notice and regulate their emotions related to L2 learning. While other students did not refer much to their emotions, Affective students acknowledged both positive and potentially negative feelings, but on balance were able to maintain an overall positive outlook. They may have the emotional maturity to understand that language learning anxiety can be overcome if it is acknowledged and dealt with, and they seem to be more willing to admit such feelings during the L2 experience interview. This self-awareness and self-regulatory capacity forms an interesting strand of the L2 learning experience, one that may be quite facilitative in the arduous and emotionally-intensive process of L2 acquisition.

Table 10.7 Profiles of L2 learning experience

L2 experience profile	Represented by	Tends to focus on (Positive z-scores)	Tends not to focus on (Negative z-scores)
Narrative	Cluster 1	Doing things, actions, events	Cognitive or perceptual processes, affect
Cognitive	Cluster 2	Learning, thinking, analyzing, discrepancies, conditional situations	Actions, events, affect
Affective	Cluster 3	Emotional regulation, learning	Discrepancies, conditional situations, actions, events

Summary of Experience Profiles

Based on the cluster analysis described above, the three profiles of successful L2 learning experience can be summarized as shown in Table 10.7.

Relationship of TOEFL Scores to Experience Profiles

To assess whether the L2 experience profiles are related to self-reported TOEFL scores, a one-way analysis of variance (ANOVA) was conducted in SPSS 20 to compare the mean TOEFL score of students in each cluster. Because not all interview participants had taken the TOEFL or were able to self-report scores, only 96 (out of 123) participants are included in this analysis. Descriptive statistics for the whole data set are shown in Table 10.8, while group means and standard deviations are shown in Table 10.9. Students in Cluster 1 had the lowest mean TOEFL score (89.310), students in Cluster 3 had the highest mean TOEFL score (96.926), and students in Cluster 2 were between the other two groups (94.950). At the time of data collection, information provided by ETS suggested that a composite score of 94 or above is considered Good, and a score of 65 to 93 is Intermediate or Fair. Therefore, the average score of students in Clusters 2 and 3 was in the Good range, while the average score for students in Cluster 1 was in the Intermediate or Fair range. Results of the ANOVA were statistically significant at the $p < 0.05$ level, with $F(2,93) = 3.865$, $p = 0.024$. Detailed results are provided in Table 10.10.

Table 10.8 Descriptive statistics for TOEFL scores

	Total population
Mean	93.802
Standard deviation	11.118
Standard error	01.135
Minimum	63.0
Maximum	119.0
N	96.0

Table 10.9 Means and standard deviations of TOEFL score by cluster

	Cluster 1 (Narrative)	Cluster 2 (Cognitive)	Cluster 3 (Affective)
Mean	89.310	94.950	96.926
Standard deviation	11.383	10.382	10.759
Minimum	63.0	71.0	73.0
Maximum	109.0	117.0	119.0
N	29.0	40.0	27.0

Table 10.10 ANOVA summary table for analysis of TOEFL scores by cluster

	Σ of squares	df	Mean square	F	Sig.
Between groups	901.281	2	450.640	3.865	0.024
Within groups	10841.950	93	116.580		
Total	11743.239	95			

The Levene's statistic (0.017) for the analysis of variance revealed that the assumption of homogeneity of variances was not met for this test. Therefore, an independent samples Kruskal-Wallis test was conducted, since this non-parametric test provides more robust results for groups that may not have homogeneous variances. The Kruskal-Wallis test was significant at the $p < 0.05$ level, with $p = 0.032$, which confirms that the mean TOEFL score does differ between clusters.

To analyze which of the three clusters differed significantly by mean, three parametric post-hoc tests (Tukey, LSD, and Bonferroni) and one non-parametric post-hoc test (Independent Samples Mann-Whitney U) were performed. All three parametric tests indicated statistical differences between Cluster 1 and Cluster 3 ($p < 0.05$), and the LSD analysis also showed a statistical difference between Cluster 1 and Cluster 2 ($p < 0.05$). (Differing results among post-hoc tests are the results of slight differences in the statistical calculations used by each test.) The Mann-Whitney U nonparametric test also indicated a statistical difference between Cluster 1 and Cluster 3 scores ($p = 0.021$) and narrowly missed significance between Clusters 1 and 2 ($p = 0.051$). It seems quite clear that students in Cluster 3 performed significantly better on the TOEFL than students in Cluster 1, and that Cluster 2 students may also have performed significantly better than Cluster 1 students. The analyses do not support a significant difference in TOEFL performance between students in Clusters 2 and 3.

The effect size for a comparison of the three clusters is negligible, $\eta^2 = 0.077$. However, the effect sizes for a comparison of individual cluster means indicates a medium or small effect. Comparing Clusters 1 and 2 results in an effect size of $d = 0.53$ (medium); comparing Clusters 1 and 3 results in an effect size of $d = 0.70$ (medium); and comparing Clusters 2 and 3 results in an effect size of $d = 0.19$ (small). This suggests, once again, that the primary difference in test performance lies between Clusters 1 and 3.

Discussion

All three of these learner profiles relate to the same experience, but they identify three different ways of perceiving that experience: (1) Narrative, as concrete actions and events; (2) Cognitive, as cognitive processes to be analyzed and explained; or (3) Affective, as a cognitive process that involves a great deal of emotional regulation. These findings result from an analysis of the words students use in L2 experience interviews and are based on pre-defined psychosocial categories applied during a software analysis. But what do they actually tell us about the ways learners talk about their learning experience?

First, we see a basic distinction in the level of abstraction with which students describe the learning process. Students in the Narrative cluster are focused on concrete events which can be narrated more or less chronologically, while students in the Cognitive and Affective clusters tend to focus less on events and more on their internalized responses to them. This distinction has been described as a deep level versus surface level approach to learning. Surface level learners tend to focus on what is immediately evident in a learning situation, while deep level learners search for meaning in the situation (Entwistle and McCune 2004). Surface level learners may accept ideas or information passively, without thoroughly reflecting on its relevance to the learning situation; deep level learners are more likely to relate new material to previous knowledge and experience, with the intention of understanding the situation for themselves (Benson and Lor 1999). This difference has been found in many types of learning situations (Marton and Booth 1997) and has been explored in the L2 learning context by Benson and Lor (1999) and Polat (2012).

As an illustration, compare the following excerpts from a Narrative learner (representing a surface level approach) and a Cognitive learner (representing a deep level approach). Both students are responding to Question 1 (Tell me about your experience learning English).

Text Samples 10.1 Narrative and Cognitive Learner Excerpts

Narrative Learner

> *Ok so, I started learning English in it's a school before the high school, and you have to stay four years in this school. And at the beginning so when you are eleven years old, you can choose if you want to study two foreign language or just one. And from six year old to eleven year old I study German, because I live in front of Germany on the border with Germany. And when I arrived in this new school I chose to study two foreign language so I selected English, too, so it will be my second foreign language. And so during the four year we had, it was two hour per week to study English. And then after that you go in the high school, you have three years, and you study, yeah, at this moment it begins to be mandatory to study two foreign language, so I continue with German and English. And so until the A-level this was the main way to learn English, it was two hour per week. So at the end of the high school you are eighteen but really you don't learn a lot during these seven years in English….*

Cognitive Learner

> *I study English start from ten year old when I was a girl, that's what most of the children in Taiwan, they go to the English school or something. And at first it's just for fun, because the teacher was playing games or something, it's funny and*

it's interesting. But when we go to the middle school or high school and the level is higher and higher, but I think in Taiwan the short part of English learning in Taiwan is that we are good at reading and writing, but actually we are not good at speaking and listening. So when I first come here it's a little hard for me to speak, I really nervous and feel embarrassed to speak English to others... especially the teenager, they speak so fast, and I cannot follow them so I just always pretending I understand but actually I don't understand. So yeah, but it's still, I think it's interesting the process to learning how to follow others speaking, so yeah I think it's interesting, to learn English.

Both responses are fairly elaborate, but there are clear differences in the level of abstraction that each learner brings to the reflection. The Narrative student describes his experiences as though telling a story, with straightforward descriptions of what occurred, when, and why (using the Space, Time, and Motion words characteristic of Cluster 1). For the most part, he focuses on providing an exact account of events. The Cognitive student, in contrast, leaves out many of the concrete details of her experience, instead describing her own reactions and looking for abstract meaning behind the concrete events. Her account includes not only external events, but also emotional reactions (*I really nervous and I feel embarrassed to speak English to others*), analysis based on learned information (*especially the teenager, they speak so fast*), and acknowledgement of the cognitive processes underlying L2 learning (*I think it's interesting the process to learning how to follow others speaking*). She uses the Cognitive Mechanism words that are quite common in Cognitive interviews. Her experience comes across as not just an accumulation of events, but also as a unified process that she thinks about and participates in. Compare these responses to the following response from an Affective student:

Text Sample 10.2 Affective Student Excerpt

It's particular because I don't have any class for learning English here. So I think it's all about my experience with the other and my interaction with the exterior, there is no really official English class. So it's difficult for me because I can work from my cassette and try to learn by myself on the other side. So I don't know I think I really really improved the first weeks. And after that I don't know maybe it stopped during a few months and it was the same level, I don't know. And yeah but that's cool, it's better than our classes in France. Because I think it's the worst country to learn English, it's horrible. So to be in a English country it helps a lot. So I think I improved.

Even though this participant is answering the same question as the two participants above ("Tell me about your experience learning English"), his response is so abstract that it is difficult to tell what question he is responding to. He provides few straightforward biographical details, instead focusing almost exclusively on his impressions and evaluations of his time as an exchange student. Interestingly, he begins his discussion not with information about learning English in his home country, but with his sojourn in the USA. And despite his assertion that "it's all about my experience with the other and the interaction with the exterior," he discusses primarily his internalized reactions and interpretations of what has happened. This Affective response is very revealing of how this group of students seems to internalize events.

We saw above that Narrative students tend to focus on biographical events and external actions rather than on analyzing the cognitive processes of learning. Although 32% of Cluster 1 students scored in the high range (94–120) on the TOEFL, their significantly lower average TOEFL score (mean = 89.21) suggests that a focus on Narrative is not as conducive to L2 learning as a focus on Cognitive. The fact that these learners speak primarily about actions and events—while avoiding analysis of thoughts and emotions—may indicate underdeveloped metacognitive attention to cognition and affect. Logically, learners who do not spend as much time thinking about learning, or who are not able to reflect deeply on the learning process, may be less likely to become adept and achieve high scores on a proficiency test. These students may not have the skills or desire necessary to think of their experience in terms of mental processes, which may in turn correspond to a lack of desire or skills needed for effective L2 learning. In this case, limited metacognition could indicate less effective language learning.

In contrast, Cognitive students are by far the most analytical group, focusing almost exclusively on cognitive and perceptual processes in their detailed descriptions of L2 learning. These learners describe their knowledge, understanding, and awareness with many modifiers, quantifiers, and hedges, suggesting an almost scientific attention to detail. Cognitive learners also have a high combined z-score for Discrepancy words such as *want*, *need*, and *would*, which appears to constitute a deeper level of analysis but also belies a hidden frustration or perceived mismatch between their desired outcome and reality. However, their intense focus on cognition may pay off, as Cognitive cluster TOEFL scores are generally higher than those of Narrative cluster (mean = 94.66). It is possible that the more highly developed metacognitive skills that enable these students to analyze their learning experience in depth and with precision may also make them better language learners (or at least enable them to perform better on an academic test of their L2).

Affective students also show evidence of advanced metacognition in their frequent use of Insight words such as *learn*, *think*, and *know*. Unlike Cognitive learners, however, Affective learners seem to spend less time analyzing the details of their cognitive processes and more time examining their emotions related to L2 learning. This is the only group of students to devote significant attention to affect, mostly in the form of Positive Emotion words (along with a few prominent Anxiety and Sadness words). In fact, Positive Emotion has by far the highest z-scores of any psychosocial feature in Affective interviews, suggesting that it is the defining feature of this group of students. Compared to Narrative and Cognitive learners, who have strongly negative z-scores for Positive Emotion, Affective learners seem very happy with their L2 learning experience.

At the same time, Affective students score significantly higher on the TOEFL than Narrative students and moderately (though not significantly) better than Cognitive students (mean = 96.68). They also had a noticeably higher proportion of high scores on the TOEFL than Cognitive students (62% compared to 51%). While a connection between positive affect and successful L2 learning is not surprising, it does beg the question of whether positive feeling produces or arises from successful learning. Either scenario (or both) seems plausible: students who feel that they are successful also feel good about their experience, or students who have a positive outlook toward L2 learning are more successful. It is important to keep in mind, however, that Affective students also express anxiety and sadness more than other students, which means that their learning experience is not one of untempered positive emotion. Rather, it seems that these learners are able to acknowledge and then overcome the emotional challenges of L2 learning, emerging from the process with overall positive feelings toward their experience. This conclusion is suggested by looking at the z-scores of these students, which show Positive Emotion at 15.2933, Anxiety at 9.092, and Sadness at 5.171. Such emotional resilience indicates that Affective learners have achieved a degree of affective self-regulation that enables them to cope with the intense effort, the emotional difficulties, and the challenges to self-image or identity necessitated by adult language acquisition.

If affective responses are so important in the learning process, it follows that awareness and regulation of affect may facilitate effective L2 learning. Thus, an important component of meta-affect is affective self-regulation, in which "the psychological self is involved in overcoming self-doubt, managing different forms of anxiety, or generating positive emotions" (Bown and White 2010, p. 434). This is exactly what Affective students appear to be doing: they acknowledge that sadness and anxiety are part of the learning process, but they still manage to generate positive emotions to keep going. Comments from two of these students (responding to question 10, How do you feel when you use English?) suggest how this might be done:

Text Samples 10.3 Comparison of Italian and Chinese Affective Learners

Affective Learner (Italian)

> *I feel pretty confident now. But I mean, I realize that when I use English I think in English and it's something very different when you're used to use another language. So I like that. And I feel confident but I used to feel obviously very sometimes embarrassed you know my skills weren't so good but then I got better.*

Affective Learner (Chinese)

> *Before I came to America I'm very confident with my English. I think oh I got a high score in the TOEFL test and I don't think language will be a problem.*

> *But when I came here I became a TA and you need to explain a lot students in the lab. So many times I feel confused about what they are talking about. And sometimes they just repeat words and sentences. And it's hard to get the whole sentence what they are trying to say. So I think I still need more time to adjust to maybe the English environment. I've got a co-workers who are senior than me, some senior student or PhD candidate, they have spent more years than me here. Some of them still have problems explaining themselves but many of them can fit in the environment quite well. So I think maybe two years or three years later I will be like that. Yeah it just need time.*

We can theorize that affective self-regulation profoundly influences the L2 learning process because the nature of language learning requires adult learners to, in a sense, give up their status as competent, sophisticated speakers and become novices who may struggle to find the right words. As one participant said, when speaking English, "I feel like I'm a little kid. I'm like five years old or something." The well-documented emotional challenges of L2 learning (e.g., Gabrys-Barker and Belska 2013) may, therefore, become an obstacle on the road to proficiency unless they are skillfully managed. Affective students seem to have adopted an approach to L2 learning that enables them to maintain a positive attitude throughout the learning process, which may in turn facilitate their English skills and produce higher TOEFL scores.

Implications for Teaching and Learning

This analysis suggests that certain aspects of the L2 learning experience, such as analyzing the learning process and maintaining positive emotions, may be instrumental in promoting more effective learning. Teachers may, therefore, try to encourage "thinking" and "feeling" in their classrooms in several ways. Crucially, they may introduce activities specifically designed to foster metacognitive awareness about not just the grammatical components of the L2 but also of L2 learning in itself as a process. Some students may believe that L2 learning "just happens" or may become demotivated when the process is not as easy as they thought it would be. They might also look at successful peers and believe that success is the result of inherent ability rather than the result of many factors, particularly hard work and a positive attitude. Teachers can play a vital role in helping students to instead see L2 acquisition as a long-term process with ups and downs, but one that almost everyone can succeed in if they believe it is important enough. If students understand the learning process as a journey of many years and much effort, they may be more likely to overcome short-term setbacks and disappointments. By helping to manage students' expectations and emotional needs, teachers may encourage an Affective experience of the L2 that could foster long-term success.

Methodological Limitations

In this study, tried-and-true techniques from fields outside of SLA were applied to non-native English speakers. This adoption of tools and methodologies from psychology into applied linguistics has many precedents, since many, if not most, of the research methods and instruments used in SLA today were first used in psychology, first language acquisition, or education (Dörnyei and Ushioda 2011). It is, therefore, important to consider whether the use of semantic content analysis is a valid methodology to use with non-native English speakers. For example, what if the psychosocial categories of LIWC did not pick up on psychosocial differences but instead measured linguistic ability? Could it be that lower-proficiency students talk about external or biographical events because it is simpler to talk about biographical subjects than about abstract or emotional topics?

One way to test the validity of differential cluster performance is to consider another traditional measure of L2 proficiency: length of utterance. In the L2 Experience Interview Corpus, Narrative-oriented students talked just as much (and in some cases more) than Cognitive- and Affective-oriented students. If Narrative learners had been constrained by their proficiency level to only discuss a few topics, we would expect them to produce less output than other students. This is not the case at all. Instead, as Table 10.11 shows, interview length for Narrative learners is very close to that of Cognitive learners and exceeds that of Affective learners. Both Narrative and Cognitive students tended to talk more than Affective students, and Narrative students had the highest median

Table 10.11 Interview length by cluster

	Cluster 1	Cluster 2	Cluster 3
Mean	1204.55	1210.21	1022.43
Median	1045.50	1028.5	913.0
Maximum	3334.0	2486.0	2673.0
Minimum	379.0	466.0	476.0
N	38.0	48.0	37.0

Table 10.12 ANOVA summary table for interview length by cluster

	Σ of Squares	df	Mean Square	F	Sig.
Between groups	888728.534	2	444364.267	1.344	0.265
Within groups	39665374.392	120	330544.787		
Total	40554102.927	122			

interview length as well as the highest maximum length. A one-way ANOVA (performed because the Levene's statistic was greater than 0.05 for the complete data set) revealed no significant differences in interview length between groups, with $F\ (2120) = 1.344$, $p = 0.265$. (See Table 10.12 for details of the ANOVA.) This suggests that Narrative students were not limited in their interviews by English proficiency.

It is also important to keep in mind that the basis of this analysis is word categories, not factors traditionally associated with proficiency level such as syntactic complexity or word sophistication. The only information LIWC provides, and on which the cluster analysis was based, is the percentage of each interview text that falls into each category. In this form of analysis, a frequent and easily learned word such as *happy* carries the same weight in the Positive Emotion category as less frequent words such as *delightful* or *magnificent*. This means that a learner who focuses on affect in her L2 experience interview can do so with few or many words at her disposal. For example, a learner who says "I so sad" would have the same effect in LIWC as another learner who says "I am filled with despair." Whether a person chooses *sad* or *miserable*, or even *melancholy*, *agony*, or *sorrow*, the semantic content related to sadness is recorded the same way.

Consideration of interview text samples serves to illustrate this point. The following two excerpts are very comparable because they come from two male participants of similar age. However, there are noticeable differences in the sophistication of their language as they respond to the same questions. Below are these participants' responses to questions 9 (Do you feel that most other people learn English in the same way that you do, or in a different way?) and 11 (Is there anything you want to change about your English learning experience?).

Text Samples 10.4 Comparison of Language Sophistication Measures

Indian Participant (Narrative Cluster)

No. I don't think so, very less people I think actually go through this kind of extensive process, but I did it just for three four months, or six months I think, just so I get into the groove, I have to learn the English language more and more words so it becomes a learning process. So what happened was after the six months now I do it often. If I read some newspaper I actually think of those words and just write them down. So now that is helping me actually I find that now it is more help, but I don't think most people actually do that. I think most people actually learn sometimes actually out of necessity, I think so. Just maybe they read and they have to read something and they have to understand it and then they go and look up those words. But if they're actually reading a newspaper and they don't actually understand a word I don't think they go and make note of it and actually meaning right away. But I think most people actually learn vocabulary by talking to each other and if they don't understand they ask what do you mean. I think most people actually do that, I don't know, that's what I think.

Yes actually there's a lot. I mean maybe pick up more on grammar, alphabet, I mean going back I would have maybe have paid more attention to grammar, not just learning new word, or maybe write a lot. I'm one person who believes constant writing actually improves your English, not only your thinking but also your English. Maybe I should have written a lot, maybe I should have read a lot more, of course I read a lot of novels and maybe I should have paid more attention to what I was actually reading, the kind of English which was actually there and how people write in different, and now when I write it's all mixed up, some of it goes in past tense and some is coming in present, and some would, may, might, this that, it's a mess, a whole lot of mess until I go back and read. So seeing all this I actually think maybe I should have paid more attention to my grammar, or maybe learned more regarding English. What to say, maybe should have continued that toastmaster club, maybe improve mostly speaking, ok. Maybe writing I could do it over time even now, maybe utilize one hour every day to sit and write anything, just anything so that I keep improving. But speaking actually I need to do it more often, speak to people, speak to a group of people, maybe I should have done it when I had a chance. Now I definitely get it but now it's more like it's academic program, but maybe just speaking on any topic. I used to do it in school, participate in this Just a Minute, there's a program called Just a Minute where they give you a topic and you need to think about it for a minute and just go and speak about it. All those actually help me. I felt after that I should have continued participating in such exercises, participating in clubs, going to some literary clubs, and maybe my English would have been much much better, that's what I feel. And now what I want to do, is yes, read a lot, that's the only thing I can do, not only my academic textbooks not only my magazines, not only that, but read much more so that, at least in two three years, once I will be staying here in the U.S., at least maybe stop being surrounded by everyone who is speaking good English. And maybe by two years I've actually reduced the gap, by speaking to them and listening to them and learning how things are done how things are spoken, how they write, it's a constant learning process, I want to do it, I always have. I should.

Chinese Participant (Cognitive Cluster)

Maybe they have learn the other way. But I think if you memory the English word sometimes you need to spend time to memory the word for not the speaking English people. So maybe everyone have their tip to learn how to memory the word.

I want to change is my speaking. I think you have to learn how to speak, you need to know the listening. Is also need to strength and helpful you can speak well.

The Narrative learner is more voluble and seems to be more at ease describing his experiences than the Cognitive learner. These excerpts help to demonstrate that the cluster analysis based on LIWC categories does not detect proficiency differences among these students, but rather differentiates based on the psychosocial focus of their interviews.

Part IV

Learner Talk in Peer Response Activities

11

Understanding Learner Talk About Writing: The Second Language Peer Response (L2PR) Corpus

In the next three chapters (Part IV, Chaps. 11, 12, and 13), we examine spoken learner language by exploring the patterns of social interaction in a corpus of university-level ESL students' spoken feedback to each other about their writing in a first-year composition course, as well as by triangulating corpus findings with student writing and student interviews. This task, called **peer response**, is widely used by practitioners and has been thoroughly examined by language learning theorists and researchers. The current chapter reviews relevant literature on learner interaction from SLA and L2 Writing traditions, and argues for a corpus-based approach to further examine these interactions. It also describes the compilation and composition of Roberson's (2015) Second Language Peer Response (L2PR) Corpus.

SLA Perspectives on the Role of Spoken Interaction in Language Development

The role of spoken output in learner language development began with the understanding that productive skills are central to this process. Swain (1993) proposed the output hypothesis based on the observation that

E. Friginal et al., *Exploring Spoken English Learner Language Using Corpora*,
DOI 10.1007/978-3-319-59900-7_11

second language learners in a French immersion setting were exposed to more than six years of comprehensible input, yet their speaking and writing skills remained surprisingly not target-like. These learners rarely had the opportunity to produce extended written or spoken discourse, and as such lacked the opportunity to control and manipulate their own language efforts. According to Swain's output hypothesis, speaking and writing serve several crucial functions in language learning. First, producing output pushes learners to notice gaps in their interlanguage system as they try to express ideas while speaking. Under pressure to create effective linguistic form and meaning, learners become aware of what they are and are not able to do in the second language. Second, producing language allows learners to test hypotheses about how the language works, especially when they work together to identify and solve linguistic problems (Swain 2000). While the output hypothesis is rooted in a cognitivist perspective on SLA, Swain's early work built the foundation for a sociocultural perspective on how speech mediates cognition.

Collaborative dialogue, in which "speakers are engaged in joint problem solving and knowledge building" (Swain 2000, p. 102), is considered an extension of the initial output hypothesis. Output serves a cognitive function and speaking mediates language learners' understanding of how lexical and syntactic systems function in the target language. One of the benefits of collaboration is that it provides opportunities for learners to engage in negotiation for meaning, treating what they have said as an object that they can continue to explore as the dialogue unfolds. Through this exploration, learners are able to co-construct their linguistic knowledge and further develop their interlanguage (Swain et al. 2002). To operationalize the concept of collaborative dialogue and its possible benefits for language learners, researchers have used two key analytical tools: language-related episodes (LREs), and patterns of interaction.

In some studies, collaborative dialogue has been explored by noting the occurrence and describing the quality of LREs, which Swain and Lapkin (1998) have described as "any part of the dialogue where the students talk about the language they are producing, question their language use, or correct themselves or others" (p. 326). That is, identifying LREs helps pinpoint and describe the parts of collaborative dialogue where co-construction of knowledge is occurring. Based on this definition, two main types of LREs have been identified: lexical and grammatical. This chapter also explores peer-peer interaction by reviewing studies that have applied a second analytic tool, Storch's (2002) patterns of interaction. This framework arose from a criticism that focusing only on the linguistic characteristics of peer-peer interaction falsely assumes that all group or pairs behave similarly, and "ignore[s] the fact that in face-to-face interactions, learners negotiate not only the basic topic but also their relationship" (Storch 2002, p. 120).

As is clear from her view on the shortcomings of an analytic approach based solely on linguistic indicators (as are LRE's), Storch was interested in exploring pair dynamics in collaborative dialogue. Specifically, she explained pair dynamics in terms of *mutuality*, or the learners' level of engagement with each other's contributions, and *equality*, or the degree of control and authority over the task. As Fig. 11.1 shows, mutuality and equality are continuums, and each can range from high to low.

The figure above includes the axes of *mutuality* and *equality*, and shows that this framework allows researchers to identify four different patterns: collaborative, dominant/dominant, dominant/passive, and expert/novice. Vygotsky (1978) noted that in order for novices to achieve what they

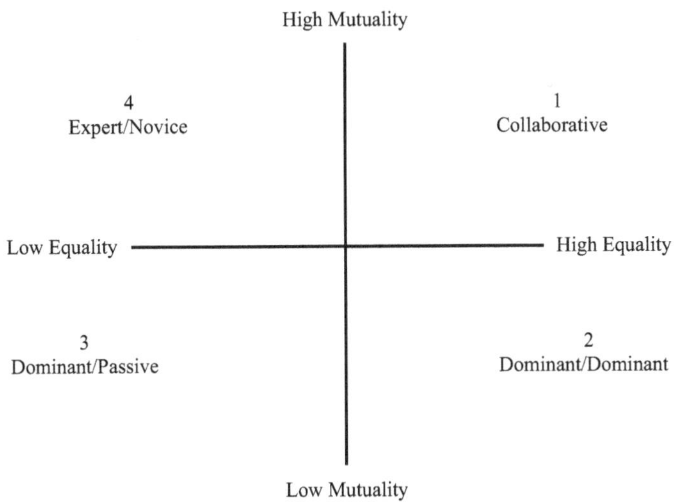

Fig. 11.1 Storch's (2002) *Patterns of Interaction*

would not be able to alone, they need support from an expert. When extending this theory to L2 learners in peer-peer interaction, peers can concurrently be experts and novices (Swain et al. 2002). Storch's (2002) *patterns of interaction* framework allows second language researchers to further describe expert and novice positionality within peer talk, and to question how it might affect the co-construction of knowledge. As Donato (1994) claims, successful collaboration involves a meaningful core activity, considers individuals as parts and accepts their contributions as useful, builds coherence within and among social relations, and co-constructs new knowledge that goes beyond any knowledge possessed by a single member in isolation. Taken together, collaborative dialogue and patterns of interaction allow SLA researchers to test claims like Donato's in natural language data.

Using this sociocultural understanding of collaboration as their base, SLA researchers have provided compelling evidence that certain kinds of peer-peer interaction are successful in contributing to language learning. While there have been socioculturally influenced SLA studies that have adopted a qualitative case study approach, this chapter focuses on those using more experimental designs; that is, studies that collect data using controlled pair tasks, and consider different variables that may affect learning outcomes. The sections below review these studies, grouping them in terms of variables they have examined. These variables include individual versus collaborative tasks, the proficiency level of learners, and the effect of patterns of interaction on collaborative dialogue.

Controlled Pair Task Studies in SLA

Several studies have examined the difference in students' performance when they complete collaborative tasks in comparison to when they work alone (Kim 2008; Storch 1999, 2007). With experimental designs that group learners into those who complete tasks individually and those who complete them in pairs, researchers in this line of inquiry have provided evidence for the benefit of pair work in fostering language development. Storch (1999) was interested in whether or not ESL students in an Australian university working in pairs and discussing their grammatical choices (during a cloze exercise, text reconstruction, and joint composition) produced more accurate written texts on these exercises than students working individually. When grammatical accuracy results for the three tasks were examined, she found that collaboration had a positive effect for all students who worked in pairs. In a later study, Storch (2007) gave students in four intact Australian ESL classes the choice of working alone or in pairs to complete a text-editing task. In contrast to the previous study, there were no significantly different scores in grammatical accuracy between pairs and individuals. However, analysis of pair talk revealed that a high proportion of the LREs that arose in pairs were resolved interactively, and Storch holds that "pair work afforded learners opportunities to pool their linguistic resources and co-construct knowledge about language" (p. 155). Kim (2008) examined the potential for collaborative dialogue to help Korean as a second language (KSL) learners acquire vocabulary in the target language. In this study, 32 adult KSL learners were randomly assigned to either the collaborative or the individual group for the completion of a dictogloss task. Students working individually were asked to verbalize their thought processes using a think aloud protocol. Kim found that while both groups produced almost the same amount of lexical LREs, the collaborative group had higher scores on the post-test and were better able to correctly resolve their LREs. Taken together, the results of Storch (1999, 2007) and Kim (2008) suggest that when peers work collaboratively, they are able to resolve language issues that may have been left unattended without the assistance of another learner.

Other studies have considered how proficiency differences of participants might affect their ability to produce collaborative dialogue that fosters language learning. Leeser (2004) examined the LREs that adult L2 learners of Spanish, of varied proficiency levels, produced during a dictogloss activity. Proficiency pairings included higher proficiency-higher proficiency pairs, higher proficiency-lower proficiency pairs, and lower proficiency-lower proficiency pairs. He found that as the overall proficiency of the dyad increased, so did the number of LREs, the proportion of grammatical LREs, and the proportion of correctly resolved LREs. Watanabe and Swain (2007) identified four "core" Japanese ESL participants, each of whom completed a text reformulation exercise with a higher and lower proficiency peer. They found that core-high pairs produced a greater frequency of LREs, but that core participants achieved slightly higher scores on the post-test after working with a lower proficiency partner. The researchers posit that core participants learned more from working with lower proficiency peers, and suggest that there is value for mixed proficiency pairing in collaborative tasks. Finally, Kim and McDonough (2008) worked with 24 KSL learners to determine how the occurrence and resolution of LREs differed based on the proficiency of the interlocutor. They found that when paired with an advanced interlocutor, intermediate KSL learners produced more lexical LREs than when paired with another intermediate proficiency partner. In addition, significantly more resolved LREs occurred when speaking with an advanced interlocutor. However, there was no significant difference in the amount of grammatical LREs produced by intermediate-advanced and intermediate-intermediate pairs in this study.

Overall, these studies on proficiency differences and collaborative dialogue suggest that learners who have a higher proficiency level are better able to produce and correctly resolve LREs than their lower proficiency counterparts. Gan's (2010) description of high performing oral assessment groups noted that these interlocutors were able to engage constructively with each other's ideas by offering suggestions, giving explanations and making challenges. Thus, it seems that as language proficiency increases, learners become better able to perform the sophisticated language functions that Gan points out, perhaps allowing them to engage more deeply with the language problems they are attempting to solve. These results seem to be true for the overall proficiency of the pair, such that pairing a less proficient interlocutor with a more advanced one results in more success during collaborative dialogue, and higher subsequent retention of the forms discussed in this setting, than would a low-low matched pairing.

Some of the studies mentioned, in addition to examining the effect of learner proficiency on collaborative dialogue outcomes, also considered Storch's (2002) framework for identifying patterns of interaction. As mentioned previously, the interaction framework identifies four possible patterns. Table 11.1 summarizes the features that Storch (2002) identified in each pattern.

Table 11.1 Features of Storch's (2002) *Patterns of Interaction*

Quadrant	Pattern	Characterized by	Features found in Storch (2002)'s data
I	Collaborative	Moderate to high equality Moderate to high mutuality	Repetition/extension of utterances Positive and negative feedback Requests for and provision of information
II	Dominant/Dominant	Moderate to high equality Moderate to low mutuality	Few requests/collaborations Peer repairs given but not accepted Raised voices
III	Dominant/Passive	Moderate to low equality Moderate to low mutuality	Dominant partner makes self-directed questions as opposed to questions for peer Little negotiation, because passive participant gives few contributions/challenges
IV	Expert/Novice	Moderate to low equality Moderate to high mutuality	Expert provides assistance that helps novice learn Expert does not impose view but rather provides explanations Novice accepts and repeats explanations Expert actively encourages novice to take part

Storch (2007) pointed out that while most instructors would perceive the collaborative stance as the one that best fosters language learning during collaborative dialogue, this pattern does not occur just because learners are asked to work in pairs. She suggests that teachers monitor pair work to ensure that beneficial collaboration occurs.

Other studies have built on Storch's observation that the collaborative pattern is linked to more successful collaborative dialogue by connecting patterns of interaction to LREs. Watanabe and Swain (2007) considered the relationship between patterns of interaction and frequency of LREs, as well as that between patterns of interaction and post-test results among 12 Japanese ESL learners. They found that pairs who adopted the collaborative pattern not only produced more lexical and grammatical LREs, but also had higher posttest scores than the other three patterns. Kim and McDonough (2008) examined patterns of interaction among

KSL learners. Examining how pair dynamics differ when intermediate KSL learners work with an intermediate interlocutor compared with an advanced one, they found that learners who adopted a collaborative stance when working with intermediate interlocutor adopted a passive or novice stance when they were paired with a more advanced speaker. Also, several learners who adopted a dominant stance with an intermediate interlocutor were collaborative when working with an advanced one.

Overall, these studies on pair dynamics suggest that a collaborative stance is most conducive to language learning. It is also clear that some learners need training and support to collaborate successfully during pair work. At the same time, SLA researchers have called for more classroom-based examinations of the relationship between peer dialogue and learning outcomes (Swain et al. 2002), and for a consideration of the role that writing plays in second language development, with the understanding that writing is a social act embedded in a particular context (Ortega 2012; Williams 2012). One such authentic classroom task is peer response, a common practice in process-oriented writing courses, where students review each other's drafts and incorporate peer feedback in revision (Ferris 2003). The L2 writing research on peer response reviewed in this chapter complements SLA findings on the importance of pair dynamics, and suggests that students who approach problems jointly and respect writer autonomy experience rich learning opportunities from this feedback activity (Zhu and Mitchell 2012).

One way to better understand collaboration during peer response, and potentially apply these findings to pedagogical materials, is to use corpus-based tools and approaches to identify linguistic patterns that occur when language learners deliver and receive feedback. While there are many linguistic features that may be indices of collaboration, one that is particularly worth exploring further is stance. Expression of stance, or the personal feelings, attitudes, value judgments, and assessments of a speaker or writer (Biber et al. 1999), plays a central role in all academic registers. Corpus analysis of stance in academic language is prevalent, but most research has focused on academic writing, although spoken lectures have also been examined (see Part II, Chaps. 3 and 4 for a review of research on stance in spoken academic language). Less is known from a linguistic standpoint, however, about how learners express stance when working together. Overall, few studies have yet employed corpus analysis to examine the linguistic features, such as stance, that may arise during collaboration among learners, and it appears that none have focused on the task of peer response. In the next section, we introduce Roberson's (2015) L2PR corpus, a collection of spoken texts from peer response sessions in an L2 writing classroom.

The Second Language Peer Response (L2PR) Corpus

The L2PR corpus is a highly-specialized collection of authentic learner-learner talk during peer response in a writing classroom. The spoken texts were collected in a special section of first-year composition for bilingual or non-native speakers of English at a large urban university. In this course, students complete writing assignments focusing on reading, writing, and revising in different academic genres such as summaries, response papers, annotated bibliographies, and research papers. The instructor for this course teaches using a process-oriented approach to writing, a common practice in university L2 writing classrooms (Casanave 2006). For three major writing assignments, students participate in peer response sessions: two summary-response papers (a one- to two-page paper that includes three components: a summary of the assigned text, a personal connection, and opinions or evaluations of the text), and one persuasive research paper (a three- to four-page paper that includes at least three academic sources in which students state their opinion on a controversial topic of their choice).

Table 11.2 describes the 10 participants from the course, who worked in five pairs to discuss their writing over the course of the semester. All names are pseudonyms.

Participants chose their own partners for completing the peer response sessions, making their selection early in the semester. During the three class sessions in which peer response data was collected, students were given a peer response handout with guiding questions, and were permitted to ask questions about the handout in a whole-group format. Guiding questions focused on global concerns such as paragraph development,

Table 11.2 Participant characteristics

Pair number	Name	Gender	First language	Length of residency in the USA (years)	Academic major
1	Dan	M	Korean	7	Undecided
	Alex	M	Mandarin	1	Finance
2	Joe	M	Swahili	6	Computing
	SongWoo	F	Korean	3	Undecided
3	HaeSun	F	Korean	3	Business
	JeeHae	F	Korean	0.5	Interior Design
4	Ivana	F	Russian	0.5	Hospitality
	Zelda	F	Russian	0.5	Biology
5	Dave	M	Korean	5	Accounting
	Jay	M	Korean	3	Marketing

transitions between different sections of the paper, and the inclusion of a thesis statement that signaled the development of the rest of the paper. Next, students exchanged papers and silently read their peer's work, while making brief notes on the draft about the guiding questions. Students were told to make enough notes so that they could remember what they would like to say, but that the majority of the feedback would be given orally when they had discussions with their partner. When students were ready to begin discussing their papers, pairs who had agreed to participate were recorded using a digital recorder. Students negotiated whose paper to discuss first, and then switched roles. They used the notes they had made on their partners' papers to discuss their responses to the questions on the handout. After each peer response session, trained research assistants transcribed each session using the conventions in Table 11.3. Transcribers referred to the first student they heard on the recording as "S1" and the second, "S2." For corpus compilation, the transcripts were cleaned of these abbreviations and converted to text files. Transcripts were also cleaned of notations that described the environment rather than student talk, such as "papers shuffling in background."

Table 11.4 presents the composition of the L2PR corpus, displaying the number of words in each text. In this corpus, each text is a transcript of a pair's discussion about one student's paper. At each peer response session, there were two papers discussed by each pair, and thus two transcripts generated by each pair. For example, in their first session,

Table 11.3 Transcription conventions for peer response transcripts (Adapted from Ellis and Barkhuizen 2005)

T:	Teacher
S 1:	Student 1
S 2:	Student 2
–	Dash indicates a short pause
Foo-	An abrupt cut-off of the prior word or sound
[	Indicates the place where overlapping talk starts
]	Indicates the place where overlapping task stops
?	Rising intonation, not necessarily a question
Yes,	A comma indicates a continuing intonation
End.	A full stop indicates falling intonation
Yea::r	Colons indicate lengthening of the preceding sound; the more colons, the greater the extent of the lengthening
(hhhh)	Laughter
(sea)	Unclear or probable item

Table 11.4 L2PR corpus composition

Pair no.	Session 1	Session 2	Session 3	Total words by pair
1	450	446	614	3269
	459	461	839	
2	604	881	469	4214
	627	1195	438	
3	807	–	572	2493
	714		400	
4	1169	1418	–	5008
	716	1705		
5	875	1104	807	6445
	1888	1259	512	
Total words by session	8309	8469	4651	**21,429**

the transcript of pair number one's discussion of the first paper was 450 words long, and their discussion of the second paper was 459 words long. Each pair participated in three peer response sessions over the course of the semester, with the exception of two pairs. Because Pair 3 missed Session 2, and Pair 4 missed Session 3, an (–) in that cell of the table represents that no transcripts were generated. As such, the corpus contains a total of 26 texts (transcripts). Row totals show the number of words generated by each pair across three sessions. Column totals show the number of words generated during each session by all five pairs. The bold number in the bottom right corner is the total number of words in the corpus: 21,429.

Comparing the total number of words produced by each pair reveals that some spoke for a longer length of time about their papers than others. For example, Pair 5 produced roughly twice the number of words that Pair 1 did. These differences are partially due to the different patterns of interaction that each pair adopted. Pairs that shared control over the direction of the task tended to need less time to discuss their papers than did those who were less cordial. In addition, the total number of words by session decreased over the course of the semester. As pairs became more comfortable with offering feedback over the course of the semester, they needed less time to negotiate the guiding questions. Also, Pair 4, whose transcripts were by far the longest on average of all the pairs, missed the last session, which may have contributed to the relatively low word count. The effect of patterns of interaction on differences in transcript length will be discussed in the next chapter.

Investigating Peer Response in the L2 Writing Tradition

Although the fields of L2 writing and SLA have, for the most part, developed separately, Liu (2002) notes that peer response is supported by cognitive SLA theories that tout the importance of spoken interaction for language development, as well as sociocultural theories that value the role of spoken interaction for the development of cognition. Because learners participating in peer response sessions are asked to use each other as sources of feedback, this activity has the potential to create collaborative dialogue as defined by the SLA studies reviewed in the first section of this chapter. Just as students who collaborate with another learner produce and resolve more LREs, peer response has been shown in some cases to result in improved writing on subsequent drafts (Ferris 2003). A separate but related writing concept, the idea of literacy development as a social act, also underlies the pedagogical practice of peer response. In the same way that collaborative dialogue researchers view spoken negotiation for meaning as crucial to language development, second language writing researchers argue that individual cognitive processes can only be understood within the unique context of learning. In an L2 writing setting, the unique context of learning may involve the kinds of spoken negotiations for meaning that occur in a peer response session and lead to the writer's improvement during later revisions.

Nelson (1993) suggests a bidirectional relationship between context and cognition in a composition classroom (citing Flower 1990), where cognition and context are dynamic and mutually influential. That is, cognition may be influenced by the context of each learner's culture and experiences, but cognition is not simply a product of these contextual factors; new cognitive knowledge might shape the individual's perception of his or her context. Flower argues that in an ESL composition classroom, this interplay of cognition and context creates a challenge for instructors: creating a classroom where social interactions (context) help students to become better individual writers (cognition).

Peer response has the potential to foster such a connection between context and cognition, or between reader-writer interactions and future individual writing development. Students who successfully participate in peer response are not simply developing their individual skills as writers; they are developing a social relationship with a peer, one in which writers feel comfortable giving and receiving constructive feedback that is beneficial for their subsequent revisions. Because it mirrors this interplay between context and cognition, peer response is promising for fostering writing development among students. However, descriptions of social interactions during peer response in the literature have shown that not all groups are successful in establishing a collaborative relationship. In addition, a smaller body of studies suggests that peer response is not always beneficial for the revision process or for longitudinal writing development. Overall, few studies have connected social interactions during peer response to revision outcomes in a way that systematically examines how this complex relationship between cognition and context develops over time. Chapter 12 aims to extend the existing knowledge about peer response by examining this neglected area: the effect that these pair dynamics may have on revision outcomes.

Exploring 'Paired' Peer Response

Some studies have described what peers do with feedback by considering both teacher and peer feedback and comparing the uptake of both in later drafts. Connor and Asenavage (1994) examined the types of revisions (text-based or surface changes) that students made based on peer comments, and how these revisions compared in number to revisions based on teacher commentary. Examining eight pairs of students, they found that although these freshman ESL students made many revisions from first to second drafts, only 5% of those could be traced to peer comments. Rabiee's (2010) study in an Iranian EFL setting placed students experimentally into three groups: those who received only teacher comments, only peer comments, or both. She found that the peer comment group showed the least gains in holistic scoring from first to second drafts. These studies seem to suggest that when L2 writing students have access to both peer and teacher comments, they are hesitant to incorporate their peers' feedback in later drafts. The students in both Connor and Asenavage and Raibee made more revisions, and more successful revisions, based on teacher feedback than on peer feedback.

Other studies have described the connection between what is said in peer response groups and what happens during revisions by quantifying the number of peer suggestions that are used in revised drafts. The 12 advanced ESL students in Mendonca and Johnson's (1994) study used only about half of their peers' comments; by audio recording peer response sessions, comparing first and second drafts, and interviewing students, the researchers conclude that writers were selective about incorporating peer feedback into their drafts. These decisions were sometimes based on whether the students saw their peer as a valuable source of feedback. Tang and Tithecott (1999) report similar results: only six of the 12 focal students in this study incorporated peer feedback in their drafts at all. In addition to the low amount of incorporated changes, a more problematic picture of peer feedback emerges in this study; some group members did not receive any suggestions, and some incorporated changes that did not result in improvements in drafts.

As mentioned previously in this chapter, some L2 writing theorists believe in a model of writing development that connects the social context of peer response to the cognitive act of individual revision. The studies reviewed above suggest that peer response sessions may not be allowing students to engage socially to give and receive comments in a way that helps them make beneficial revisions. Based on the studies, it appears that the connection between context (peer response suggestions) and cognition (the individual incorporation of these comments after the peer response session) may not be exploited successfully in all peer response sessions.

Revision outcomes can be seen as a short-term effect of peer response sessions. Perhaps a more important outcome might be the effect of peer response on long-term development in student writing. One study attempted to uncover this connection by examining student progress over the course of a semester. Lundstrom and Baker (2009) consider whether giving or receiving feedback is more beneficial to improving student writing. Their experimental design divided students into two groups: one that commented on others' papers, but did not receive any feedback on their own writing, while the other group received peer feedback, but did not give any to others. The authors report that over the course of the semester, the givers benefitted more than the receivers. Tsui and Ng's (2000) investigation of student attitudes toward peer review and how these affect revision efforts also examines the possible long-term effects that peer response sessions can have on writing development. By conducting semi-structured interviews with students and administering questionnaires, the authors conclude that peer comments serve four main functions: to develop a sense of audience, to enhance learners' awareness of their strengths and weaknesses, to encourage collaborative learning, and to create a sense of ownership over the text. The authors suggest that these functions of peer comments may affect writers' development beyond the peer response session, although they acknowledge that longitudinal studies should further investigate these claims. Another method that can be used to uncover writing development beyond the comments made in peer response sessions is to consider whether or not students make self-revisions that originate in peer response sessions, and go beyond what was suggested there. Villamil and De Guerrero (1998) note that the 14 Spanish-speaking ESL students in their study made further revisions in the paper they discussed with a peer, which were "adopted in the session and further revised at home" (p. 497) and self-revisions, which were "performed at home and not discussed in the session" (p. 497). The researchers take the presence of further revisions and self-revisions as evidence that "certain linguistic or rhetorical processes which were in a state of development or instability may have had an opportunity to mature and consolidate, and new knowledge may have been generated" (p. 504). That is, the process of talking about writing with a peer may have contributed to the writers' ability to make further improvements when revising alone.

The studies reviewed in this section have quantified the extent to which peers incorporate each other's suggestions, have compared the amount of peer feedback relative to teacher feedback that is incorporated in revisions, and considered revisions that occur beyond the peer response session. Overall, they paint a somewhat inconclusive picture of the effects of peer response on revision outcomes and on writing development. It seems that some peer response groups (e.g., Villamil and De Guerrero 1998) are more willing to incorporate changes than are others (e.g., Connor and Asenavage 1994). What remains to be addressed in more detail, though, is why this is so. It seems reasonable that students who choose not to incorporate their peers' suggestions do not see these contributions as valuable or accurate, but a more compelling question is why students have this view about peer feedback. This question can be examined with methodologies such as think-aloud protocols that ask students to explain their choices (as Hyland 2008, suggests).

Contextual Factors in Peer Response

The following studies focus primarily on the contextual factors that are involved in peer response. These include individual student factors, such as their attitudes toward the practice of peer response. Taken together, these studies provide a detailed view of what students talk about in peer response groups and how they negotiate the relationship between reader and writer. Understanding these contextual factors is an important step toward describing effective peer response groups, and linking these interactions to later positive revision outcomes.

A large body of research has addressed the question of how students feel about peer response. Some studies on student views of peer response used questionnaires and concluded that students do value peer response as one source of feedback (Jacobs et al. 1998). Other investigations have asked students to further explain their opinions after they participated in peer response, thus deepening researchers' understandings of the reasons why students value peer feedback. One of these is that peers can identify areas of student writing that are clear (Rollinson 2004; Mendonca and Johnson 1994), as well as those that are less so (Mendonca and Johnson 1994; Tang and Tithecott 1999). In addition, students in peer response groups have stated that they are exposed to new ways of expressing their own ideas after reading those of a peer (Mendonca and Johnson 1994). In the case of intact peer response groups that meet over time, peers may even come to rely on their readers to identify problems, and be upset if they miss them (Rollinson 2004).

However, not all research on student attitudes has revealed that they value and enjoy the process of peer response. Students have expressed reservations about their ability to respond effectively to another student's writing, and stated that they feel more comfortable when a teacher fills this role (Tang and Tithecott 1999; Rollinson 2004). Students who receive feedback from their peers have also expressed hesitations about this feedback source, because they feel their partner lacks the background knowledge necessary to make effective comments (Mendonca and Johnson 1994), or because they are hesitant to accept grammar feedback from another learner when there was no consensus on whether to do so (Carson and Nelson 1996). In Tang and Tithecott's (1999) study, students were asked to read their papers aloud, and peer responders expressed difficulty with listening comprehension during such long stretches of discourse.

It is difficult to draw overall conclusions about student attitudes toward peer response because the research about student attitudes summarized above has been conducted in a variety of settings (EFL and ESL) at a variety of levels (pre-university, university, and graduate). However, it seems that some of the claims about the benefits and drawbacks of peer response for students mentioned in the pedagogical literature are borne out in research about student attitudes. For example, students may not know what to look for in their peers' writing, as Liu (2002) mentions, and they may be unsure about the accuracy of their peers' advice (Leki 1990). However, not all students have negative views about peer response; Ferris' (2003) claim that peers can provide developmentally appropriate feedback is echoed by students who note that their peers are able to identify problems that they are not able to alone (Mendonca and Johnson 1994; Tang and Tithecott 1999).

Another important contextual variable in peer response is how students interact with their peer reviewer. Nelson and Murphy (1993) define the social dimension of peer response groups as "the way participants perceive, relate to, and interact with each other" (p. 181). The studies reviewed below describe the social dimension of peer response groups in terms of: group and individual roles (Nelson and Murphy 1992); learner stances toward the peer response task (Mangelsdorf and Schlumberger 1992; Lockhart and Ng 1995); learner revision profiles (Rollinson 2004); and the sociocultural theory concepts of scaffolding (De Guerrero and Villamil 2000; Hyland 2008) and mediation (De Guerrero and Villamil 2000).

Nelson and Murphy (1992) examine four L2 writers who were part of a writing group and describe their interaction processes and dynamics. Although coding for the task dimension of peer response in this study is encouraging in that nearly three-quarters of group talk was devoted to the study of language, Nelson and Murphy report more discouraging results in terms of the social dimension of this group. They write that perhaps an "apt metaphor for describing the group participation patterns is a duel" (p.181), as there was one student who positioned herself in the role of "attacker" (p. 182) by dominating floor time and giving negative comments to other students in the group.

Instead of describing students' roles in peer response groups, other studies have focused on their stances toward the task. Mangelsdorf and Schlumberger (1992) asked 60 ESL freshman composition students to write comments on an essay written the previous semester by the same kind of student, and found that the most common type of response letter was coded as prescriptive. The authors suggest that students who wrote prescriptive letters valued a "traditional pedagogic approach" (p. 247) to writing, in which the focus is on correctness rather than expression of meaning, and that these students may need to be guided toward adopting a more collaborative stance, and toward focusing on global concerns in peer response sessions. Lockhart and Ng (1995) analyzed transcripts of 27 peer response groups and identified four reader stances. In the authoritative stance, readers have preconceived ideas of what the essay should be, and tell the writer what changes to make; in the interpretive stance, readers present personal responses to writers' text, focus on what they like, and give reasons; in the probing stance, readers try to puzzle out meaning in the text, ask the writer for clarification, and focus on confusing areas; and in the collaborative one, readers negotiate with the writer to discover the writer's intention and build meaning. Students who adopted probing and collaborative stances tended to focus more on the rhetorical concerns of ideas, audience, and purpose, and tended to give suggestions rather than state opinions.

Other studies have described the social dimension of peer response groups by utilizing the concept of scaffolding to explain how learning occurs in these groups. In their investigation of two Spanish-speaking ESL students in a peer response session, De Guerrero and Villamil (2000) posit that scaffolding, or supportive behaviors adopted by the more competent learner to facilitate the less competent learner's progress (Ohta 2000) allowed peer response interaction to evolve. Specifically, participants moved from reader-dominated to more active participation between reader and writer toward the end of the session.

Hyland (2008) was also interested in analyzing how learners in peer response groups scaffold each other. By examining the ways that two different teachers structured peer interaction in writing workshops, Hyland found that students in both classes provided verbal scaffolding to each other, suggesting that students "felt a need for such interaction" (p. 186). One instructor openly encouraged students to use each other as resources, and thus fostered scaffolding. The other created "micro-communities" (p. 186) of writers that were stable over the course of the semester, fostering a sense of security in sharing ideas and writing. Sharing one's writing often involves personal vulnerability and the threat of being criticized.

It is perhaps not surprising, then, that the studies on the social dimension of peer response groups reviewed here seem to suggest that those which function more collaboratively are more successful.

Summary and Outlook

In this chapter, we explored SLA findings about collaborative dialogue in language learning and reviewed peer response studies in the context of L2 writing. While both bodies of literature suggest that working collaboratively is beneficial for learners, SLA and L2 writing researchers alike have identified gaps in our current knowledge about how students experience collaboration in ecologically valid settings. There is a need for continued systematic analysis of the linguistic and social features of productive talk during peer response. This chapter also outlined the collection and composition of the L2PR corpus, a classroom-based collection of spoken learner language that will be examined in the next two chapters.

Chapter 12 presents the results of a qualitative analysis of patterns of social interaction in the corpus, drawing upon our coding as well as stimulated recall interviews with students. It also explores the relationship between these patterns of interaction and revision outcomes, asking if students in some patterns use more feedback or write better second drafts than others. Next, to explore the linguistic features of collaboration, Chap. 13 explores the use of modal verbs as stance markers in two sub-sections of the L2PR Corpus: collaborative and non-collaborative talk. Frequencies and communicative functions of six modals and semi-modals are presented, and differences in modal use between the two subcorpora are explored. Part IV concludes with a consideration of future directions in spoken learner corpora as well as a discussion of the pedagogical implications of our findings.

12

Social Dynamics During Peer Response: *Patterns of Interaction* in the L2PR Corpus

This chapter explores the social dynamics of peer conversations in the L2PR Corpus (Roberson 2015) using Storch's (2002) patterns of interaction framework to understand how learners share control over the direction of the task, and how they engage with each other's feedback on writing. We first provide a description of the data sources used in the analysis (peer response transcripts; stimulated recall interview transcripts; and first and second drafts of student writing), and then examine the relationship between patterns of interaction and revision practices. Chapter 13 will further explore one linguistic feature of the patterns of interaction analyzed in this chapter: the use of modal verbs as stance markers by collaborative and non-collaborative pairs.

Data Sources and Analysis

The first data source drawn upon in this analysis is the L2PR Corpus. As described in Chap. 11, participants were recorded as they orally discussed their feedback on a partner's writing, and these conversations were transcribed and collected to form the corpus. The coding scheme used to analyze transcripts, *patterns of interaction* (Storch 2002), was created

E. Friginal et al., *Exploring Spoken English Learner Language Using Corpora*,
DOI 10.1007/978-3-319-59900-7_12

to describe how students position themselves during pair work in a university ESL writing course. It describes pair interactions based on the extent to which learners engage with each other's suggestions (*mutuality*) and the extent to which they share control over the direction of the task (*equality*). Chapter 11 provided an extensive description of Storch's coding scheme and a review of the empirical studies that have applied it to pair talk. Briefly, pairs that adopt *collaborative* patterns experience more positive learning outcomes than those who adopt other patterns (Storch 2002; Watanabe and Swain 2007; Kim and McDonough 2008).

When applying Storch's coding scheme to the L2PR Corpus, transcripts were first divided into episodes, understood as a section of the peer response transcript where students discussed a single topic of the paper being reviewed. When students moved on to another topic, another episode began. Each episode was coded as exhibiting one of four *patterns of interaction* (collaborative, dominant/passive, expert/novice, or dominant/dominant), by identifying instances of the features found in two studies of pair interaction: Storch (2002) and Zheng (2012). Table 12.1 summarizes the features from both studies that were identified in the L2PR Corpus. Features from Zheng (2012) are marked with (*), and unmarked features are from Storch (2002):

Table 12.1 Patterns of interaction in the L2PR corpus (Features from Storch 2002; Zheng 2012)

Pattern	Features
Collaborative	Reader and writer discuss optional revisions together*
	Students discuss alternative views, and reach resolution
	Students request and provide information
Dominant/Dominant	Students engage in disputes
	Each student insists on own opinion; no consensus reached*
	Teasing/hostility
Dominant/Passive	Dominants do not try to involve passives to help them learn*
	Little negotiation because passives give few Contributions/challenges
	Dominants take authoritative stance, while passives are subservient
Expert/Novice	Experts are authoritative and provide scaffolding/direct instruction*
	Novices admit failure or error*
	Experts do not impose view but provide suggestions

After a pattern of interaction was identified for each episode of each transcript, the transcript was assigned a single pattern of interaction by identifying the most frequently occurring one; in order for it to be assigned, the pattern must have occurred in at least 75% percent of the total episodes. A trained independent second rater also coded the transcripts. After the second coding, inter-rater reliability was consistent on 23 out of 26 patterns, or 85%. For those patterns where the coders did not agree, they re-read the transcript episode by episode, referring repeatedly to the coding scheme to agree on a pattern for each, and finally for each transcript. After this discussion, 100% intercoder reliability was reached.

In addition to transcriptions of peer response sessions, stimulated recall interviews with participants provide an additional data source. These interviews use stimuli such as audio or video recordings to "prompt participants to recall thoughts they had while performing a task or participating in an event" (Gass and Mackey 2000, p. 17). In the current study, stimuli used were recordings of peer response sessions and revised second drafts. Before interviews, which occurred no more than two days after students received feedback and made revisions, the interviewer used both peer response transcripts and second drafts to create a list of questions that might be asked. The goal of these questions was to understand the following: how the participant perceived the social dynamics at particular segments of the recording, how they felt about giving or receiving feedback at particular segments, how they understood their partner's suggestions at particular segments, and how they decided to accept or reject suggested revisions. Participants were also asked to stop the peer response recording at any moment where they felt they had something to say about what they were thinking or feeling at the time they were participating in the session. Student-initiated comments were prioritized over prepared questions, and students sometimes chose to talk about segments of the peer response recording or of their revised drafts that had not been previously selected.

The next data sources used in this analysis are first (pre-peer response) and second (post-peer response) drafts of student writing. Two different measures were used to quantify the improvement in student writing from first to second drafts: (1) calculating the amount of comments provided during peer response, and the percent of these that were accepted in revision, and (2) rating each pair of first and second drafts with a rubric. Analysis of comments was limited to those where it seemed possible to identify implementation in the second draft (a similar procedure was used in Liu and Sadler (2003)). For example, during their second peer response session, Dan (the reader) had the following feedback for Alex, his partner: "I think summary, you need, um, to introduce the article, like the title of the article or the author." This comment is specific and revision-oriented. However, not all revision-oriented comments are captured in this analysis, because some comments were too vague, or too general, for their implementation to be directly observable in the second draft. In addition, stimulated recall transcripts often provided insight into the writer's decisions to implement or ignore comments received. The rubric used for rating drafts is adapted from Paulus (1999), and includes four analytical categories (organization/unity; development; structure; and vocabulary) with 5 possible points for each one, such that each essay could be given a maximum score of 20 points. Using the rubric, first and second drafts were assigned a score out of 20 total points, and then the gain in score for that participant was calculated. Trained independent raters also scored each first and second draft. Inter-rater reliability for all drafts was calculated at 94%, such that third rating was not necessary for any drafts.

Results and Discussion

A single *pattern of interaction* (collaborative, dominant/passive, dominant/dominant, or expert/novice) was identified for each peer response transcript, where one transcript consists of a pair's discussion of one of their drafts. Table 12.2 shows the pattern of interaction that was identified for each pair during each session of peer response. There are three sessions that correspond with three different writing assignments. For each session, there are two *patterns of interaction* listed: one for the discussion of the first paper, and one for the discussion of the second.

Table 12.2 Patterns of interaction for each transcript, across three sessions

Pair	Participants	Session One	Session Two	Session Three
1	Dan and Alex	Collaborative Expert/novice	Collaborative Expert/novice	Expert/novice Collaborative
2	Joe and SongWoo	Expert/novice Collaborative	Expert/novice Collaborative	Expert/novice Collaborative
3	HaeSun and JeeHae	Dominant/passive Collaborative	(Did not complete)	Dominant/passive Dominant/dominant
4	Ivana and Zelda	Expert/novice Collaborative	Collaborative Collaborative	(Did not complete)
5	Dave and Jay	Dominant/passive Dominant/dominant	Dominant/passive Dominant/dominant	Dominant/passive Dominant/dominant

As Table 12.2 shows, each of Storch's four *patterns of interaction* were identified in this study. For all transcripts, the predominant *pattern of interaction* occurred in an average of at least 77% of the transcript. That is to say, although coding by episode accounted for variability within the session, each transcript did seem to exhibit a strong tendency toward one of the four patterns. The most common pattern is the collaborative one, which occurs in close to half of the peer response transcripts (10 out of 26). The second most common pattern is the expert-novice one, which was identified in about one quarter (seven). The remainder of the transcripts are split almost evenly between dominant/passive (five) and dominant/dominant (four).

The predominance of the collaborative pattern in the current study is in line with most other studies that have examined *patterns of interaction* with a single experimental group (Storch 2002; Watanabe 2008; Watanabe and Swain 2007). Other studies had two groups of participants, and found that the collaborative pattern was the most common in one of the groups: students in Kim and McDonough's (2011) study. Those students who received pre-task modeling of the collaborative pattern demonstrated it more than their classmates who had not received modeling. Tan et al. (2010) found that the collaborative pattern was more common among students completing peer response using a computer as opposed to those conducting the activity face-to-face. The only study to date that has not identified mostly collaborative

Table 12.3 Mean number of turns and length of turns by pattern of interaction

Pattern of Interaction (number of transcripts)	Mean turn length in number of words (SD)	Mean turns (SD)	Mean total words (SD)	Mean transcript length in minutes (SD)
Collaborative (10)				
Student 1	20.3 (5.1)	60.1 (6)	1222.4 (334.5)	20.8 (3)
Student 2	18.8 (6.5)	59.6 (5.8)	1108.6 (350.6)	
Expert/Novice (7)				
Expert	26.9 (3.9)	61.6 (9.6)	1647 (248.5)	22.4 (4.1)
Novice	13.8 (2.3)	61.3 (9.4)	828.4 (15.3)	
Dominant/Passive (5)				
Dominant	23.3 (3.3)	52 (3.4)	1213.6 (193.4)	16.9 (3.1)
Passive	12 (1)	52 (3.4)	624	
Dominant/Dominant (4)				
Student 1	19.3 (4.4)	61.8 (3.4)	1196.5 (319)	21.3 (2.7)
Student 2	19.6 (4.7)	61.5 (2.5)	1211.5 (329.5)	

patterns is Zheng (2012), where the dominant/dominant pattern was most common.

The patterns of interaction displayed in Table 12.2 were identified using the transcript coding process. In order to triangulate the differences among *patterns of interaction*, an additional analysis was conducted: a calculation of the average number and length of turns by pattern of interaction. Table 12.3 displays these results.

Table 12.3 illustrates several trends that corroborate the identification of *patterns of interaction* in the current study. In the two patterns with relatively low equality, expert/novice and dominant/passive, experts and dominant students take turns that are roughly twice as long as their novice and passive counterparts. In fact, experts took the longest turns of any of the student roles, and expert/novice transcripts were the longest of all four patterns. This stands to reason, considering that a feature of the expert/novice pattern is the expert's tendency to ask clarifying questions of their novice partners, and to provide detailed explanations of their comments. All in all, the word- and turn- count analysis supported the identification of *patterns of interaction* that were made based on coding of transcripts. The next sections will further discuss each of the four patterns identified in the L2PR Corpus, providing excerpts from both peer response transcripts and stimulated recall interviews to illustrate and explain some of the characteristic features of each pattern.

Collaborative Pattern

The excerpt below, where Zelda is reviewing Ivana's summary-response paper about the class book, *Outcasts United*, represents the collaborative pattern. Ivana wrote about a couple of instances where the refugees in the novel experienced discrimination in their American community. She is expressing that she thinks the paragraph needs to be expanded:

Text Sample 12.1 Summary-Response Paper

Ivana: Here I stop because I have no idea, because I have no clue (laughing)
Zelda: (laughing) I'll just write you some notes here about just "church and store" and, um, "stories", and "your opinion" about it.
Ivana: Because maybe I can say that they had to be thankful for escaping from war, um, and don't be so aggressive …
Zelda: Mhm.
Ivana: to the new life
Zelda: You can keep going, saying about the church and the store and what happened in your opinion …
Ivana: Yes, there I will say about it [should not happen
Zelda: Yes, that it's not] supposed to be to happen …
Ivana: Mhm.
Zelda: because it is in United States. And in conclusion, you can just say that *although in theory it sounds [so easy …*
Ivana: Perfect, yeah]
Zelda: uh, *but in reality …*
(Zelda and Ivana, Peer Response Session One, February 2013)

In this episode, Ivana and Zelda engage in collaborative brainstorming that results in the generation of language that Ivana might use in her second draft. Rather than wait for Zelda to point out problematic aspects of her paper, Ivana begins the episode by sharing that she is stuck. Both women then participate in generating new ideas, thus showing that they are sharing control over the direction of the task and engaging meaningfully with each other's suggestions.

Stimulated recall interviews provided further insight into the collaborative pattern. In the excerpt below, SongWoo speaks about the impact of being a reader on her own writing process. Rather than see peer response solely as an opportunity to receive suggestions on their own papers, collaborative participants like SongWoo see the learning potential in giving feedback:

Text Sample 12.2 Stimulated Recall Interview

> Okay, I like, as I'm giving, by giving him a suggestion, I also learn … cause to give a suggestion I have to understand it, and have to have some ideas. Other ideas or some different ways to say, like other opinion, I guess. I have to have some idea, some different idea to suggest him, right? So I'm, I, by giving suggestion, I learned, like I got suggestion also? (SongWoo, Stimulated Recall Interview Two, March 2013)

Storch (2002) also found that students who reported positive attitudes toward group work were more likely to adopt a collaborative *pattern of interaction.* In addition, several researchers (Allwright 1984; van Lier 1996; Webb 1989) have confirmed what SongWoo identified in her own experience as a peer responder: that providing an explanation is beneficial for learning because the learner must first clarify and organize her own knowledge (as cited in Storch 2002).

Dominant/Dominant Pattern

The excerpt below presents an example of a dominant/dominant episode, where Jay is reviewing Dave's research paper about organ trafficking. In his paper, Dave has included China as an example of a country where this practice is problematic. Jay questions this choice, and also maintains that statistics should be included:

Text Sample 12.3 Dominant/dominant Peer Response

Jay:	Why do you say China? Why do you include China?
Dave:	Well, China is the major country. Where it happens a lot, you know?
Jay:	No.
Dave:	You do know.
Jay:	No, I don't know. Did you look it up?
Dave:	I look it up.
Jay:	Then, where's the statistic of it?
Dave:	Well, I didn't put it, though. That's not the point. So, next.
Jay:	How do I know it's true or not?
Dave:	Well, whether you believe or not, it's true. Okay, move on.
Jay:	No, you must, you have to convince me. Or like, try to make me trust you, or …
Dave:	Well, that's not the point, so …
	(Dave and Jay, Peer Response Session Three, April 2013)

This episode is a clear example of the disputes that can occur in the dominant-dominant pattern. Each participant clings to his own view, such that no consensus about whether to include statistics is reached: Dave ends the episode by saying that convincing the reader, as Jay suggests he do, is "not the point." These two are engaged in trying to control the direction of the task, but are unwilling to engage with each other's discourse, exhibiting the high *equality* but low *mutuality* that characterizes the dominant-dominant pattern. Dave's stimulated recall interview revealed more complexity in his relationship with Jay. In this segment of the interview, Dave had just listened to a recording of Jay laughing at his [Dave's] second paragraph and telling him, "you have only three sentences, man. Why do you think that's enough?"

Text Sample 12.4 Stimulated Recall: Dave

Dave:	Um, it was kind of fun … kinda, like, I was trying to, like, attack him, like offend him, and he's kinda defending his opinion, so

Interviewer: Okay ... do you think it felt fun to Jay?
Dave: Yeah, he's, he's yeah cause he was laughing too ... we couldn't stop laughing.
(Dave, Stimulated Recall Interview One, February 2013)

The insight gained from stimulated recall for the dominant/dominant pattern highlights the need for these kinds of interviews. Relying on the transcript alone, one might have assumed that the interaction was unpleasant for the participants. However, Dave revealed that he enjoyed "trying to attack him, to offend him." Likewise, Jay revealed in his first stimulated recall interview that Dave "knows I'm not serious about it [the teasing comments]" and that "he [Dave] does that to me too."

Dominant-Passive Pattern

In this pattern, while one participant controls the direction of the task, the other demonstrates little engagement. In the following excerpt, HaeSun is giving JeeHae feedback on a research paper on same-sex marriage. JeeHae does not ask any clarifying questions about HaeSun's feedback, and it is not clear from the transcript whether or not she understands or agrees with it:

Text Sample 12.5 Dominant-Passive Pair

HaeSun: Your position ... I think it is clear, but, like, a little more clear.
JeeHae: Okay.
HaeSun: And then [background
JeeHae: Mhm]
HaeSun: Paragraph. I mean, you had a little background information, but ... little more.
JeeHae: Yeah.
(HaeSun and JeeHae, Peer Response Session Three, April 2013)

JeeHae's stimulated recall interview shed light on why she contributed so little during the discussion. She revealed, "I didn't understand what the background information would be." When asked why she responded "okay" if the feedback was actually unclear, JeeHae responded, "I didn't even, I mean, I don't know how to write in detail …I don't know much information about my paper and I was so confused how to write my argument."

Interviews with JeeHae also suggest that passive students may be quieter because they do not feel confident as writers, and they view themselves as less proficient in English than their dominant partners. When HaeSun read JeeHae's first paper, a summary response that asks students to make a personal connection to some aspect of the class book, HaeSun told her, "I think your personal connection should be how, how hard it was for you fitting into America as a refugee," to which JeeHae responds "okay." In the stimulated recall interview after that session, she further explains her response:

Text Sample 12.6 Stimulated Recall: JeeHae

Interviewer:	Here she says your personal connection should be about being a refugee. Are you a refugee?
JeeHae:	No, I'm an international student.
Interviewer:	Okay. So you said 'okay' to her suggestion, but do you remember what you were thinking?
JeeHae:	I think she meant, um, the hard experience when first came into the United States as the foreign student, and most other students think I'm Asian so I can speak English and stuff. Yeah, so I think she wanted me to write about that because she wrote about things like that in her paper.
Interviewer:	But that's not what you wanted to write about?
JeeHae:	No, I tried to think of something and think back but I couldn't really find anything … and I say okay because I really like her personal connection and she is better English than me. I think I was confused. I'm just lack of speaking skills so when I start speaking I feel confused.
	(JeeHae, Stimulated Recall Interview One, February 2013)

Something as individual as a personal connection is appropriated by the dominant reader, and the passive writer says nothing to change the course of the discussion. JeeHae revealed that she is hesitant to challenge HaeSun's suggestion because she sees herself as having relatively lower English proficiency.

Stimulated recall interviews with dominant readers like Dave further deepened my understanding of why students adopt these roles when doing peer response. After listening to his recorded peer response session and concluding that he sounded "offensive," he had the following to say:

Text Sample 12.7 Stimulated Recall: Dave

Interviewer:	Okay, how do you think that affects doing peer review?
Dave:	Mm, I think if I did it, like, nicer way, he would be like, 'okay, whatever' and stuff, but if I did it, like, straightforward, then he would listen. So I try to help him out.
Interviewer:	Oh, okay. So you think actually if you were nicer, he wouldn't listen to you.
Dave:	Yeah, yeah.
	(Dave, Stimulated Recall Interview One, February 2013)

It seems that while Dave is aware that his tone and comments sound hostile, he may not be behaving this way out of malice. He thinks that if he made comments in a "nicer way," Jay would not listen to him. Instead, he makes comments in a way that he sees as more direct to "help him out."

Expert-Novice Pattern

In this pattern, the expert ensures that the novice is engaged in the discourse and understands the suggestions for revision. In the excerpt below, Joe is reviewing SongWoo's summary paper about an article she read on cultural adjustment. He identifies a sentence that is confusing to him and guides SongWoo toward choosing a clearer way to express her idea:

Text Sample 12.8 Expert-Novice Pattern

Joe: I didn't understand what you meant, like this you write ["they had a …"

SongWoo: "They had a way] they could to understand each other"? Yeah, I don't know is there a word for it …

Joe: Yeah, what did you mean by that? Maybe you mean without words?

SongWoo: You know, like, they have a, they speak different languages, but they could understand each other … but the way I write is confused.

Joe: Okay, so basically they could understand each other even though they speak different languages? Like, they do gesture and things like that?

SongWoo: Yes, like that.

Joe: Okay so for that we can say *the body language. Using the body language*. That's what you're trying to say?

SongWoo: Yeah, using the body language, yeah.

Joe: Yeah, using the body language, I like that idea.

(Joe and SongWoo, Peer Response Session One, February 2013)

Joe begins this episode by pointing out an unclear sentence in SongWoo's paper. Although it seems clear from the end of the episode that Joe knows an appropriate phrase she can use, rather than supply it for SongWoo, he asks her to first explain what she was trying to express.

In the following excerpt, SongWoo (the novice writer) is asking Joe (the expert reader) to give her a suggestion on how to revise a sentence that she admits has confused her:

Text Sample 12.9 Expert-Novice Pattern: Giving a Suggestion

Joe: Do you want to, like, restructure the sentence? Like you could structure

SongWoo: Could you …

Joe: Oh, write it down?

SongWoo: Yeah, ah, you just give me a suggestion, cause that sentence always confused .... I don't know how to make it.
Joe: Yeah, you could say, like, *the Fugees have a connection between each other*. Yeah, that'd be better. Is that what you want to say?
SongWoo: Instead of *they love each other*. That'd be better.
(Joe and SongWoo, Peer Response Session One, February 2013)

In an attempt to scaffold novice writers toward making revisions that improve their papers, one expert used his own paper as a model. In the excerpt below, Dan is giving Alex feedback on his persuasive research paper. At the end of the session, Dan calls attention back to Alex's draft and suggests a possible revision, using his own paper as a model:

Text Sample 12.10 Suggesting Revision

Dan: Oh, like what I told you about using, like, how to catch, like, the readers?
Alex: Mhm.
Dan: Like, um, my first sentence? It says *in today's society, going to college after high school seems to be the way the river flows.* Right?
Alex: Mhm.
Dan: I could have just said *In today's societies most people go to college after high school*. But, you know, I said in a different way to like, unusual way, to like
Alex: I got you. Catch the attentions.
Dan: So you could do something like that.
Alex: Okay. I can ... I will try.
(Dan and Alex, Peer Response Session Three, April 2013)

Further contributions to understanding this pattern come from stimulated recall interviews with expert readers. These students seem to believe that writing development is best fostered when students have to correct their own mistakes. In the following excerpt, Dan is talking about how he tries not to fix Alex's problems, but, rather, to simply point them out:

Text Sample 12.11 Decisions About Areas for Improvement

> So, I know, like I know his weaknesses, and I guess his strengths … I know and he knows that he has grammar issues, so I try not to comment on that as much cause he knows he has problems and he tries to fix them … I try to focus on, like, the main ideas he's missing, or something like that … [I'm] getting to know his style of writing

As the expert reader, Dan is making thoughtful decisions about the areas for improvement in his novice partner's paper. Dan believes that the process of correcting his own grammar errors is beneficial for Alex, and he wants to give him room to do this.

Patterns of Interaction and Revision Outcomes

Table 12.4 displays the total number of specific comments, and the number and percent of those comments that were implemented in the second draft, by pattern of interaction role of the writer. The numbers reported are an average of all peer response transcripts and corresponding second drafts that occurred for each role.

Relatively fewer comments were provided in the dominant/dominant and collaborative patterns, and examining peer response and stimulated

Table 12.4 Provision and implementation of specific, revision-oriented comments, by writer role

Writer role	Comments received	Comments implemented	Percent implemented
Collaborative (10)			
Mean	5.1	3.9	76.50%
SD	2.4	2.1	
Dominant (4)			
Mean	6	1.2	20%
SD	2.2	1.3	
Passive (5)			
Mean	12	7.8	64.60%
SD	6.8	2.1	
Novice (7)			
Mean	12.4	10.6	85.10%
SD	3.4	3.3	

recall transcripts helps to explain why. In the excerpt below, Jay is giving Dave feedback on a paper about the class book. Jay is asking Dave why he did not mention Luma, the soccer coach in the story, in his summary paragraph. Earlier in this session, the two had argued about whether or not a summary should include personal opinion; Dave thought this was permissible, and Jay held the opposite view:

Text Sample 12.12 Dominant/dominant Pattern

Jay: Why, why didn't you put about Luma?
Dave: It's, you know, it's a summary, so I just summarize, the, uh, the most important parts.
Jay: So you, you think that Luma is not important?
Dave: I didn't say [that
Jay: She's not taking an important role?]
Dave: I didn't say Luma is not important, but the [the
Jay: I don't know, man, I don't see any "L" in this sentence]
Dave: The soccer team is more important in my opinion so I put just the basic
[information
Jay: So another opinion] right here, man. See?
Dave: That's not an opinion.
(Dave and Jay, Peer Response Session One, February 2013)

Because these two are locked in a dominant/dominant pattern, they spend time arguing with each other's suggestions and explanations, which may cause them to lose opportunities to generate more comments. This excerpt suggests that one of the potential effects of high equality in a peer response context is that students in these patterns may give relatively fewer comments than students in patterns where one student has more control over the task.

Students in a collaborative pattern also exhibit high equality relative to other patterns, although high equality manifests differently than in the dominant/dominant pattern. Rather than battling for control over the task, students in the collaborative pattern seem to agree to share it. In the excerpt below, Alex has read Dan's research paper, and Dan asks for feedback about cohesion. Alex suggests that maybe Dan needs to include more transitional devices in his revisions:

Text Sample 12.13 Collaborative Pattern

Dan: Oh, maybe we should focus on transition, I mean
Alex: You mean the transitions?
Dan: Between each paragraph.
Alex: Okay, like, uh transition to the paragraph. Better one. Uh, lemme see, do you want to do each paragraph like individual?
Dan: Uh, I like my essay to like, really, you know, flow. Does it flow, the paragraphs?
Alex: Oh, okay. So you can maybe just put transitions here.
Dan: Yeah. Where's the paper, like, thingie
Alex: Huh?
Dan: With the list of words she gave us, [for the flow
Alex: oh, the flow] the transitioning words.
Dan: Yeah, never mind I'll find it after.
Alex: Yeah, you can just use that one for ideas.
(Dan and Alex, Peer Response Session Three, April 2013)

These two take a relatively long amount of time (13 turns) to discuss transition devices in Dan's paper, and take the time to mention class handouts they might use in revision. Because they spend a longer amount of time on each episode, collaborative participants give fewer specific revision-oriented comments, but the ones they do give are reasoned and thoughtful.

Two other patterns, dominant/passive and expert/novice, display a relatively low amount of equality, because one student (the dominant and expert student, respectively) has more control over the task than the other. Dominant and expert students' motivations are different: the dominant student moves quickly through a list of things that the writer should "fix" in revisions, while the expert student directs the task in order to ensure that the novice understands how to implement comments during revision.

Dominant readers tend to give direct comments to their passive partners without pausing to foster engagement, the result of which is that passive students receive a fairly large amount of comments without necessarily understanding them. In the episode below, HaeSun is reading JeeHae's persuasive research paper, which should include a thesis statement of opinion that makes clear the writer's position on a controversial topic. HaeSun moves quickly through a series of suggestions with little input from JeeHae:

Text Sample 12.14 Suggestions with Little Input

HaeSun: And then um … you had a thesis statement but it wasn't very clear enough.
JeeHae: Oh, okay.
HaeSun: Yeah, so. I want you to be more detail about it.
JeeHae: [Mhm
HaeSun: and] focus on, like, what your paper is going to be. And then, yeah, you have a side that you are supporting, you're not supporting the discrimination.
JeeHae: Yeah, [it's terrible
HaeSun: But,] yeah it's … I, I want, I think it should be more detail, also more descriptive. And then, um, your position
JeeHae: Mhm
HaeSun: I think it's clear, but, like … a little more clear
JeeHae: Okay.
HaeSun: I guess, And then [background
JeeHae: Mhm]
HaeSun: paragraph. I mean, you did had it a little, but … little more.
JeeHae: Yeah.
(HaeSun and JeeHae, Peer Response Session Three, April 2013)

Over 14 turns, HaeSun gives JeeHae at least three specific revision-oriented comments: make her thesis statement clearer and more detailed, make her stance on the issue clearer, and expand her background paragraph. It is not apparent from the transcript, however, that JeeHae understands these comments or intends to use them. JeeHae revealed in the stimulated recall interview after this session that she was indeed confused about how to revise her thesis statement of opinion.

In terms of the number of comments that readers give, the expert/novice pattern aligns with the dominant/passive one. The nature of these comments, however, is strikingly different from that of dominant reader comments: experts take time to ensure that their novice partners understand and intend to implement the feedback.

Experts produce longer turns, and more turns, than do any other roles. In the excerpt below, Zelda is giving Ivana feedback on her summary-response paper about the class book. In the paper, Ivana has cited a theory of cultural adjustment that relates to immigrants, and Zelda is questioning whether Ivana needs to make a more explicit connection between the theory and the refugee boys in the book:

Text Sample 12.15 Longer Turns from Experts

Zelda: We are talking right now only about immigrants. Do you want to talk about boys too? How it is connected to them? You can tell it's …

Ivana: Oh, actually I thought since the boys are immigrants? So talking about immigrants, it's in, in general. But now I think maybe is confusing.

Zelda: So you mean it's including these boys, right?

Ivana: Yeah.

Zelda: So yeah, I can see that. But you may want to, yeah, because you are, um, summarizing this whole part about the whole immigration, you want to say that the refugee boys are same as immigrants.

Ivana: Yeah?

Zelda: So if you want to you can include it.

Ivana: Mhm.

Zelda: It's up to you.

Ivana: But why would I … just to make it more connected to the *Outcasts United*? Do you mean like add some sentence?

Zelda: Yeah if you want to, [but

Ivana: but I don't have to].

Zelda: You don't have to, but I think would be good to say more about the connection. Because it is so good, this theory.
Ivana: Mhm. I see now, just a little more direct the connection.
Zelda: Do you think so? Right?
Ivana: Yeah. Okay, okay.
(Zelda and Ivana, Peer Response Session One, February 2013)

Like collaborative readers, experts take time to make sure that their novice partners understand and agree with their suggestions. Rather than wait for Ivana to ask for feedback on areas of her paper, like collaborative writers do, Zelda took control of the task and pointed out an area of the paper that they should discuss. She does so skillfully, asking clarifying questions before making a recommendation, and making sure that Ivana understands her suggestion while ultimately respecting Ivana's ownership over her own paper.

While the number of comments that readers give aligns with the concept of equality in patterns of interaction, the percentage of comments that writers use in their revisions seems related to mutuality. In patterns with higher mutuality, collaborative and expert/novice, writers use more comments in their revisions than in other patterns. Collaborative and novice writers implement 76.5% and 85.1% of the comments they receive, while dominant and passive writers use only 20% and 64.6%, respectively.

An analysis of all stimulated recall transcripts from collaborative writers helps explain why these writers are more likely to use feedback when revising than dominant or passive writers: students in collaborative patterns attend not only to the task but also to their relationship. In Ivana's second stimulated recall interview, she reflected on her personal relationship with Zelda and how it may be associated with her receptivity to Zelda's feedback:

Text Sample 12.16 Receptivity to Feedback

> It was very effective. First, it's, um, like, difference a lot from, for example what was in the last semester when I was peer reviewing. Uh, I trust Zelda, and we have a connection, like, uh, I like her, like, like a friend ... so that's why I accept ideas from her, and I can adequately react to critique from her

… I like our process of working, so I really try to make her paper better, and she tries to make my paper better. (Ivana, Stimulated Recall Interview Two, March 2013)

Novice writers, the group that incorporated the highest amount of feedback (85.1%) also revealed a unique motivation for doing so. The theme that emerged from these interviews is that novice writers view their partners as being better at writing. For this reason, they assume that the feedback they are receiving is sound, and they are likely to implement it during revisions. In our second stimulated recall interview, Alex was asked why he chose to use Dan's suggestion that he expand the second paragraph of his summary response paper. He said the following:

Text Sample 12.17 Stimulated Recall: Alex

Um, I think because he come here, like really long time, I mean his grammar, I mean his English is better than me, so he can advise me more better than what I thought, and he knew much more than me, so I just respect his opinion … yeah, um, because he comes here like I think seven years or six years. (Alex, Stimulated Recall Interview Two, March 2013)

Alex seems to trust Dan's opinions of his writing more than he trusts his own, and it appears that his assessment of Dan's English proficiency influenced his decisions to be receptive to his feedback.

Relative to other roles, dominant writers use roughly a third of the amount of comments that collaborative and novice writers do; they incorporate only 20% of the comments that they receive during peer response. As discussed earlier, dominant writers also receive fewer comments than other patterns. Because their priority sometimes seems to be gaining control over the direction of the task, dominant writers may miss opportunities to ask clarifying questions that could leave them with clearer suggestions. Dominant readers in this pattern also may not be taking the time to thoroughly explain their comments because they are distracted by arguing.

Passive writers spoke about not understanding the comments they received in peer response sessions. In a stimulated recall interview, JeeHae revealed that while she was receptive to her partner's suggestions, she did not understand them. HaeSun says, "And I think you'll be very good if you put some examples of same sex guy." She stopped the recording to reflect on this episode, revealing the following:

Text Sample 12.18 Stimulated Recall: JeeHae

JeeHae:	She's trying to help me out with it, by using examples like how their struggles in the real life. Yeah, I think that's what she's talking about.
Interviewer:	But you're not sure?
JeeHae:	No, now I don't know. But I haven't found any articles on the same sex couple. Maybe on their struggles in the real life.
Interviewer:	Yeah, in your second draft I don't see that. So did you, did you think about other ways to add detail here?
JeeHae:	I found some of them but I don't think that goes with my paper. Some that is credible. And other ways, I don't know what is those ways.
	(JeeHae, Stimulated Recall Interview Three, April 2013)

JeeHae thinks that her partner suggested that she find articles on "their [same sex males'] struggles in the real life." Interestingly, it does not seem like JeeHae considered finding another way to expand the paragraph in question, because, she says, "I don't know what is those ways." This episode illustrates that, like dominant writers, passive ones may be at a disadvantage when implementing comments. Their lower rate of implementation of comments relative to the two patterns with high mutuality (collaborative and novice) suggests that the lack of engagement that is characteristic of the dominant/passive pattern may leave writers with comments that they do not understand.

In summary, readers in patterns with low equality, dominant/passive and expert/novice, give more comments than do readers in the other two patterns. When examining the amount of feedback that writers use in their second drafts, on the other hand, groups seem to align along the dimension of mutuality. Novice and collaborative writers, who are situated in patterns with relatively high mutuality, use more of their partners' feedback during revisions, relative to dominant and passive writers. This advantage for writers in high mutuality patterns may mean that students benefit from the engagement that happens there. The majority of other studies that have measured the amount of feedback that writers use after peer response sessions have reported that they use between half and three quarters of the feedback they receive (Nelson and Murphy 1993; Mendonca and Johnson 1994; Tang and Tithecott 1999; Tsui and Ng 2000; Liu and Sadler 2003; Zhao 2010). In this study, students in the collaborative and passive patterns used 76.5% and 64.6%, respectively. This amount of feedback use puts them in line with students in the studies mentioned above. Novice writers, who used 85.1% of the feedback they received, have a higher percentage of feedback use than has been previously reported. Dominant writers, who used only 20% of the feedback received, are below the average rate of use in most other peer response studies.

While measuring the amount of comments that students include in second drafts is helpful for understanding what they do with reader suggestions during revision, these figures do not paint a full picture of revision outcomes. This is true in part because comments that students implement may not necessarily improve their papers, and because students whose first drafts are relatively strong may not implement as many comments as other students, but may still experience gains in score. In this study, first and second drafts were scored out of 20 points with an analytic rubric, and gain in score was calculated. Table 12.5 displays the results of this analysis.

All patterns of interaction showed a score increase from first to second drafts, which is encouraging for peer response. Looking at point gains by pattern of interaction, however, shows that some writers fared better than others: collaborative writers improved more (1.9 point gain) than dominant (0.9 point gain) and passive (1.4 point gain) writers. Novice writers gained the most points from first to second draft, with a 2.9 point gain, which is roughly three times the gain of dominant writers, and roughly twice the gain of passive ones.

Because writers started with a range of first draft scores, it also helpful to examine percent gain from first to second draft. Doing so yields a slightly different order of improvement than looking at average point gain. Passive writers have a slightly higher percent gain (13.5) than do col-

Table 12.5 Mean score gains from first to second draft, by writer role

Writer role	Draft one	Draft two	Point gain	Percent gain
Collaborative (10)				
Mean	14.5	16.4	1.9	13.1
SD	0.7	1.9	1.7	
Dominant (4)				
Mean	11.7	12.6	0.9	7.7
SD	1.6	1.4	0.6	
Passive (5)				
Mean	10.4	11.8	1.4	13.5
SD	1.6	1.8	0.7	
Novice (7)				
Mean	12.8	15.7	2.9	22.7
SD	2.3	0.6	2.2	

laborative writers (13.1), because the former started with the lowest average score for draft one (10.4 points), while collaborative writers started with the highest (14.5 points). Finally, and also encouragingly, percent gains in score by writer role align almost exactly with the amount of comments these students used in their second drafts: novice writers improved the most, followed by passive, collaborative, and dominant writers.

The amount of comments offered and used, as well as gains in score from first to second draft, when taken together, show that some patterns of interaction do lead to better revision outcomes than others. If we consider average point gains and average second draft scores alone, collaborative writers are the strongest. It should be considered, though, that the collaborative group also had the highest average scores on the first draft of their papers. It might be true, then, that highly proficient students are more likely to adopt a collaborative role than are other students. These students' better writing ability might also partially explain their lower rates of uptake of comments compared to novice writers. Because their drafts are already strong, they are able to be more discerning in the feedback from their peers that they decide to use. For novice writers, there is a clearer picture of improvement from first to second drafts. These students show the highest percent gain in score, as well as out-performing other writers according to percent uptake of comments. Writers who assume this position benefit from the relatively high amount of comments they receive from their expert readers. Perhaps because they see themselves as less proficient than their partners, they implement a large number of their comments, use them to make more revisions, and improve the most from first to second drafts. Dominant writers (in the dominant/dominant pattern), on the other hand, perform poorly on all indices, relative to their classmates.

It should be noted that patterns of interaction is not the only factor that influences how students choose to implement the comments they receive; proficiency might also be an important variable to consider in peer response. It is impossible to know, for example, if collaborative writers experienced good revision outcomes because of the social relationship they developed, or because they were already more proficient writers relative to their classmates. By and large, however, it does appear that the collaborative and expert/novice patterns are associated with better revision outcomes than the other two patterns.

13

Linguistic Features of Collaboration in Peer Response: Modal Verbs as Stance Markers

Chapters 11 and 12 have demonstrated the need for a corpus-based approach to further understand spoken learner-learner (peer response) interactions, and described one way of addressing this need: the L2PR corpus. We have also explored the results of a qualitative analysis of social dynamics in the corpus, and considered the relationship between these dynamics and learning outcomes. In sum, our analysis in Chap. 12 found that pairs who assume a collaborative or expert-novice stance, as opposed to a dominant-dominant or dominant-passive one (Storch 2002), experience better revision outcomes after peer response sessions. In the current chapter, we analyze one feature of learner stance in two sub-sections of the corpus: collaborative talk and non-collaborative talk. Comparing frequencies in the use of modal verbs across the two sub-corpora, we explore how the two groups of learners use these devices to deliver and respond to feedback during peer response sessions.

E. Friginal et al., *Exploring Spoken English Learner Language Using Corpora*,
DOI 10.1007/978-3-319-59900-7_13

Describing and Researching Modal Verbs as Stance Markers

Expression of stance (see also Part II), or the personal feelings, attitudes, value judgments, and assessments of a speaker (Biber et al. 1999), plays a central role in all academic registers. To emphasize, while analysis of stance in academic language is prevalent, most research studies have focused on academic writing contexts. Classroom talk, primarily instructor lectures or teacher-student interactions, has also been examined. Less is known, however, about how learners express stance when working together in language classrooms. In peer response, a common writing classroom task where students review each other's drafts and offer feedback that is later used in revisions (Ferris 2003), thoughtful expression and interpretation of stance is crucial. Qualitative research in L2 writing suggests that students who approach problems jointly and respect writer autonomy experience rich learning opportunities from peer response (Zhu and Mitchell 2012). However, to our knowledge, no studies have yet employed corpus analysis to examine the linguistic features of this type of collaboration.

Stance can be understood as expressions of speakers' or writers' thoughts and feelings toward information, their understanding of its veracity, how they accessed it, and the perspective they are taking toward it (Biber 2006b). While stance can be expressed paralinguistically (e.g., using intonation), non-linguistically (e.g., using body position), or with lexical items like evaluative adjectives, academic language often marks stance grammatically, using function words like modal verbs. To date, the focus of many linguistic explorations of academic stance has been that it is important for academic writers and for the spoken language of instruction, because stance markers can suggest how readers and listeners should interpret this information (Biber 2006b).

Many studies of stance marking in spoken academic language have focused on the use of these devices by instructors during lectures and in other classroom settings (see Chaps. 4, 5, and 6 for a review of instructor use of stance in spoken academic language). Relatively fewer studies have examined learner use of stance markers in the spoken mode, but exceptions include investigations of stance in an ELF context and comparisons of learner to native speaker use of stance markers. Kecskés (2007), examining an ELF corpus, found stance markers to be scarce in learner talk, because talk was more focused on reaching communicative goals to complete tasks than they were on attending to the generation of shared knowledge. While one study confirmed this underuse of modals by comparing Japanese EFL learners to native speakers (Shirato and Stapleton 2007), another found that Chinese EFL students used more modal verbs when making suggestions than a comparison group of native English speakers in MICASE (Gu 2014).

As we previously mentioned in Chap. 3, a notable exception to the lack of corpus-based studies on stance in spoken learner-learner interaction is O'Boyle's work using the English Language Learner Classroom Task Talk (ELLTTALK) Corpus (2010), which is composed of learners' spoken interactions during collaborative tasks in a university setting. Comparing this corpus to a reference corpus of learner-tutor talk, O'Boyle found that while learners often used the pronouns *you* and *I* in clusters due to hesitations and false starts under the demands of speaking in real time, tutors used the same pronouns less frequently and more skillfully to build common ground with their tutees (2014). While this study did not examine modal verbs in particular, O'Boyle notes that personal pronouns are "little words [that] do a great deal" (p. 40) of stance marking in spoken language.

Overall, these studies suggest that when they are speaking, learners may underuse different types of stance markers, overuse them, or use them in unexpected ways compared to native speakers. In particular, while modals are by far the most frequent spoken stance markers identified in Biber's (2006b) large-scale analysis of university language, they have primarily been understood and researched as devices for instructors to accomplish directive purposes. Because stance markers are also critical for establishing and maintaining relationships in spoken learner-learner discourse, however, it is worthwhile to further examine their use in learner corpora, and to consider the learning outcomes associated with their use.

Analytical Procedure

As previously described, the L2PR Corpus (Roberson 2015) is composed of transcripts of learner-learner talk as they complete a peer response task in a second language composition course at a large urban university in the USA. Transcripts come from five pairs of students with a range of gender, home country, and first language backgrounds. Each pair completed three peer response sessions, discussing two papers at each session (with two sessions missed due to absence from the class). Supporting data include stimulated recall interviews after the task, which will occasionally be referenced in this chapter, although they are not included in the corpus.

To examine whether learners who work collaboratively use modals in different ways than their less collaborative counterparts, we divided the L2PR Corpus into two sub-corpora: collaborative talk (L2PR_C) and non-collaborative talk (L2PR_NC). The collaborative talk sub-corpus is comprised of transcripts that were coded as either the collaborative or expert-novice pattern, and the non-collaborative sub-corpus is comprised of transcripts coded as either dominant-dominant or dominant-passive patterns (as described in Chap. 12, based on Storch 2002). It should be noted that transcripts were coded qualitatively, following Storch's dimensions of mutuality (the degree to which students engage each other's ideas) and equality (the degree to which they share control over the direction of the task). That is, learner use of modal verbs was not an explicit focus during transcript coding. Table 13.1 shows the composition of the sub-corpora.

While these sub-corpora are relatively small compared to other collections of classroom talk, working with such specialized corpora allows for both quantitative comparisons of frequencies and detailed qualitative analyses of concordance lines (O'Boyle 2014). Unlike other spoken academic corpora, the L2PR_C and L2PR_NC are composed of talk from a single task in a single classroom. An understanding of the unique context in which patterns of modal verb use are embedded, therefore, can enrich the interpretation of their communicative purpose.

To examine the use of modal verbs in the two sub-corpora, each one was searched for instances of all 14 modals and semi-modals listed in

Table 13.1 Sub-corpora of the L2PR corpus (Roberson 2015)

Sub-corpus	Number of texts	Number of tokens
L2PR_C	17	12,587
L2PR_NC	9	8376

Biber's (2006a) *University Language* book: *can, could, may, might, must, should, (had) better, have to, got to, ought to, will, would, shall,* and *be going to*. Contacted forms with pronouns (e.g., *I'll, you'll*) and negatives (e.g., *can't, won't*) were also searched. Concordance lines with these modals were manually examined to ensure that each occurrence was used as a modal verb instead of as a different lexical class (i.e., *can* as a noun), but very few instances were eliminated. Modals that were not used to complete the task of peer response were also eliminated. For instance, one group veered away from giving feedback to discuss the topic of a paper, which was salaries for professional athletes: *you've got Ronaldo and Messi on the same team. They* ***will*** *lose*. This non-task use of modals was also very infrequent. Frequencies of all instances of these modals in both sub-corpora were then calculated, grouping them by type (possibility/permission/ability; necessity/obligation; and prediction/volition), and norming frequencies per 10,000 words to ensure comparability across the slightly different sized corpora. This frequency distribution provides an overall picture of the use of different types of modals.

Next, we take a deeper look at the context of the most frequently occurring modals within each class. In order to be included in this analysis, a modal needed to occur at least 20 times in one of the sub-corpora. This cut-off number generated a list of six modals: *can, could, should, have to, will* and *would*. Concordance lines of these six modals were then qualitatively analyzed for patterns in meaning, with special attention given to the tone readers used to deliver feedback, and to the position writers adopted when they acknowledged the feedback and indicated how they might use it to revise. This process of both quantitative and qualitative corpus analysis allowed for a thorough understanding of the differences in frequency and use of modals across the two sub-corpora (Conrad 2002).

Results and Discussion

Table 13.2 shows frequencies for the modals that occurred in L2PR_C and L2PR_NC. Six of the 14 from Biber (2006a) are not present in either sub-corpus: *may, (had) better, got to, ought to, shall,* and *be going to*; there are thus no frequencies displayed for these modals.

Table 13.2 Distribution of modals by class, raw/normed per 10,000 words

Modals by class	L2PR_C	L2PR_NC
can	80/63.6	33/39.4
could	28/22.2	8/9.6
might	1/0.8	5/6
Total: possibility/permission/ability	109/86.6	46/54.9
must	0/0	1/1.2
should	62/43.9	25/29.8
have to	27/21.5	12/14.3
Total: necessity/obligation	89/70.7	38/45.4
will	37/29.4	3/3.6
would	22/17.5	1/1.2
Total: prediction/volition	59/46.9	4/4.8
Total: all modals	257/204.2	88/105.1

Overall, modals occur roughly twice as much in the collaborative sub-corpus when normed frequencies are compared. The eight modals that occur represent all three classes of modals, but the distribution of individual modals within classes varies across the sub-corpora. Patterns of distribution by class, however, were the same in both sub-corpora. Modals of possibility, permission, or ability were the most frequent, followed by modals of necessity or obligation. As a class, modals of prediction or volition were the least frequent.

This pattern of modal class distribution differs from Biber's (2006a) corpus of university language (T2K-SWAL Corpus), where prediction/volition modals are most common in spoken registers (classroom teaching, class management, labs, office hours, study groups, and service encounters). In the T2K-SWAL Corpus, modals of prediction like *will* are commonly used during class management to announce future actions or events. The distinct distribution of modal classes in the L2PR Corpus may reflect that student talk about peer response is generally more focused on the present conversation, and it does not entail future orientation in the same way that instructor class management speech does.

Table 13.3 shows the six frequently occurring modals that were selected for further contextual analysis. To be included in this analysis, a modal had to occur at least 20 times (raw frequency) in at least one of the sub corpora.

Table 13.3 Distribution of frequent modals (raw/normed per 10,000 words)

Modal	L2PR_C	Rank	L2PR_NC	Rank
can	80/63.6	1	33/39.4	1
could	28/22.2	4	8/9.6	4
should	62/49.3	2	25/29.8	2
have to	27/21.5	5	12/14.3	3
will	37/29.4	3	3/3.6	5
would	22/17.5	6	1/1.2	6
All frequent modals	256/203.4		82/97.9	

Overall, the selected modals were relatively frequent. In fact, *can*, which occurs 80 times in the collaborative sub-corpus, ranks number 31 on a frequency list of all word types in the sub-corpus. The six selected modals in L2PR_C and L2PR_NC also have a similar rank order, with *can* occurring most frequently, *should* being the second most frequent, and *would* being the least frequent of all. Modals overall, however, were almost twice as frequent in the collaborative sub-corpus as in the non-collaborative one. We now further explore the use of frequent modals, discussing how each modal appears in collaborative and non-collaborative talk, to attempt to understand why and how students are using them during peer response. Throughout this section, we refer to utterances made by readers (who are giving feedback) and writers (who are receiving or requesting it), because these roles seem to influence the way students mark stance during the task.

We begin this contextual exploration with the most frequently occurring modal in both L2PR_C and L2PR_NC, *can*. One feature of the collaborative pattern in this corpus is that writers often use modals of ability to ask their readers for feedback on segments of their papers, rather than place this responsibility on their readers:

Text Samples 13.1 (1–15) Occurrences of *can*

(1) <u>**Can**</u> you understand what I mean here?
(2) <u>**Can**</u> you see the reasons why I said no?

The examples above come from a writer who is asking for global feedback on areas of his paper, and the ensuing conversation is about the general clarity of ideas. Writers also use this modal in the sense of possibility, to ask their readers for more specific advice on sentence-level elements of their papers:

(3) **Can** I ask you a question? Should I move this [thesis statement] to here?
(4) **Can** you just give me a suggestion, because that sentence always confused .... I don't know how to make it.

A feature of the expert/novice pattern (which is included in the L2PR_C) is that expert readers often ensure that they understand their novice partner's intent before offering suggestions, as in:

(5) And I don't, uh, **can** you explain to me what that means, [reading from paper] *that they so skinny, they turn sideways they disappear*?

In the session where the example above occurred, the reader continued to ask the writer to first explain the idea that she had been trying to express before offering suggestions. This pair spent time arriving at this type of understanding, often using modals of ability to politely ask for clarification of the writer's intent.

Another reason why there may be frequent use of the modal *can* in L2PR_C is that readers use this modal to give suggestions about how the writer might revise (7):

(6) S2: Mhmm. How do you think, what sentences should I take out?
(7) S1: I was thinking that first two sentences are all right, even the third one. You **can** cut this one because you already said, like, what is it about.

The effect of using the modal *can* to signal possibility in this example is that the suggestion is softened, and some autonomy about how to revise remains with the writer. This type of attention to the interpersonal relationship is common in the collaborative pattern in this study. In fact, as Chap. 12 discussed, being aware of the writer's feelings and creating a sense of trust is something that collaborative readers pay deliberate attention to. While *can* was also the most frequently occurring modal in the L2PR_NC, it was used for different communicative purposes. Instead of asking for feedback, clarification, or softening suggestions, *can* appeared to express writer autonomy:

(8) S1: When I read this paper, I have a question over this thing. Here. What is the difference between … *donors* and *donators*?
(9) S2: Same thing.
(10) S1: Then why did you use *donator* in this sentence?
(11) S2: Well, it's the same thing so I **can** use … whatever I want.

Here, the writer in a pair that often argued during peer response sessions uses *can* as a modal of ability to assert that he is not going to follow his partner's suggestion. In a tense exchange, another writer also used *can* in this way:

(12) S1: You have to say the other side. It is the other side for persuasive research paper.
(13) S2: There is no support side! Not even China will support now. You think we should to support him?
(14) S1: For the thesis statement of opinion you have to show the both sides. You don't have.
(15) S2: I **can** not have!

In line 12, the reader begins by telling the writer that the opposing view was missing from her thesis statement of opinion, in a paper about North Korea's use of nuclear weapons. The writer seems to have misunderstood this comment as a suggestion that she personally should support further militarization, and ends the segment with a vehement assertion that she does not agree with supporting a dictator, using *can* as a modal of ability.

After *can*, *should* was the most frequently occurring modal in both sub corpora. The main distinction in the use of this modal between L2PR_C and L2PR_NC, though, appears to be that collaborative students use it to ask questions about their own papers, while non-collaborative readers use it to direct writers about how to revise their papers.

In the excerpt below, a collaborative pair discusses whether the writer should add more background information in his revision of a paper about the class book:

Text Samples 13.2 (16–31) Occurrences of *should*

(16) S1: Um, I think it's really good, but I think you need to put more detail about what's going on in the background, the background of the novel. Where they come from ...
(17) S2: Like everybody? I was ... I didn't know if I **should** put all the people.
(18) S1: Yeah, that was hard for my paper too. I think not like everybody, you know, just key people. Like the background of the novel, like what kind of team it is.

In the example below (23), another writer asks her partner questions about his paper, and ponders whether she should follow a similar structure in her own:

(19) S1: So, in your essay, you introduced this whole article first?
(20) S2: Mhmm.
(21) S1: And you, 'cause she said summary, then critique, right?
(22) S2: Mhmm.
(23) S1: So I **should** use my introduction as my critique?
(24) S2: Yeah, I think this paragraph will work as your critique.

While collaborative writers ask for validation about their own ideas for revision by using *should* as a modal of necessity, excerpts from L2PR_NC show that readers in this section of the corpus are more likely to use *should* in an obligatory sense (25 and 30):

(25) S1: You said you want me to focus on main thesis statement and argument but the, here, the thesis statement is kind of clear, but I think it **should** be longer and give a reason.
(26) S2: [Uh huh.
(27) S1: Briefly in the thesis statement]

(28) S2: And, but your supporting point is only focused on the opposing idea.
(29) S1: Mhmm.
(30) S2: Um, you said you are ready to accept, um, same-sex marriage but not, included supporting idea about why he should pass the law, so I think you **should**, um, put something on detail.

The same pair whose excerpt is featured above often adopted this stance, where the reader seems to be giving directives to the writer about revision, without much input from her partner:

(31) I want you to be more detail about it, and focus on, like, what your paper is going to be … I think it **should** be more detail, also more descriptive.

The next frequently occurring modal, *will*, ranked number three in L2PR_C, but number five in L2PR_NC. A look at concordance lines of collaborative pairs reveals that writers in this section of the corpus commonly used *will* to mark future tense when indicating how they plan to revise:

Text Samples 13.3 (32–37) Occurrences of *will*

(32) S1: That racial discrimination is unfair for different reasons but happens in this country? It's not from the book, right?
(33) S2: Yeah, but I think it was, uh … I **will** put in the last [paragraph
(34) S1: Yeah] maybe in another paragraph. But it's not wrong. It's just not summary is what I'm saying.

Another writer in L2PR_C used *will* repeatedly over a long turn, as she essentially thought out loud about her revision plans. She also uses the semi-modal *be going to* [*gonna*]:

(35) Uh, somehow, I **will** put these sentences … I **will** focus on this sentence and I **will** make it more relevant, to uh, like, critique part. **I'm gonna** focus on this information.

Readers in L2PR_C also used will in a predictive sense to encourage writers about positive revision outcomes:

(36) Just to make clear and you agree, you disagree, or what. And it **will** be, it **will** be a very good thesis statement.
(37) Switch this here, just this one, and it **will** be nice.

As for L2PR_NC, it is possible that *will* does not appear nearly as frequently (only three times) because writers are not engaged in the same kind of thinking out loud about what they will do with feedback during revisions. As we discussed in Chap. 12, writers in this pattern tend to be argumentative about the feedback they receive, or speak very little relative to their readers. This relative lack of modals of prediction may underscore the lack of opportunities for non-collaborative writers to benefit from the feedback they receive.

The next frequently occurring modal, *could*, was ranked number four in L2PR_C and in L2PR_NC. Collaborative pairs used this modal to express both possibility and ability:

Text Samples 13.4 (38–46) Occurrences of *could*

(38) S1: Do you want to, like, restructure the sentence? Like you **could** [structure
(39) S2: **Could**] you ....
(40) S1: Oh, write it down?
(41) S2: Yeah, ah, can you just give me a suggestion, because that sentence always confused .... I don't know how to make it.
(42) S1: Yeah, you **could** say, like, *the Fugees have a connection between each other*. Yeah, that'd be better. Is that what you want to say?

In the excerpt above, the reader (S1) uses *could* to describe the types of revision that the reader might choose to make, while the writer (S2) uses it to ask for additional support in restructuring a sentence. Other instances of *could* in L2PR_C function as counterfactuals, like the excerpt below where a writer uses his own paper as a model:

(43) S1: I **could** have just said *in today's societies most people go to college after high school*, but, you know, I said it in a different way to, like, unusual way, to, like
(44) S2: I got you. Catch the attentions.
(45) S1: So you **could** do something like that.

In the first instance of *could* in the example above (43), the writer uses a counterfactual statement to illustrate an alternative (and in the writer's mind, less catchy) way to phrase one of the sentences in his own paper. He then suggests, using *could* as a modal of possibility, that his partner similarly change the wording of his sentences during revision.

In L2PR_NC, *could* appears only eight times, so it is difficult to draw conclusions about trends in the way it is used. The example below, however, shows that readers use *could* to tell writers how to revise. The way that *could* is used seems similar to the way it appears in L2PR_C:

(46) Yeah, I think you **could** take this part out. And I think you **could** fix this.

While *could* did not occur frequently in L2PR_NC, the semi modal *have to* ranks third in the list of six modals selected for qualitative analysis. In the excerpt below, *have to* is used to express obligation as well as to reject it:

Text Samples 13.5 (47–60) Occurrences of *have to*

(47) S1: Where's the statistic of it?
(48) S2: Well, I didn't put it, though. That's not the point. So, next.
(49) S1: Well, how do I know it's true or not?
(50) S2: Well, whether you believe it or not, it's true. Okay, move on.
(51) S1: No you must, you **have to** convince me. Or, like, try to make me trust you,
or ....
(52) S2: Well, that's not the point, so I don't **have to**.
(53) S1: You totally **have to**.

As this excerpt shows, readers in this section of the corpus use *have to* in order to express obligations to the writers, who repeat the semi-modal with negative particles to express their unwillingness to do so. It should be noted here that *have to* occurs a total of 12 times in L2PR_NC. There were fewer modals overall used in this section of the corpus, so we should exercise caution when generalizing about trends and patterns of use. Because *have to* can be used as a modal of necessity or obligation, we might assume that it would occur less frequently in L2PR_C, where students are generally more careful about the way that they deliver feedback. Interestingly, though, this semi-modal occurs nearly twice as much in L2PR-C as in L2PR_NC, when relative frequencies are compared. A look into the concordance lines shows that *have to* is often used by readers in a negative sense, to express that writers are not obligated to follow their suggestions:

(54) S1: Do you mean, like, add some sentence?
(55) S2: Yeah, if you want to, [but
(56) S1: but I don't **have to**].
(57) S2: You don't **have to**, but I think it would be good to say more about the connection. Because it is so good, this theory.

In the excerpt above, the writer (S1) fills in the reader's thought by supplying *have to*, which the reader confirms. Readers also use *have to* negatively after suggesting specific revisions:

(58) S1: Can I say *as time goes by … goes along* or something?
(59) S2: *As time goes by*, yeah you can say that. *As time goes by, the Fugees has*
become a good team. You don't **have to** use this, you can …
(60) S1: Yeah, it's like you know, to be a good team, the teamwork is very important, yeah that's what I meant.

In this way, the force of suggestions is softened. The reader in the segment above is offering language that the writer might include in revisions. He appears to be mindful that ultimately, doing so will be the writer's decision.

The final modal that we consider in this qualitative analysis is *would*. Because this modal only occurred once in L2PR_NC, it will not be considered for that segment of the corpus. In L2PR_C, *would* was the least frequent modal selected for further analysis, but it still occurred almost as much as the second most frequent modal in L2PR_NC. Interestingly, when readers in L2PR_C use *would*, they often do so with the first person pronoun *I*:

Text Samples 13.6 (61–63) Occurrences of *would*

(61) The only thing I **would** change is, I **would** make it clear where the critique part starts.
(62) And I **would** probably even in conclusion when you say *where there is a smoke there is a fire*, I **would** say something about your personal experience.

We can infer from the examples above that the reader is putting herself in the shoes of the writer, essentially saying if *I were you, I would do this*. The effect of this conditional aspect is that there is some solidarity and common ground established between reader and writer.

Similar to the way that they use *will*, collaborative readers also rely on the counterfactual force of *would* to express how a writer's paper might improve during revisions:

(63) If you use a higher vocabulary, that **would** make the entire paper really good.

As Biber (2006a) notes, this use of *would* has a polite tone, so it stands to reason that collaborative readers, who attend more overtly to the social dynamics of peer response, make use of this device to soften their feedback.

Summary of Findings

In sum, we have seen that collaborative readers and writers make more use of modals as stance markers, and they do so in a variety of ways. Often the effect of modal use in L2PR_C is to lessen the intensity of suggestions, or to create a polite tone. They do this by using modals of possibility like *could* and *can*, and modals of obligation like *have to* with negative particles. Using modals in this way grants autonomy to the writer and removes any obligation to revise in a certain way. Collaborative readers also use modals of prediction to encourage writers about the revision process. Finally, they use hypothetical counterfactuals to put themselves in the shoes of writers, establishing a sense of shared experience.

Non-collaborative readers and writers use nearly half the amount of modals that collaborative ones do. Modals of ability like *can* are used in a distinct way, to express that the writer does not plan to follow the reader's advice. In addition, modals of necessity and obligation (*should, have to*) rank higher in L2PR-NC than in L2PR_C. They are used by readers to make more firm, direct suggestions to writers about how they should revise, as well as by writers with a negative particle to affirm their autonomy (e.g., *I don't have to*). In sum, non-collaborative students are not taking advantage of the full range of modality in the way that collaborative ones appear to be.

Perhaps most interestingly, these trends in use of modals parallel almost all of the research that has been done on instructor and student spoken stance marking in an academic setting. With very few exceptions, investigations of learner use of modals have found that these devices are used less frequently or in less effective ways compared to native speakers, or compared to instructors (e.g., Shirato and Stapleton 2007; Gu 2014). In fact, our exploration of hedges and boosters in classroom discourse (Chap. 4) found that overall, instructors make more frequent use of these devices. In the L2PR corpus, it is collaborative students who seem to parallel instructor or native speaker use, while non-collaborative ones appear to be using modals in a way that matches studies of learner talk. Because collaborative students are more successful at delivering and receiving feedback, their use of stance may match that of instructor discourse: the reader is scaffolding the writer's understanding and encouraging the writer to make positive changes during revision.

Part V

Conclusion and Future Directions

14

Corpus-Based Studies of Learner Talk: Conclusion and Future Directions

This book explored learner oral production in university-level ESL (and specifically, EAP) classrooms in the USA from a corpus-based approach, utilizing specialized corpora of learner talk. We described and interpreted the structure of learner (and teacher) spoken language in the classroom, language experience interviews, and peer response/feedback activities. Our discussions also focused on ideas related to corpus design and development, implications for SLA, semantic content analysis, and some methodological limitations of current research. A summary of our concluding remarks, suggestions for pedagogy and practice, and future research directions is presented below.

Conclusion

Learner (and Teacher) Talk in the Classroom

Part II (Chap. 4) explored the ways in which EAP learners and teachers mark their stance toward propositional content and each other, specifically focusing on hedges and boosters. The results indicate that the dis-

E. Friginal et al., *Exploring Spoken English Learner Language Using Corpora*,
DOI 10.1007/978-3-319-59900-7_14

tribution of these interpersonal resources in learner and teacher discourse differ in significant ways. Combined with their greater use of hedges and relatively fewer boosters, teachers seem to more effectively balance caution and certainty than learners. Learners, in contrast, appear to be more committed to the statements they make. They also seem to lack the range of possible linguistic options available for expressing uncertainty and certainty. However, among the top five hedges and boosters found in both sub-corpora, the specific linguistic realizations of these interpersonal resources in learners' and teachers' discourse are strikingly similar. There may be a few possible reasons for this similarity. One possibility is that language learners are using linguistic resources similar to that used by their teachers due to their frequency and saliency. If language emerges from interactions between people, then it seems reasonable to suggest that learners imitate the discourse practices of their teachers to a certain degree, or as far as their linguistic abilities allow. It is also possible that these hedges and boosters are simply those that are most widely used in spoken discourse in general and classroom discourse in particular. As learners are still in the process of developing their linguistic and communicative abilities, however, it is more likely that they lack the range of vocabulary to express certainty or lack thereof. In order to help learners develop their linguistic repertoires, we suggest that teachers need to use and emphasize other hedging and boosting devices to a greater degree in order for learners to notice them and use them appropriately in the classroom. Doing so, we argue, might enhance students' linguistic repertories to mark their stance and to engage in more sophisticated interactions in the classroom.

In Chap. 5, we explored the use of personal pronouns in learner and teacher talk. As our comparative analysis shows, both learners and teachers use *I* and *you* far more frequently than *we*, suggesting that EAP classrooms are highly involved, interpersonal, and interactive communicative sites. The analysis also reveals the varying ways in which learners and teachers use these pronouns to position each other in the conversational space. When they use *we*, teachers tend to include the learners in the dialogue to establish rapport and signal to learners that the classroom lesson is a jointly accomplished endeavor (Lee 2016); however, learners prefer to exclude the teachers in their use of *we*. Teachers also use *you* to refer to the students directly in their efforts to not only involve the learners in the interactive classroom experience but also to provide students with explicit instructions on carrying out pedagogic tasks. Even though learners clearly favor the audience-*you*, especially in seeking assistance from teachers, they use the generalized-*you* significantly more frequently than teachers, mostly when demonstrating their understanding or knowledge of content and language matters. While teachers use *you* and *we* more frequently to increase learner involvement, engagement, and participation, learners use more *I*, thus locating themselves at the center of the conversational space. Supporting O'Boyle (2014), our findings suggest that learners make fewer attempts at "connect[ing] with the informational space of others" (p. 54), in this case the teacher. Additionally, like O'Boyle, we suggest that teachers need to raise students' awareness of their use of personal pronouns so that they not only express their ideas more proficiently but also focus on establishing and maintaining greater interpersonal and intersubjective relations and shared experiences in the classroom in preparation for university classes in which such features are considered crucial.

In Chap. 6, we examined the ways in which learners and teachers use spatial deixis to conceptualize classroom space. Supporting previous findings that demonstratives are the primary spatial deictics used in face-to-face interactions (e.g., Biber et al. 1999), we found that *that* was the most common demonstrative used by EAP teachers. However, our findings also deviate from previous studies. Even though *that* was the most common spatial deictic in teacher talk, *this* was also greatly utilized by EAP teachers. Furthermore, unlike O'Boyle (2014), *this* was the most frequent demonstrative used in the learner sub-corpora. Also diverging from previous studies, *here* was the preferred locative adverb in both learner and teacher talk. Similar to Bamford (2004), we propose that these differences lie in the fact that classroom lessons and interactional patterns in language classrooms differ from those of other types of registers and genres since the purpose, content, participants, and context of L2 classrooms are dissimilar to other communicative situations.

Our findings also suggest that learners and teachers conceptualize the perceived space of the classroom in different ways. Learners seem to use spatial deictics to contract the classroom space by positioning objects and class participants within their speaker territory. Comparable to their use of personal pronouns in Chap. 5, learners appear to primarily focus on their own individual informational space. On the other hand, teachers attempt to expand and connect with the informational space of learners by shifting the focal referent proximally to and distally from their territory in their effort to create a more inclusive classroom climate. We propose that EAP teachers need to provide classroom instruction that encourages EAP learners to expand their informational space to connect with that of others, as such an association is considered to be vital in university classroom interaction. We argue that doing this would assist learners in developing their abilities to engage in more dynamic interpersonal interactions in the "locally relevant features of the [classroom] environment" (Sidnell and Enfield 2016, p. 218).

Learner Talk in Language Experience Interviews

In Chaps. 8, 9, and 10 (Part III), we conducted three analyses on the detailed interview texts of the L2 Experience Interview Corpus, resulting in three related but different views of the L2 learning experience. We now consider what these three studies together can tell us about the L2 learning experience.

The first two studies examined the corpus horizontally to identify themes or dimensions of L2 learning that are experienced by most learners. In Chap. 8, we saw the three salient themes of Classroom, Communicating, and Studying. In Chap. 9, we found four psycho-social dimensions of L2 learning, which we named Positive-Learning, Negative-Anxious, Social-Participatory, and Education. The third study shifted into an analysis of individual learners, resulting in three clusters of learners: Narrative, Cognitive, and Affective. We can, therefore, modify our chart from the section introduction (Chap. 7) to include the findings of each study (see Table 14.1).

The summary of findings for Part III clearly shows a pattern in the outcomes of these studies. Whether we are looking at the L2 experience common to all learners or at differences between learners, the salient themes are quite similar. For example, the biographical details of the

Table 14.1 Summary of analyses and findings of Chaps. 8, 9, and 10

Chapter	Analysis	Conducted with	Performed on	Identifies	Findings
8	Cluster analysis	T-Lab	Keywords	General themes of the L2 learning experience common to all learners	3 themes: Classroom, Communicating, Studying
9	MDA	SPSS	LIWC scores	Psychosocial dimensions of the L2 learning experience common to all learners	4 dimensions: Positive-Learning, Negative-Anxious, Social-Participatory, Education
10	Cluster analysis	SPSS	LIWC scores	Groups of learners who share a similar L2 learning experience	3 clusters: Narrative, Cognitive, Affective

learning process appear in Chap. 8 in the Classroom cluster, in Chap. 9 in the Education dimension, and in Chap. 10 as a Narrative tendency among learners. The Cognitive cluster of Chap. 10 draws on many of the same lemmas as the Studying theme of Chap. 8 and the Positive-Learning theme of Chap. 9, while the Affective cluster of Chap. 10 is similar to Communicating in Chap. 8 and the Negative-Anxious and Social-Participatory dimensions of Chap. 9.

Although it would be redundant and reductive to draw exact equations between clusters and dimensions in the three analyses, this consistency does provide an important triangulation for the semantic content analysis methodology. When approached from different angles and with different analytical techniques, the corpus and methodology yield similar overarching themes. This triangulation also confirms the acceptability of using LIWC to measure psychosocial themes in the L2 Experience

Interview Corpus, since the two studies conducted with LIWC resulted in findings similar to those of T-Lab's content-neutral analysis.

At the same time, the clustering of individual interview texts seemed to occur along the same general themes and clusters found in the corpus as a whole, indicating that learners tended to focus on one of these salient dimensions of experience. While all learners might experience the Classroom, Communicating, and Studying aspects of L2 learning, some appear to focus more on the classroom, some on communicating, and some on studying. These three themes from the T-Lab analysis correspond very closely to the three groups of students identified in the LIWC cluster analysis. We also saw that L2 performance (as measured by self-reported TOEFL scores) seemed significantly related to which theme learners focused on in their interviews. It therefore appears likely that, while most learners experience all three themes in their L2 learning, they might tend to focus more on one than others. This focus, perhaps for reasons explored in Chap. 10, could lead to differential performance results.

The exploratory nature of these studies in Part III means that further research is required to confirm and expand the value of semantic content analysis as a methodology in L2 studies. In particular, several limitations were described that should continue to be investigated in future studies. However, we believe that, paired with the L2 Experience Interview Corpus and other large corpora of learner speech, this content analysis technique can provide important insights into how and why the learning process occurs. By combining the benefits of quantitative and qualitative research at the level of data collection and then introducing new programs for data analysis, we can explore the words that L2 learners themselves use to describe their experience.

Learner Talk in Peer Response Activities

Chapter 11 explored SLA findings on collaborative dialogue in language learning and reviewed peer response studies in the L2 writing tradition. We argue that there is a need for continued systematic analysis of the linguistic and social features of productive talk during peer response. We also suggest that working collaboratively is beneficial for learners, even as

SLA and L2 writing researchers alike have identified gaps in our current knowledge about how students experience collaboration in ecologically valid settings.

Some studies have suggested that training students to participate effectively in peer response leads to the delivery of more helpful comments (see, e.g., Min 2005, 2008). In Part IV of this book, some participants gained valuable insight into their participation in peer response through the stimulated recall interviews. For example, one of our student participants thought that he sounded "mean" on the recording and stated that he would like to change his manner of delivery. Others identified areas where they assessed their participation in peer response as helpful for their partner. Asking students to reflect on their peer response sessions may be a way to achieve the goal of ongoing training for peer response.

In the future, there is a need to continue to investigate the relationship between social interaction and peer response outcomes in more narrow as well as broader ways. From a qualitative research paradigm, more case studies that describe in rich detail the writing classrooms where peer response occurs will allow for fuller understanding of the sociocultural dimension of this practice. This approach, especially when employed in longitudinal studies, has the potential to reveal new insights into areas that seem to have been neglected in peer response research, which attempts to connect social dynamics to revision outcomes. In addition to studies that describe the social dimension of peer response in ways that are context-specific, there is also a need for more quantitative studies that lead to generalization about features of the social dimension of peer response associated with favorable revision outcomes. A corpus-based approach investigating linguistic features such as personal pronouns, stance markers, or hedging devices, for example, could help practitioners and students understand the language of collaboration in writing classrooms.

As with any interpretation of what linguistic patterns mean, we acknowledge that caution is necessary when trying to understand why and how modals are used in L2PR_C and L2PR_NC as presented in Chap. 13. Frequency is just that: a measure of how often different words and phrases occur, and it cannot tell us with certainty why these linguistic features are being used, or what their effect is. This is especially true for the L2PR corpus, which is relatively small and composed of the speech of only 10 learners. Some trends in the qualitative analysis are based on one or two pairs, so it is highly possible that they mark not general ways that learners use modals, but rather are idiosyncratic to a handful of speakers. On the other hand, our deep understanding of the context in which conversations occurred, and the supporting data in the form of stimulated recall interviews, lend credibility to qualitative findings. It would be interesting to see investigations of spoken learner stance marking with larger corpora to see if trends hold.

Chapter 13 identified linguistic features of stance in learner talk that could inform the creation of classroom materials that guide students to deliver and interpret feedback successfully. There is growing evidence in the L2 writing literature that training students to participate effectively in peer response leads to the delivery of more substantive and constructive comments (see, e.g., Min 2005, 2008). Based on these two studies, Min recommends a multi-step peer response training sequence that involves various in-class activities where students are trained to adopt collaborative stances during peer response. In the future, this training in the classroom might involve corpus-based findings like the ones presented in Part IV, to explicitly guide students in using the language of collaboration. Stance markers like modal verbs could be worthwhile structures to focus on. As Chap. 13 presented, modals are central in adopting the stance of a successful reader or writer in a peer response setting.

Future Directions

Multi-modal Annotation of Learner Talk

What is now becoming increasingly popular in corpus-based research is the multi-modal annotation of spoken interactions in various setting such as classrooms and workplaces. Together with enhanced prosodic and acoustic mark-ups of spoken corpora, multi-modal transcripts linking video recordings to non-linguistic features that play a crucial role in communication, such as facial expressions, hand gestures, and body position, can be highlighted and automatically extracted (Friginal and Hardy 2014). These annotations can then be interpreted alongside frequency data and other learner demographic information. We hope to see many of these projects focusing on learner oral production in the future. As briefly discussed in Chap. 2, EUROCAT and other audio/video corpora (e.g., the LeaP Corpus, The LONGDALE Project, YOLECORE, and the Multimedia Adult ESL Learner Corpus) have been developed for the purpose of including video or audio-based information in corpus analyses.

In his March 2017 plenary lecture at the American Association for Applied Linguistics (AAAL) Conference, Suresh Canagarajah of Penn State University emphasized the role of spatiotemporal dimensions of communicative activity to show language as a self-defining grammatical system. He pointed out that developments in mobility, globalization, and technology (including corpus-based technology) have motivated a realization that meanings and grammatical forms are co-constructed in situated interactions, much like the classroom, in an expansive context of social networks, ecological affordances, and material objects. Canagarajah briefly presented data and video clips from the International Teaching Assistants Corpus (ITACorp) collected by his research team and colleagues at Penn State. The ITACorp has video recordings with over 500,000 words of language from a variety of spoken classroom tasks: lectures, office hours, role plays, presentations, discussions from international teaching assistants. His conclusions, in part, focused on important dimensions such as "boardwork" (how an ITA utilized the blackboard in writing mathematical equations), movement, and use of space in the classroom. Students may have immediately noticed the ITA's heavy L2 accent or expressed difficulty in understanding some utterances, but the ITA's effective use of space may have also enhanced the classroom experience for his students. As one student (native speaker of English) pointed out, "some ITAs might talk more fluently, but if the boardwork is poor, it will not work at all." In sum, important non-linguistic data will have to be added to linguistic frequencies in exploring learner language in academic settings.

Canagarajah added that students and teachers are now becoming more sensitive to space as a defining and generative resource in communicative success. "A competence for such success involves one's emplacement in relevant spatiotemporal scales to strategically align with diverse semiotic features beyond language, participate in an assemblage of ecological and material resources, and collaborate in complex social networks." He argued that such a consideration compels us to revise traditional notions about the autonomy of language, separation of labeled languages, primacy of cognition, and agency of individuals. We believe that these are all related to the future of corpus-based approaches that are merged with annotations and evidence from multimedia sources.

Phonetically Transcribed Corpora of Learner Talk

We briefly mentioned in Part I along with other corpus studies of spoken discourse (e.g., Friginal and Hardy 2014; Friginal 2009) that the study of accent and pronunciation is difficult to accomplish with traditional corpus-based methods. This difficulty, however, may already be changing with new transcription and captioning technology, including "notetaking software and equipment" (e.g., a company called Titan has a product called Titan Note launched in late 2017, recording and converting audio to text "accurately" and will "distinguish who is speaking, summarize, translate, share and edit notes"). The annotation of spoken corpora for prosody, for example, with the Hong Kong Corpus of Spoken English (HKCSE) and more detailed contextual transcriptions and annotations of spoken texts continue to influence researchers to pursue more innovative research paradigms, painting a promising future for capturing some socio-phonetic features of speech in orthographic transcripts (Friginal and Hardy 2014). Although not necessarily considered corpora in the traditional sense, available databases of speech that are designed to be analyzed phonetically, phonologically, or acoustically point to a possible framework and model for developing a phonetically annotated corpus.

The *Speech Accent Archive* (http://accent.gmu.edu/) (Weinberger 2013), currently with over 1700 speech samples, is an online database of speakers and speech samples from around the world using crowdsourcing techniques. Speakers can submit their speech patterns and accents digitally as they read aloud a single paragraph:

> *Please call Stella. Ask her to bring these things with her from the store: Six spoons of fresh snow peas, five thick slabs of blue cheese, and maybe a snack for*

> *her brother Bob. We also need a small plastic snake and a big toy frog for the kids. She can scoop these things into three red bags, and we will go meet her Wednesday at the train station.*

This paragraph was designed to elicit many of the possible sounds and sound combinations occurring in English.

The audio samples from the *Speech Accent Archive* are then transcribed (manually, by researchers) phonetically using the International Phonetic Alphabet (IPA), in essence forming a "corpus" of IPA-transcribed texts. Nearing 2000 participants, this project offers views into English variation, both native and non-native, across the world. Although the sample is read and not naturally occurring, the database offers the beginning of what could be possible in phonetically transcribing a corpus. Generalizations (in pronunciation patterns of a speaker), and vowel/syllable structures are provided in various links together with the audio sample. Every speech sample in the archive is annotated for birthplace, native language, other language known, age, age when first learning English, method of English learning (in school or not), and length of time having lived in an English-speaking country (and which country, if that is the case). All of these variables are also searchable on the website. This makes it easy for a teacher, phonetician, speech pathologist, or anyone interested in accents to search for a group of speakers to explore phonetic and phonological processes. Another useful feature of the *Speech Accent Archive* is that its website allows users to search for audio and transcript by categories of phonetic characteristics as they differ from General American English (GAE). Phonetic generalizations for the samples can be searched by vowel, consonantal, and syllabic differences from the GAE.

More Well-Designed, Well-Collected Spoken Learner Corpora

Biber (1993) defines representativeness in corpus design as "the extent to which a sample includes the full range of variability in a population" (p. 243). In more general sense beyond corpus linguistics, representativeness refers to the idea that one can collect a smaller sample than the population as a whole, but that that smaller sample could show as much variability in the subset as in the overall population (Friginal and Hardy 2014). The collection of spoken learner language will have to continue to focus on important design considerations such as representativeness, effective sampling procedures, and register coverage. Because a spoken L2 corpus should sufficiently represent a particular group of learners, designers must be aware of the kinds of questions they would like to answer or think about what others who will use their corpora might ask. Learner-spoken corpora will have to include many sub-registers that directly show L2 language production. Most data, so far, focuses on classroom settings but other contexts (outside of the classroom) will have to be added in future text collections. Learner interview samples, such as those in Part III, LINDSEI interviews, and peer response (in Part IV), are promising areas of focus in current research, but more situational contexts, interview questions, and peer response topics or paired activities will have to be considered and added.

For design consideration, sampling strategies (especially random sampling designs) will have to continue to be effectively operationalized in corpus collection. Related to sampling is the concept of *balance* in corpus design. Not only must we choose our spoken texts using appropriate sampling techniques, corpus researchers also need to think about how sampling of different types of learner oral production could affect the final composition of the corpus. A corpus is said to be balanced if the full range of registers associated with the target population is represented in the sample. One way that balance is achieved is by proportional sampling. That is, sampling that is done relative to the frequency of register use in the population (Friginal and Hardy 2014).

Representativeness is not easily planned and verifiable at the onset of a study. Instead, it is an iterative process that can only begin after data has been collected. While a corpus collector can plan his or her corpus to be balanced and appropriately sampled, there is no way of knowing if that plan will work until the corpus begins to be built. Tagliamonte (2006) describes how ethnographic methods of qualitatively investigating a population can be useful in understanding the population, and getting to know how language is used. This also applies to the collection of L2 speech samples across various settings. Often in corpus-based research, the size of the corpus is described. Some might think "the bigger, the better" when it comes to corpus size. However, corpus creation should consider where the spoken data comes from and not just how much data can be collected. Defining the learner population being focused on and describing how samples will systematically be taken from that group as a whole are, arguably, more important.

Teaching Applications: Publication and Sharing of Results

Finally, teachers need easy access to accurate and effective models of academic speech in order to make curricular decisions, design effective teaching materials, plan lessons, and coach L2 students as they work toward mastery of the spoken genres of the academic world. As emphasized by Simpson-Vlach (2013), the emerging body of research on L2 spoken discourse in academic settings has provided teachers with a wealth of valuable resources for materials production in the classroom. Frequency-based vocabulary and grammar studies, keyword analyses, concordances and collocations from various learner corpora, in addition to more qualitative discourse and pragmatic research findings are very relevant as they inform the linguistic content knowledge of teachers and provide insights into the characteristic features of academic speech that are distinct from academic writing or ordinary conversation.

As discussed in different sections of this book, MICASE, LINDSEI, and T2K-SWAL Corpus studies have included a wide range of pedagogical suggestions for incorporating corpus-based exercises and research findings into classroom teaching. More textbook treatments of these corpora and their resulting datasets directly written for teachers and their L2 students, in addition to an increased number of analyses and experimental studies would be necessary in moving the field forward. We hope that the three analytical sections of this book also provided ideas for teachers in further incorporating corpus-based data and findings in their classrooms.

Appendix A: Transcription Conventions for the L2CD (Adapted from Jefferson 2004; Simpson et al. 2002)

T	Teacher
S1, S2, etc.,	Identified student
SU	Unidentified student
Ss	Several or all students at once
-	Interruption; abruptly cutoff sound
,	Brief mid-utterance pause of less than one second
.	Final falling intonation contour with 1-2 second pause
?	Rising intonation, not necessarily a question
(P: 02)	Measured silence of greater than 2 seconds
x	Unintelligible or incomprehensible speech; each token refers to one word
<LAUGH>	Laughter
( )	Uncertain transcription
{ }	Verbal description of events in the classroom
(( ))	Nonverbal actions
Italics	Non-English words/phrases
/ /	Phonetic transcription; pronunciation affects comprehension
ICE	Capitals indicate names, acronyms, and letters

E. Friginal et al., *Exploring Spoken English Learner Language Using Corpora*,
DOI 10.1007/978-3-319-59900-7

Appendix B: Hedges and Boosters Investigated (Adapted from Hyland 2005, pp. 221–223)

Hedges

Content-oriented: Accuracy-oriented

about, almost, apparent, apparently, approximately, around, bit, broadly, certain amount, certain extent, certain level, could, couldn't, could not, doubt, doubtful, essentially, estimate, estimated, fairly, frequently, generally, guess, in general, in most cases, in most instances, just, kind of/kinda, largely, likely, little, mainly, may, maybe, might, mostly, often, on the whole, perhaps, plausible, plausibly, possible, possibly, presumable, presumably, pretty probable, probably, quite, rather X, relatively, roughly, slightly, sometimes, somewhat, sort of/sorta, tend to, tended to, typical, typically uncertain, uncertainty, unclear, unclearly, unlikely, usually

Content-oriented: Speaker-oriented

argue, argued, appear, appeared, assume, assumed, claim, claimed, indicate, indicated, postulate, postulated, seem, seemed, suggest, suggested, suppose, supposed, suspect, suspected

Audience-oriented

believe, believed, feel, felt, from my perspective, from our perspective, from this perspective, in my opinion, in our opinion, in my view, in our view, in this view, ought, should, think, thought, to my knowledge, would, wouldn't, would not

E. Friginal et al., *Exploring Spoken English Learner Language Using Corpora*,
DOI 10.1007/978-3-319-59900-7

Boosters

Emphatics

actually, beyond doubt, certain, clear, definite, demonstrate, demonstrated, doubtless, establish, established, evident, find, found, in fact, incontestable, incontrovertible, indeed, indisputable, know, known, must (possibility), no doubt, obvious, of course, prove, proved, realize, realized, really, show, showed, shown, sure, truly, true, undeniable, without doubt, without a doubt

Amplifiers

a lot/lots, absolutely, always, certainly, clearly, completely, conclusively, decidedly, definitely, evidently, incontestably, incontrovertibly, indisputably, never, obviously, so, surely, too, totally, undeniably, undisputedly, undoubtedly, very

References

Aijmer, K. (2011). Well I'm not sure I think...the use of well by non-native speakers. *International Journal of Corpus Linguistics, 16*(2), 231–254.

Allen, P., Fröhlich, M., & Spada, N. (1984). The communicative orientation of language teaching: An observation scheme. In J. Handscombe, R. A. Orem, & B. P. Taylor (Eds.), *On TESOL '83: The question of control* (pp. 231–252). Washington, DC: TESOL.

Allwright, R. L. (1984). The importance of interaction in classroom language learning. *Applied Linguistics, 5*, 156.

Anthony, L. (2014). *AntConc (Version 3.4.3)* [Computer software]. Tokyo: Waseda University. Accessed 9 July. http://www.laurenceanthony.net/

Baker, P. (2010). *Sociolinguistics and corpus linguistics.* Edinburgh: Edinburgh University Press.

Bamford, J. (2004). Gestural and symbolic uses of the deictic *here* in academic lectures. In K. Aijmer & A. Stenström (Eds.), *Discourse patterns in spoken and written corpora* (pp. 113–138). Amsterdam: John Benjamins.

Barbieri, F. (2008). Patterns of age-based linguistic variation in American English. *Journal of SocioLinguistics, 21*(1), 58–88.

Barlow, M. (2012). *MonoConc Pro 2.2 (MP2.2)* [Software]. Available from http://www.monoconc.com/

Basturkmen, H. (2009). *Developing courses for English for specific purposes.* London: Palgrave Macmillan.

E. Friginal et al., *Exploring Spoken English Learner Language Using Corpora*,
DOI 10.1007/978-3-319-59900-7

Benson, P., & Lor, W. (1999). Conceptions of language and language learning. *System, 27*, 459–472.

Biber, D. (1988). *Variation across speech and writing*. Cambridge: Cambridge University Press.

Biber, D. (1993). Representativeness in corpus design. *Literary and Linguistic Computing, 8*(4), 243–257.

Biber, D. (2006a). Stance in spoken and written university registers. *Journal of English for Academic Purposes, 5*(2), 97–116. doi:10.1016/j.jeap.2006.05.001.

Biber, D. (2006b). *University language: A corpus-based study of spoken and written registers*. Amsterdam: John Benjamins.

Biber, D. (2009). A corpus-driven approach to formulaic language in English: Multi-word patterns in speech and writing. *International Journal of Corpus Linguistics, 14*(3), 275–311. doi:10.1075/ijcl.14.3.08bib.

Biber, D., Conrad, S., & Reppen, R. (1998). *Corpus linguistics: Investigating language structure and use*. Cambridge: Cambridge University Press.

Biber, D., Johansson, S., Leech, G., Conrad, S., & Finegan, E. (1999). *Longman grammar of spoken and written English*. London: Longman.

Biber, D., Conrad, S., & Cortes, V. (2004a). *If you look at…*: Lexical bundles in university teaching and textbooks. *Applied Linguistics, 25*, 371–405.

Biber, D., Conrad, S., Reppen, R., Byrd, P., Helt, M., Clark, V., Cortes, V., Csomay, E., & Urzua, A. (2004b). *Representing language use in the university: Analysis of the TOEFL 2000 spoken and written academic language corpus* (ETS TOEFL monograph series, MS-25). Princeton: Educational Testing Service.

Biber, D., Reppen, R., & Friginal, E. (2010). Research in corpus linguistics. In R. B. Kaplan (Ed.), *The Oxford handbook of applied linguistics* (2nd ed., pp. 548–570). Oxford: Oxford University Press.

Bown, J., & White, C. (2010). Affect in a self-regulatory framework for language learning. *System, 38*, 432–443.

Brand, C., & Götz, S. (2011). Fluency versus accuracy in advanced spoken learner language: A multi-method approach. *International Journal of Corpus Linguistics, 16*(2), 255–275.

British Academic Spoken English and BASE Plus Collections. (2017). *The British Academic Spoken English*. Available from http://www2.warwick.ac.uk/fac/soc/al/research/collections/base/

Brown, P., & Levinson, S. (1987). *Politeness*. Cambridge: Cambridge University Press.

Burns, R., & Burns, R. (2008). *Business research methods and statistics using SPSS*. Thousand Oaks: Sage.

Buysse, L. (2012). So as a multifunctional discourse marker in native and learner speech. *Journal of Pragmatics, 44*(13), 1764–1782.

Cairns, B. (1991). Spatial deixis: The use of spatial co-ordinates in spoken language. *Lund University, Department of Linguistics, Working Papers, 38*, 19–28.

Canagarajah, S. (2017, March 22). *'The smartest person in the room is the room': Emplacement as language competence*. Paper presented at the AAAL 2017 Conference, Portland.

Carson, J. G., & Nelson, G. L. (1996). Chinese students' perceptions of ESL peer response group interaction. *Journal of Second Language Writing, 5*(1), 1–19.

Casanave, C. P. (2006). *Controversies in second language writing: Dilemmas and decisions in research and instruction*. Ann Arbor: University of Michigan Press.

Cheng, S. W. (2012). "That's it for today": Academic lecture closings and the impact of class size. *English for Specific Purposes, 31*, 234–248.

Cheng, W., Greaves, C., & Warren, M. (2006). From n-gram to skipgram to concgram. *International Journal of Corpus Linguistics, 11*(4), 411–433.

Cheng, W., Greaves, C., & Warren, M. (2008). *A corpus-driven study of discourse intonation*. Amsterdam: John Benjamins.

Connor, U., & Asenavage, K. (1994). Peer response groups in ESL writing classes: How much impact on revision? *Journal of Second Language Writing, 3*(3), 257–276.

Conrad, S. (2002). Corpus linguistic approaches for discourse analysis. *Annual Review of Applied Linguistics, 22*, 75–95.

Cortes, V. (2004). Lexical bundles in published and student disciplinary writing: Examples from history and biology. *English for Specific Purposes, 23*, 397–423.

Coxhead, A. (2000). A new academic word list. *TESOL Quarterly, 34*, 213–238.

Coxhead, A. (2011). The academic word list 10 years on: Research and teaching implications. *TESOL Quarterly, 45*(2), 355–361.

Crashborn, O. (2008). Open access to sign language corpora. In O. Crashborn, T. Hanke, E. Efthimiou, I. Zwitserlood, & E. Thoutenhoofd (Eds.). *Construction and exploitation of sign language corpora* (Third workshop on the representation and processing of sign language, pp. 33–38). Paris: European Language Resources Association (ELRA).

Crawford Camiciottoli, B. (2005). Adjusting a business lecture for an international audience: A case study. *English for Specific Purposes, 24*, 183–199.

Csomay, E. (2007). A corpus-based look at linguistic variation in classroom interaction: Teacher talk versus student talk in American university classes. *Journal of English for Academic Purposes, 6*, 336–355.

Cullen, R. (2002). Supportive teacher talk: The importance of the F-move. *ELT Journal, 56*, 117–127.

De Cock, S. (2004). Preferred sequences of words in NS and NNS speech. *Belgian Journal of English Language and Literatures, 2*, 225–246.

De Guerrero, M., & Villamil, O. S. (2000). Activating the ZPD: Mutual scaffolding in L2 peer revision. *The Modern Language Journal, 84*(1), 51–68.

De Haan, P. (1989). *Postmodifying clauses in the English noun phrase: A corpus-based study*. Amsterdam: Rodopi.

Donato, R. (1994). Collective scaffolding in second language research. In J. P. Lantolf & G. Appel (Eds.), *Vygotskian approaches to second language research* (pp. 33–56). Norwood: Ablex Publication Corporation.

Dörnyei, Z., & Ushioda, E. (2011). *Teaching and researching motivation*. Harlow: Pearson Education Limited.

Duriau, V., Reger, R., & Pfarrer, M. (2007). A content analysis of the content analysis literature in organization studies: Research themes, data sources, and methodological refinements. *Organizational Research Methods, 10*(5), 5–34.

Ellis, R., & Barkhuizen, G. (2005). *Analysing learner language*. Oxford: Oxford University Press.

Entwistle, N., & McCune, V. (2004). The conceptual bases of study strategy inventories. *Educational Psychology Review, 16*(4), 325–345.

Fanselow, J. (1977). Beyond Rashomon – Conceptualizing and describing the teaching act. *TESOL Quarterly, 11*, 17–39.

Ferris, D. R. (2003). *Response to student writing: Implications for second language students*. New York: Routledge.

Firth, J. (1957). *Papers in linguistics*. Oxford: Oxford University Press.

Flower, L. (1990). Introduction: Studying cognition in context. In L. Flower, V. Stein, J. Ackerman, M. J. Kantz, K. McCormick, & W. C. Peck (Eds.), *Reading-to-write: Exploring a cognitive and social process* (pp. 3–32). New York: Oxford University Press.

Fortanet, I. (2004). The use of 'we' in university lectures: Reference and function. *English for Specific Purposes, 23*, 45–66.

Francis, D., Rivera, M., Lesaux, N., Kieffer, M., & Rivera, H. (2006). *Practical guidelines for the education of English language learners: Research-based recommendations for instruction and academic interventions*. Portsmouth: RMC Research Corporation, Center on Instruction.

Friginal, E. (2009). *The language of outsourced call centers: A corpus-based study of cross-cultural interaction*. Amsterdam: John Benjamins.

Friginal, E. (2013). 25 years of Biber's multi-dimensional analysis: Introduction to the special issue. *Corpora, 8*(2), 137–152.

Friginal, E. (2015). Concordancers. In J. Bennet (Ed.), *The Sage encyclopedia of intercultural communication* (pp. 109–111). Thousand Oaks: Sage.

Friginal, E., & Hardy, J. A. (2014). *Corpus-based sociolinguistics: A guide for students*. New York: Routledge.
Friginal, E., & Polat, B. (2015). Linguistic dimensions of learner speech in English interviews. *Corpus Linguistics Research, 1*, 53–82.
Friginal, E., Li, M., & Weigle, S. (2014). Revisiting multiple profiles of learner compositions: A comparison of highly rated NS and NNS essays. *Journal of Second Language Writing, 23*, 1–14.
Friginal, E., Pickering, L., & Bruce, C. (2016). Narrative and informational dimensions of AAC discourse in the workplace. In L. Pickering, E. Friginal, & S. Staples (Eds.), *Talking at work: Corpus-based explorations of workplace discourse* (pp. 27–54). London: Palgrave-Macmillan.
Gabrys-Barker, D., & Belska, J. (Eds.). (2013). *The affective dimension in second language acquisition*. Bristol: Multilingual Matters.
Gan, Z. (2010). Interaction in group oral assessment: A case study of higher-and lower-scoring students. *Language Testing, 27*(4), 585–602.
Gass, S. (1997). *Input, interaction, and the second language learner*. Mahwah: Erlbaum.
Gass, S. M., & Mackey, A. (2000). *Stimulated recall methodology in second language research*. New York: Routledge.
Gass, S., Mackey, A., & Ross-Feldman, L. (2005). Task-based interactions in classroom and laboratory settings. *Language Learning, 55*, 575–611.
Gilquin, G. (2008). Hesitation markers among EFL learners: Pragmatic deficiency or difference? In J. Romero-Trillo (Ed.), *Pragmatics and corpus linguistics: A mutualistic entente* (pp. 119–149). Berlin: Mouton de Gruyter.
Gilquin, G., De Cock, S., & Granger, S. (Eds.). (2010). *The Louvain international database of spoken English interlanguage, handbook and CD-ROM*. Louvain-la-Neuve: Presses Universitaires de Louvain.
Goo, J. (2012). Corrective feedback and working memory capacity in interaction-driven L2 learning. *Studies in Second Language Acquisition, 34*, 445–474.
Granger, S. (1983). *The BE + past participle construction in spoken English (with special emphasis on the passive)*. Amsterdam: Elsevier.
Granger, S., Gilquin, G., & Meunier, F. (2015). *The Cambridge handbook of learner corpus research*. Cambridge: Cambridge University Press.
Grant, L., & Ginther, A. (2000). Using computer-tagged linguistic features to describe L2 writing differences. *Journal of Second Language Writing, 9*(2), 123–145.
Greenbaum, S. (Ed.). (1996). *Comparing English worldwide: The international corpus of English*. Oxford: Clarendon Press.

Grieve, J., Biber, D., Friginal, E., & Nekrasova, T. (2010). Variation among blogs: A multi-dimensional analysis. In A. Mehler, S. Sharoff, & M. Santini (Eds.), *Genres on the web: Corpus studies and computational models* (pp. 45–71). New York: Springer.

Gu, T. (2014). A corpus-based study on the performance of the suggestion speech act by Chinese EFL learners. *International Journal of English Linguistics, 4*(1), 103.

Hammadou, J., & Bernhardt, E. (1987). On being and becoming a foreign language teacher. *Theory into Practice, 26*, 301–306.

Handford, M. (2010). *The language of business meetings*. Tokyo: Cambridge University Press.

Hardy, J., & Friginal, E. (2012). Filipino and American online communication and linguistic variation. *World Englishes, 31*(2), 143–161.

Hinkel, E. (2002). *Second language writers' text: Linguistic and rhetorical features*. Mahwah: Lawrence Erlbaum Associates.

Hofstede, G. (2001). *Culture's consequences: Comparing values, behaviors, institutions, and organizations across nations* (2nd ed.). Thousand Oaks: Sage.

Holmes, J. (2006). Sharing a laugh: Pragmatic aspects of humor and gender in the workplace. *Journal of Pragmatics, 38*, 26–50.

Hong, H., & Cao, F. (2014). Interactional metadiscourse in young EFL learner writing: A corpus-based study. *International Journal of Corpus Linguistics, 19*, 201–224.

Horwitz, E. (2010). Foreign and second language anxiety. *Language Teaching, 43*, 154–167.

Hyland, K. (1996). Writing without conviction? Hedging in science research articles. *Applied Linguistics, 17*, 433–454.

Hyland, K. (2004). Disciplinary interactions: Metadiscourse in L2 postgraduate writing. *Journal of Second Language Writing, 13*, 133–151.

Hyland, K. (2005). *Metadiscourse: Exploring interaction in writing*. London: Continuum.

Hyland, F. (2008). Scaffolding during the writing process: The role of informal peer interaction in writing workshops. In D. D. Belcher & A. Hirvela (Eds.), *The oral-literate connection: Perspectives on L2 speaking, writing, and other media interactions* (pp. 168–190). Ann Arbor: University of Michigan Press.

Hyland, K. (2009). *Academic discourse*. London: Continuum.

Hyland, K., & Milton, J. (1997). Qualification and certainty in L1 and L2 students' writing. *Journal of Second Language Writing, 6*, 183–205.

Jacobs, G. M., Curtis, A., Braine, G., & Huang, S. Y. (1998). Feedback on student writing: Taking the middle path. *Journal of Second Language Writing, 7*(3), 307–317.

Jefferson, G. (2004). Glossary of transcript symbols with an introduction. In G. H. Lerner (Ed.), *Conversation analysis: Studies from the first generation* (pp. 13–31). Amsterdam: John Benjamins.

Johansson, S., & Hofland, K. (1989). *Frequency analysis of English vocabulary and grammar* (Vols. 1–2). Oxford: Clarendon Press.

Johnston, T., & Schembri, A. (2006). Issues on the creation of a digital archive of a signed language. In L. Barwick & N. Thieburger (Eds.), *Sustainable data from digital fieldwork* (pp. 7–16). Sydney: University of Sydney Press.

Kamio, A. (2001). English generic *we, you*, and *they*: An analysis in terms of territory of information. *Journal of Pragmatics, 33*, 1111–1124.

Kaneko, T. (2007). Why so many article errors? Use of articles by Japanese learners of English. *Gakuen, 798*, 1–16.

Kaneko, T. (2008). Use of English prepositions by Japanese university students. *Gakuen, 810*, 1–12.

Kecskés, I. (2007). Formulaic language in English Lingua Franca. In I. Kecskés & L. R. Horn (Eds.). *Explorations in pragmatics: Linguistic, cognitive and intercultural aspects* (Vol. 1), (pp. 191–218). Berlin/New York: Walter de Gruyter.

Kennedy, G. (2003). Amplifier collocations in British National Corpus: Implications for English language teaching. *TESOL Quarterly, 37*, 467–487.

Kim, Y. (2008). The contribution of collaborative and individual tasks to the acquisition of L2 vocabulary. *The Modern Language Journal, 92*(1), 114–130.

Kim, Y., & McDonough, K. (2008). The effect of interlocutor proficiency on the collaborative dialogue between Korean as a second language learners. *Language Teaching Research, 12*(2), 211–234.

Kim, Y., & McDonough, K. (2011). Using pretask modelling to encourage collaborative learning opportunities. *Language Teaching Research, 15*(2), 183–199.

Knight, D., Evans, D., Carter, R., & Adolphs, S. (2009). HeadTalk, HandTalk and the corpus: Towards a framework for multi-modal, multi-media corpus development. *Corpora, 4*(1), 1–32.

Koester, A. (2010). *Workplace discourse*. London: Continuum.

Kučera, H., & Francis, W. N. F. (1967). *Computational analysis of present-day American English*. Providence: Brown University Press.

Lancia, F. (Ed.). (2004). *Strumenti per l'analasi dei testi* [Tools for textual analysis]. Rome: Franco Angeli.

Lancia, F. (2016). *T-Lab online user manual*. http://tlab.it/en/allegati/help_en_online/fare.htm

Larsen-Freeman, D., & Long, M. (2014). *An introduction to second language acquisition research*. New York: Routledge.

Lee, Y.-A. (2007). Third turn position in teacher talk: Contingency and the work of teaching. *Journal of Pragmatics, 39*, 180–206.

Lee, J. J. (2009). Size matters: An exploratory comparison of small- and large-class university lecture introductions. *English for Specific Purposes, 29*, 42–57.

Lee, J. J. (2010). The uniqueness of EFL teachers: Perceptions of Japanese learners. *TESOL Journal, 1*, 23–48.

Lee, J. J. (2011). *A genre analysis of second language classroom discourse: Exploring the rhetorical, linguistic, and contextual dimensions of language lessons*. Unpublished doctoral dissertation, Georgia State University, Atlanta.

Lee, J. J. (2016). "There's intentionality behind it…": A genre analysis of EAP classroom lessons. *Journal of English for Academic Purposes, 23*, 99–112.

Lee, J. J., & Casal, J. E. (2014). Metadiscourse in results and discussion chapters: A cross-linguistic analysis of English and Spanish thesis writers in engineering. *System, 46*, 39–54.

Lee, J. J., & Deakin, L. (2016). Interactions in L1 and L2 undergraduate student writing: Interactional metadiscourse in successful and less-successful argumentative essays. *Journal of Second Language Writing, 33*, 21–34.

Lee, J. J., & Subtirelu, N. (2015). Metadiscourse in the classroom: A comparative analysis of EAP lessons and university lectures. *English for Specific Purposes, 37*, 52–63.

Leeser, M. J. (2004). Learner proficiency and focus on form during collaborative dialogue. *Language Teaching Research, 8*(1), 55–81.

Leki, I. (1990). Potential problems with peer responding in ESL writing classes. *CATESOL Journal, 3*, 5–17.

Levinson, S. C. (1983). *Pragmatics*. Cambridge: Cambridge University Press.

Li, T., & Wharton, S. (2012). Metadiscourse repertoire of L1 Mandarin undergraduates writing in English: A cross-contextual, cross-disciplinary study. *Journal of English for Academic Purposes, 11*, 345–356.

Lin, C. Y. (2012). Modifiers in BASE and MICASE: A matter of academic cultures or lecturing styles? *English for Specific Purposes, 31*, 117–126.

Lindemann, S., & Mauranen, A. (2001). "It's just real messy": The occurrence and function of *just* in a corpus of academic speech. *English for Specific Purposes, 20*, 459–475.

Liu, J. (2002). *Peer response in second language writing classrooms* (Michigan series on Teaching Multilingual Writers). Ann Arbor: University of Michigan Press.

Liu, J. & Sadler (2003). *Peer response in second language writing classrooms* (Michigan series on Teaching Multilingual Writers). Ann Arbor: University of Michigan Press.

Lockhart, C., & Ng, P. (1995). Analyzing talk in ESL peer response groups: Stances, functions, and content. *Language Learning, 45*(4), 605–651.

Long, M. H. (1983). Native speaker/non-native speaker conversation and the negotiation of meaning. *Applied Linguistics, 4*, 126–141.

Long, M. H. (1996). The role of the linguistic environment in second language acquisition. In W. C. Ritchie & T. K. Bhatia (Eds.), *Handbook of language acquisition (Vol. 2): Second language acquisition* (pp. 413–468). New York: Academic Press.

Lundstrom, K., & Baker, W. (2009). To give is better than to receive: The benefits of peer review to the reviewer's own writing. *Journal of Second Language Writing, 18*(1), 30–43.

MacArthur, F., Alejo, R., Piquer-Piriz, A., Amador-Moreno, C., Littlemore, J., Ädel, A., Krennmayr, T., & Vaughn, E. (2014). *EuroCoAT. The European corpus of academic talk*. http://www.eurocoat.es

Mackey, A. (1999). Input, interaction, and second language development. *Studies in Second Language Acquisition, 21*, 557–587.

Mangelsdorf, K., & Schlumberger, A. (1992). ESL student response stances in a peer-review task. *Journal of Second Language Writing, 1*(3), 235–254.

Marra, M. (2012). English in the workplace. In B. Paltridge & S. Starfield (Eds.), *The handbook of English for specific purposes* (pp. 67–99). Chichester: Wiley.

Marton, F., & Booth, S. (1997). *Learning and awareness*. Mahwah: Lawrence Erlbaum and Associates.

Mauranen, A. (2001). Reflexive academic talk: Observations from MICASE. In J. M. Swales & R. C. Simpson (Eds.), *Corpus linguistics in North America: Selections from the 1999 symposium* (pp. 165–178). Ann Arbor: University of Michigan Press.

Mauranen, A. (2003). The corpus of English as lingua franca in academic settings. *TESOL Quarterly, 37*(3), 513–527.

McCarthy, M., & Handford, M. (2004). Invisible to us: A preliminary corpus-based study of spoken business English. In U. Connor & T. A. Upton (Eds.), *Discourse in the professions: Perspectives from corpus linguistics* (pp. 167–201). Amsterdam: John Benjamins.

McEnery, T., & Hardie, A. (2012). *Corpus linguistics*. Cambridge: Cambridge University Press.

McEnery, T., Xiao, R., & Tono, Y. (2006). *Corpus-based language studies: An advanced resource book*. New York: Routledge.

Mendonca, C. O., & Johnson, K. E. (1994). Peer review negotiations: Revision activities in ESL writing instruction. *TESOL Quarterly, 28*, 745–769.

Min, H. T. (2005). Training students to become successful peer reviewers. *System, 33*(2), 293–308.

Min, H. T. (2008). Reviewer stances and writer perceptions in EFL peer review training. *English for Specific Purposes, 27*(3), 285–305.

Morell, T. (2004). Interactive lecture discourse for university EFL students. *English for Specific Purposes, 23*, 325–338.

Moskowitz, G. (1971). Interaction analysis – A new modern language for supervisors. *Foreign Language Annals, 5*, 211–221.

Mukherjee, J. (2009). The grammar of conversation in advanced spoken learner English: Learner corpus data and language-pedagogical implications. In K. Aijmer (Ed.), *Corpora and language teaching* (pp. 203–230). Amsterdam: John Benjamins.

Mur-Dueñas, P. (2011). An intercultural analysis of metadiscourse features in research articles written in Spanish and English. *Journal of Pragmatics, 43*, 3068–3079.

Nation, P. (2001). *Learning vocabulary in another language*. Cambridge: Cambridge University Press.

Nelson, G. (1993). Reading and writing: Integrating cognitive and social dimensions. In J. Carson & I. Leki (Eds.), *Reading in the composition classroom: Second language perspectives* (pp. 315–330). Boston: Heinle & Heinle.

Nelson, G. (1996). The design of the corpus. In S. Greenbaum (Ed.), *Comparing English worldwide: The international corpus of English* (pp. 27–35). Oxford: Clarendon Press.

Nelson, G. L., & Murphy, J. M. (1992). Peer response groups: Do L2 writers use peer comments in revising their drafts? *TESOL Quarterly, 27*(1), 135–141.

Nelson, G. L., & Murphy, J. M. (1993). An L2 writing group: Task and social dimensions. *Journal of Second Language Writing, 1*(3), 171–193.

O'Boyle, A. (2010). *The dialogic construction of knowledge in university classroom talk: A corpus study of spoken academic discourse*. PhD thesis, Queen's University Belfast.

O'Boyle, A. (2014). "You" and "I" in university seminars and spoken learner discourse. *Journal of English for Academic Purposes, 16*, 40–56.

O'Keeffe, A., Clancy, B., & Adolphs, A. (2011). *Introducing pragmatics in use*. London: Routledge.

Ohta, A. S. (2000). *Second language acquisition processes in the classroom setting: Learning Japanese*. Mahwah: Lawrence Erlbaum.

Ortega, L. (2012). Epilogue: Exploring L2 writing–SLA interfaces. *Journal of Second Language Writing, 21*(4), 404–441.

Patton, M. Q. (2005). *Qualitative research*. New York: Wiley.

Paulus, T. M. (1999). The effect of peer and teacher feedback on student writing. *Journal of Second Language Writing, 8*(3), 265–289.

Pennebaker, J., Booth, R., & Francis, M. (2007a). *Linguistic inquiry and word count: LIWC* [Computer software]. Austin: LIWC.net.

Pennebaker, J., Chung, C., Ireland, M., Gonzales, A., & Booth, R. (2007b). *The development and psychometric properties of LIWC2007 [LIWC manual]*. Austin: LIWC.net.

Pica, T., Holliday, L., Lewis, N., & Morgenthaler, L. (1989). Comprehensible output as an outcome of linguistic demands on the learner. *Studies in Second Language Acquisition, 11*, 63–90.

Pickering, L., & Bruce, C. (2009). *AAC and non-AAC workplace corpus (ANAWC)*. Atlanta: Georgia State University.

Plonsky, L., & Gass, S. (2011). Quantitative research methods, study quality, and outcomes: The case of interaction research. *Language Learning, 61*, 325–366.

Polat, B. (2012). Experiencing language: Phenomenography and second language acquisition. *Language Awareness, 22*(2), 111–125.

Polat, B. (2013a). *The L2 experience interview corpus*. Atlanta: Georgia State University.

Polat, B. (2013b). L2 experience interviews: What can they tell us about individual differences? *System, 41*, 70–83.

Poos, D., & Simpson, R. (2002). Cross-disciplinary comparisons of hedging: Some findings from the Michigan corpus of academic spoken English. In R. Reppen, S. Fitzmaurice, & D. Biber (Eds.), *Using corpora to explore linguistic variation* (pp. 3–23). Amsterdam: John Benjamins.

Rabiee, M. (2010). Facilitating learning together in Iranian context: Three collaborative oral feedback models in EFL writing classes. *Sino-US English Teaching, 7*(3), 9–22.

Rayson, P. (2003). *WMatrix: A statistical method and software tool for linguistic analysis through corpus comparison*. Unpublished doctoral dissertation, Lancaster University, Lancaster.

Rayson, P. (2008). From key words to key semantic domains. *International Journal of Corpus Linguistics, 13*(4), 519–549. doi:10.1075/ijcl.13.4.06ray.

Rayson, P. (n.d). Log-likelihood calculator [Computer Software]. UK: Lancaster University. http://ucrel.lancs.ac.uk/llwizard.html. Accessed 9 July.

Riazi, A. (2016). Innovative mixed-methods research: Moving beyond design technicalities to epistemological and methodological realizations. *Applied Linguistics, 37*(1), 33–49.

Roberson, A. (2015). *The second language peer response (L2PR) corpus*. Atlanta: Georgia State University.

Rollinson, P. (2004). Experiences and perceptions in an ESL academic writing peer response group. *Estudios Ingleses de la Universidad Complutense, 12*, 79–108.

Römer, U. (2010). Establishing the phraseological profile of a text type: The construction of meaning in academic book reviews. *English Text Construction, 3*(1), 95–119. doi:10.1075/etc.3.1.06rom.

Römer, U., & Wulff, S. (2010). Applying corpus methods to written academic texts: Explorations of MICUSP. *Journal of Writing Research, 2*(2), 99–127.

Rounds, P. L. (1987a). Characterizing successful classroom discourse for NNS teaching assistant training. *TESOL Quarterly, 21*, 643–671.

Rounds, P. L. (1987b). Multifunctional personal pronoun use in education setting. *English for Specific Purposes, 6*, 13–29.

Saito, K., & Akiyama, Y. (2017). Video-based interaction, negotiation for comprehensibility, and second language speech learning: A longitudinal study. *Language Learning, 67*(1), 43–74.

Scott, M. (1997). PC analysis of key words – And key key words. *System, 25*(2), 233–245.

Scott, M. (2012). *WordSmith Tools (Version 6)* [Software]. Available from http://lexically.net/wordsmith/

Seedhouse, P. (2004). *The interactional architecture of the language classroom: A conversation analysis perspective*. Malden: Blackwell.

Seidlhofer, B. (2007). Common property: English as a lingua franca in Europe. In J. Cummins & C. Davison (Eds.), *International handbook of English language teaching* (pp. 137–153). New York: Springer.

Seidlhofer, B. (2012). Anglophone-centric attitudes and the globalization of English. *Journal of English as a Lingua Franca, 1*(2), 393–407. doi:10.1515/jelf-2012-0026.

Sheen, Y. (2007). The effects of corrective feedback, language aptitude and learner attitudes on the acquisition of English articles. In A. Mackey (Ed.), *Conversational interaction in second language acquisition: A collection of empirical studies* (pp. 301–322). Oxford: Oxford University Press.

Shirato, J., & Stapleton, P. (2007). Comparing English vocabulary in a spoken learner corpus with a native speaker corpus: Pedagogical implications arising from an empirical study in Japan. *Language Teaching Research, 11*(4), 393–412.

Sidnell, J., & Enfield, N. J. (2016). Deixis and the interactional foundations of reference. In Y. Huang (Ed.), *The Oxford handbook of pragmatics* (pp. 217–239). Oxford: Oxford University Press.

Simpson, R., Briggs, S., Ovens, J., & Swales, J. (2002). *The Michigan corpus of academic spoken English*. Ann Arbor: The Regents of the University of Michigan.

Simpson-Vlach, R. (2013). Corpus analysis of spoken English for academic purposes. In C. Chapelle (Ed.), *The encyclopedia of applied linguistics* (pp. 452–461). Malden: Wiley Blackwell.

Simpson-Vlach, R., & Leicher, S. (2006). *The MICASE handbook*. Ann Arbor: University of Michigan Press.

Sinclair, J. (2005). Corpus and text – Basic principles. In M. Wynne (Ed.), Developing linguistic corpora: A guide to good practice (pp. 1–16). Oxford: Oxbow Books. Retrieved from http://www.ahds.ac.uk/creating/guides/linguistic-corpora/chapter1.htm

Sinclair, J. M., & Coulthard, R. M. (1975). *Towards an analysis of discourse: The English used by teachers and pupils*. London: Oxford University Press.

Spada, N., & Fröhlich, M. (1995). *COLT observation scheme*. Sydney: The National Centre for English Language Teaching and Research, Macquarie University.

Staples, S. (2015). *The discourse of nurse-patient interactions: Contrasting the communicative styles of U.S. and international nurses*. Philadelphia: John Benjamins.

Staples, S. (2016). Identifying linguistic features of medical interactions: A register analysis. In L. Pickering, E. Friginal, & S. Staples (Eds.), *Talking at work: Corpus-based explorations of workplace discourse* (pp. 179–208). London: Palgrave-Macmillan.

Staples, S., Laflair, G., & Egbert, J. (2017). Comparing language use in oral proficiency interviews to target domains: Conversational, academic, and professional discourse. *The Modern Language Journal, 101*(1), 1–20.

Storch, N. (1999). Are two heads better than one? Pair work and grammatical accuracy. *System, 27*(3), 363–374.

Storch, N. (2002). Patterns of interaction in ESL pair work. *Language Learning, 52*(1), 119–158.

Storch, N. (2007). Investigating the merits of pair work on a text-editing task in ESL classes. *Language Teaching Research, 11*(2), 143–159.

Stubbe, M., Lane, C., Hilder, J., Vine, E., Vine, B., Marra, M., Homes, J., & Weatherall, A. (2003). Multiple discourse analyses of a workplace interaction. *Discourse Studies, 5*(3), 351–388.

Swain, M. (1993). The output hypothesis: Just speaking and writing aren't enough. *Canadian Modern Language Review, 50*(1), 158–164.

Swain, M. (2000). The output hypothesis and beyond: Mediating acquisition through collaborative dialogue. In J. P. Lantolf (Ed.), *Sociocultural theory and second language learning* (pp. 97–114). Oxford: Oxford University Press.

Swain, M., & Lapkin, S. (1998). Interaction and second language learning: Two adolescent French immersion students working together. *Modern Language Journal, 82*(3), 320.

Swain, M., Brooks, L., & Tocalli-Beller, A. (2002). Peer-peer dialogue as a means of second language learning. *Annual Review of Applied Linguistics, 22*, 171–185.

Swales, J. M. (1990). *Genre analysis: English in academic and research settings*. Cambridge: Cambridge University Press.

Swales, J. M., & Burke, A. (2003). "It's really fascinating work": Differences in evaluative adjectives across academic registers. In P. Leistyna & C. F. Meyer (Eds.), *Corpus analysis: Language structure and language use* (pp. 1–18). Amsterdam: Rodopi.

Swales, J. M., & Malczewski, B. (1999). Discourse management and new episode flags in MICASE. In R. C. Simpson & J. M. Swales (Eds.), *Corpus linguistics in North America: Selections from the 1999 symposium* (pp. 145–164). Ann Arbor: University of Michigan Press.

Tagliamonte, S. A. (2006). *Analysing sociolinguistic variation*. Cambridge: Cambridge University Press.

Tan, L. L., Wigglesworth, G., & Storch, N. (2010). Pair interactions and mode of communication: Comparing face-to-face and computer mediate communication. *Australian Review of Applied Linguistics, 33*(3), 27.

Tang, G. M. (1999). Peer response in ESL writing. *TESL Canada Journal, 16*(2), 20–38.

Tang, G. M., & Tithecott, J. (1999). Peer response in ESL writing. *TESL Canada Journal, 16*(2), 20–38.

Tausczik, Y., & Pennebaker, J. (2010). The psychological meaning of words: LIWC and computerized text analysis methods. *Journal of Language and Social Psychology, 29*(1), 24–54.

Tsui, A. B. M. (1985). Analyzing input and interaction in second language classrooms. *RELC Journal, 16*, 8–32.

Tsui, A., & Ng, M. (2000). Do secondary L2 writers benefit from peer comments? *Journal of Second Language Writing, 9*(2), 147–170.

van Lier, L. (1996). *Interaction in the language curriculum: Awareness, autonomy and authenticity*. New York: Longman.

Villamil, O. S., & De Guerrero, M. C. (1998). Assessing the impact of peer revision on L2 writing. *Applied Linguistics, 19*(4), 491–514.

Vine, B. (2009). Directives at work: Exploring the contextual complexity of workplace directives. *Journal of Pragmatics, 41*(7), 1395–1405. doi:10.1016/j.pragma.2009.03.001.

Vine, B. (2016). Pragmatic markers at work in New Zealand. In L. Pickering, E. Friginal, & S. Staples (Eds.), *Talking at work: Corpus-based explorations of workplace discourse* (pp. 1–26). London: Palgrave-Macmillan.

Vine, B. (forthcoming). Just, actually at work in New Zealand. In E. Friginal (Ed.), *Studies in corpus-based sociolinguistics*. New York: Routledge.

VOICE. (2013). *The Vienna-Oxford International Corpus of English (Version 2.0 Online)*. http://voice.univie.ac.at (date of last access).

Vygotsky, L. S. (1978). *Mind in society: The development of higher psychological processes*. Cambridge: Harvard University Press.

Walsh, S. (2002). Construction of obstruction: Teacher talk and learner involvement in the EFL classroom. *Language Teaching Research, 6*, 3–23.

Warren, M. (2004). //So what have YOU been WORking on REcently//: Compiling a specialized corpus of spoken business English. In U. Connor & T. A. Upton (Eds.), *Discourse in the professions: Perspectives from corpus linguistics* (pp. 115–140). Philadelphia: John Benjamins.

Watanabe, Y. (2008). Peer–peer interaction between L2 learners of different proficiency levels: Their interactions and reflections. *Canadian Modern Language Review, 64*(4), 605–635.

Watanabe, Y., & Swain, M. (2007). Effects of proficiency differences and patterns of pair interaction on second language learning: Collaborative dialogue between adult ESL learners. *Language Teaching Research, 11*(2), 121–142.

Webb, N. M. (1989). Peer interaction and learning in small groups. *International Journal of Educational Research, 13*(1), 21–39.

Weinberger, S. H. (2013). *The speech accent archive*. George Mason University. Retrieved from http://accent.gmu.edu

Weisser, M. (2016). *Practical corpus linguistics: An introduction to corpus-based language analysis*. Malden: Wiley Blackwell.

Williams, J. (2012). The potential role (s) of writing in second language development. *Journal of Second Language Writing, 21*(4), 321–331.

Yang, S. (2014). *Investigating discourse markers in Chinese college EFL teacher talk: A multi-layered analytical approach*. Unpublished doctoral dissertation, Newcastle University, Newcastle upon Tyne.

Yeo, J.-Y., & Ting, S.-H. (2014). Personal pronouns for student engagement in arts and science lecture introductions. *English for Specific Purposes, 34*, 26–37.

Zhao, H. (2010). Investigating learners' use and understanding of peer and teacher feedback on writing: A comparative study in a Chinese English writing classroom. *Assessing Writing, 15*(1), 3–17.

Zheng, C. (2012). Understanding the learning process of peer feedback activity: An ethnographic study of exploratory practice. *Language Teaching Research, 16*(1), 109–126.

Zhu, W., & Mitchell, D. A. (2012). Participation in peer response as activity: An examination of peer response stances from an activity theory perspective. *TESOL Quarterly, 46*(2), 362–386.

Ziegler, N. (2015). Synchronous computer-mediated communication and interaction: A meta-analysis. *Studies in Second Language Acquisition, 38*, 553–586.

Index

E. Friginal et al., *Exploring Spoken English Learner Language Using Corpora*,
DOI 10.1007/978-3-319-59900-7

K

L

M

N

O

Kolibri 360 GmbH
Ferdinand-Jühlke-Straße 7
99095 Erfurt, Deutschland
produktsicherheit@kolibri360.de